An illustrated history of

Stamp Design

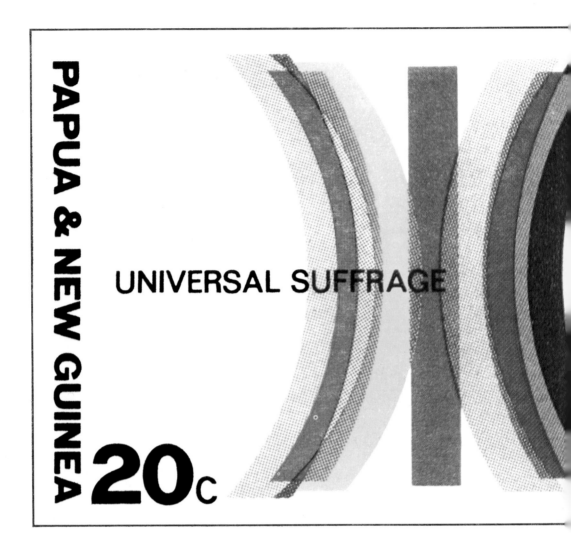

PAPUA & NEW GUINEA

UNIVERSAL SUFFRAGE

20c

One of a series of four abstract designs used in 1968 by Papua New Guinea to symbolize Human Rights Year and Universal Suffrage (36 × 28mm). After designing stamps for many years in a more orthodox style based on realistic motifs, George Hamori began applying abstract treatments to his designs for Australia, Papua and other countries in the mid-1960s.

An illustrated history of

Stamp Design

by William Finlay

Peter Lowe

ROSS
DEPENDENCY

18c

1

2

4

1967

Picea excelsa

0,40+0,07
SUOMI·FINLAND

5

ZEHN JAHRE
VERTRAG ÜBER DIE
DEUTSCH-FRANZÖSISCHE
ZUSAMMENARBEIT 1963-1973
Xᵉ ANNIVERSAIRE DU TRAITÉ
SUR LA COOPERATION
FRANCO-ALLEMANDE
1963-1973

Muster

40

DEUTSCHE BUNDESPOST

7

支那

8

POSTES

2c

SOUDAN
FRANÇAIS
A.DELZERS

10

AFRIQUE OCCIDENTALE FRANÇAISE

RF

1c

GUINÉE

11

25

RÉPUBLIQUE TUNISIENNE

EDITOR'S NOTE
Most of the stamps illustrated in this book
have been enlarged in the same proportion,
and are half as big again as the originals.
Where a different enlargement or reduction
has been necessary, the original dimensions
of the stamp are given in the caption.
Where there is a perforation edge, this
is included in the measurement.

ISBN 0 85654 609 7

Printed in Spain

Contents

Introduction 10

1 The beginning of stamp design 12

2 The printing processes 18

3 The old masters 26

4 The primitives 46

5 Nineteenth-century typography 54

6 Fin de siècle pictorialism 74

7 The influence of art nouveau 86

8 The influence of art deco 102

9 Early twentieth-century pictorialism 118

10 Twentieth-century phenomena 142

11 Pictorialism today 150

12 The age of the gimmick 164

Books for further reading 182

Glossary 183

Index 184

1. Ross Dependency, 18 cents, 1972
2. Bulgaria, 5 stotinki, 1902
3. Western Australia, 5 pence, 1885
4. Finland, 40 + 7 pennia, 1967
5. West Germany, 40 pfennigs, 1973
6. Sweden, 85 öre, 1971
7. Japan (P.O. in Korea), 3 sen, 1900
8. French Sudan, 2 centimes, 1931
9. Austria, 5 groschen, 1949
10. French Guinea, 1 centime, 1906
11. Tunisia, 25 millièmes, 1970
12. Jamaica, 2 pence, 1860

Introduction

The earliest stamp collectors, on acquiring a
new specimen, were likely to ask 'Where has
it come from?' A later generation of collectors
were more likely to ask, 'What is it worth?'
Naturally these questions are still prominent in
the minds of philatelists, but nowadays the
collector is just as likely to ask, 'Who designed
and printed it?' The increasing emphasis on
thematic or topical collecting and the decline
in country collecting have made collectors
more conscious of the subject matter on their
stamps. At the same time postal administrations
and philatelic bureaux, in a bid to secure
increased revenue from collectors, have devoted
greater care than ever before to the design and
execution of stamps.

Postage stamps are such commonplace
objects nowadays that we tend to forget that
they have only been in existence for little more
than a century and a quarter. They did not
materialize out of nothing, and their
subsequent developments have not arisen
haphazardly. This book is concerned with the
design of postage stamps. It begins with the
evolution of the small, upright format of the
Penny Black, the world's first stamp, and traces
the development of design right up to the
present day.

The design of such an essentially utilitarian
object is often a prosaic matter, governed
primarily by political necessity and the
limitations of the printing process employed.
That the postage stamp should ever have risen
above that mundane level, and have some
pretension to be an art form in its own right, is

almost miraculous. It is true to say that the earliest designers and printers strove to produce an article which embodied the elements of fine art—sensitive portraiture and delicate engraving—since these elements minimized the possibility of forgery; but advances in production techniques lessened the fear of forgery, and 'artistry' as such diminished in importance as the nineteenth century progressed. This, by and large, explains the pedestrian nature of so many of the stamps used throughout the world at the turn of the century.

In recent years there have been numerous attempts to inject aesthetic qualities into postage stamp design; here and there, in Czechoslovakia and Japan, in Britain and Scandinavia, designs are produced which may be considered as artistic in themselves, without having to fall back on the reproduction of existing works of art in other media. But these attempts are still very much in the minority. The modern multicoloured postage stamp, representing the acme of technical excellence, tends to be either a photograph or a poster in miniature, with scant attention devoted to the style and positioning of lettering, denomination and other incidental features.

Although there are artistically conceived postage stamps at the present time, few of them can be said to be inspired or influenced by prevailing ideas in the world of the fine arts. One or two isolated examples of stamps derived from non-figurative, abstract, surrealist or pop art may be cited, but they do not add up to any distinct trend in modern stamp design. In the past, the influence of such movements as Art Nouveau at the turn of the century, and Art Deco in the interwar period, could be detected here and there, but again such influence was sporadic and usually felt only after such styles had passed their peak in other branches of the applied and decorative arts.

It has to be admitted that art has played relatively little part in the development of postage stamps, but—good, bad or indifferent—stamps have still had to be designed. This book is concerned with the history of stamp design: the establishment of conventions in heraldry and portraiture, the various attempts to produce a more pictorial approach, and the dominant factors influencing design at different times, from the fear of forgery in the 1840s and the obsession with minimizing costs in the 1880s, to the propaganda and didactic style of the present day.

Obviously it would require several volumes to discuss adequately all the approaches to the problems of stamp design, and analyse even a fraction of the designs used for the stamps of the world, more than a quarter of a million of which have been produced since 1840. I have attempted an overall survey of stamp design, showing the trends and patterns dictated by practical or political necessity. One picture is worth a thousand words, and for this reason the illustrations have been carefully selected to show the significant features of global stamp design from the sublime to the ridiculous, from the serenity of the early line-engraved stamps to the gimmickry of the present day.

Charles F. Whiting of Beaufort House, Strand, London, produced at least seven of the essays submitted to the Treasury Competition of 1839. These bi-coloured essays were printed by the Congreve method using a multiple plate process invented by Sir William Congreve. This type of printing, patented in 1821, was used at Somerset House in the production of medicine tax stamps and other security items. The intricate background was an anti-forgery device.

I
The beginning of stamp design

THE ADHESIVE postage stamp is such a common-place article nowadays that most people take it for granted. They seldom spare a thought, as they lick the back and stick it on the corner of the card or envelope, for the tiny piece of printed paper, the smallest form of official document or negotiable security, nor wonder how and why such a thing came into being. The basic function of the stamp is, and always has been, to indicate the prepayment of postage, a fact often lost sight of, since postage stamps have long since acquired many other purposes. More than a century ago the prepayment of postage had to be effected in other ways. The sender would have to take the letter to a receiving house or post office; there the letter would be weighed or, more probably, the number of sheets comprising it would be counted; then the distance the letter was to travel would be laboriously computed and the appropriate rate of postage multiplied by the number of sheets. There might even be an additional charge, to cover tolls levied on certain types of conveyance on certain roads, and when this complicated sum had been worked out the postal official would mark the cost of the letter on the cover—in red if the letter was prepaid, in black if the money was to be recovered from the addressee on receipt. Prepaid letters were also marked with a 'Paid' handstamp, usually applied in red, so that the postmen at the destination would know that no further charge was to be collected from the recipient.

Apart from business correspondence, it was not considered polite to prepay postage on letters. The recipient was supposed to be glad to pay the cost of getting a letter from a friend or relative. Nevertheless it was quite common for letters to be refused by the would-be recipient, and in such cases the postal authorities had to stand the loss. The inflation which hit Europe in the aftermath of the Napoleonic Wars grievously affected postal rates everywhere. By the 1830s the cost of sending letters was prohibitive and revenue from postal services was in decline—despite the fact that better standards of literacy and expanding commerce made letter writing a greater necessity. In many parts of Europe men concerned themselves

with ways and means of reforming the outmoded postal system. In Britain the foremost champion of postal reform was Rowland Hill, a Kidderminster schoolmaster, and he devised a scheme for Uniform Penny Postage. He realized that the cumbersome accountancy involved in transmitting letters was at the heart of the problem, and he proposed that the assessment of postage according to the number of sheets (with the wrapper counting as an extra sheet) and the distance travelled should be scrapped. Instead, letters should be charged at a flat rate irrespective of distance, although he felt that it was reasonable to charge extra for overweight letters, a criterion that has ever since been retained. The establishment of uniform tariffs eliminated the complicated system of charges and also encouraged prepayment, which he hoped would become the rule rather than the exception. To this end he also proposed the adoption of stamped letter sheets and wrappers, which the public could purchase in advance. Thus a letter could be posted at any time, and not just when the post office or receiving house happened to be open—though it should be noted that Britain lagged behind many European countries in erecting postal boxes on convenient street corners.

Almost as an afterthought Rowland Hill suggested that, in addition to the stamped sheets, there ought to be small adhesive labels in cases where the stamped sheets were not readily available. In his pamphlet advocating postal reform, published in February 1837, he wrote: 'Perhaps this difficulty might be obviated by using a bit of paper just large enough to bear the stamp, and covered at the back with a glutinous wash, which the bringer might, by the application of a little moisture, attach to the back of the letter so as to avoid the necessity of re-directing it.' It is this casual sentence which gives to Rowland Hill the credit for being the father of the adhesive postage stamp, but like so many other great inventions no one person can be accorded all the honour. The Dundee bookseller and publisher, James Chalmers, is often given this title, because of assertions (made many years later) that he had proposed adhesive stamps in 1834—three years before Hill's pamphlet was published. Chalmers certainly produced experiments for adhesive stamps, but the earliest substantiated examples seem to date from 1838. Chalmers himself went on record as saying that he first suggested 'slips' to Robert Wallace (a member of Parliament interested in postal reform) at the end of 1837; but it is quite possible that he had come to this solution independently of Hill since he was not at that time aware of Hill's pamphlet of the previous February. Samuel Roberts of Llanbrynmair claimed (many years later) to have devised adhesive stamps in 1827, and Francis Worrel Stevens, a fellow schoolmaster of Hill's, claimed (in 1876) that he submitted proposals of this nature to the Chancellor of the Exchequer in 1833. Dr. John Gray of the British Museum also claimed to have thought of adhesive stamps in 1834; but though he later became one of the foremost pioneers of philately, his claim to be the father of the stamp is unsupported by any documentary evidence.

Adhesive stamps were also proposed by an Austrian civil servant named Laurenc Kosir (or Koschier) in 1836, and for this reason Austria and Yugoslavia claim him as the 'ideological creator' of the adhesive stamp; but the Austro-Hungarian authorities did nothing to implement his proposals. In 1938 a letter,

from Spittal to Klagenfurt, was discovered in Austria and created considerable furore in philatelic circles. It bore an adhesive 1-kreuzer label which experts subsequently pronounced to be genuine. It had been devised (unofficially) by Ferdinand Egarter, postmaster of Spittal and father of the lady who had written the letter. At that time it was the practice for postmen to get a tip of one kreuzer for delivering letters and Herr Egarter apparently devised this method of collecting his dues. Thus the 'stamp' was nothing more than a collecting-fee label and has no real status as a postage stamp. It bore the letters o.p.—once thought to signify *Österreichische Post* (Austrian Post), but now regarded as meaning *Orts Post* (local post). Since no other examples have so far come to light this stamp's authenticity is doubted.

Adhesive stamps for the prepayment of postage, in fact, go back much farther than Hill's reforms of the nineteenth century. Renouard de Villayer established an urban postal service in Paris in 1653. Known as the *Petit Poste*, it operated on an ingenious system of prepaid postage. Letters were franked with labels called *billets de port payé* and dropped into street collecting boxes for onward transmission to other parts of the city. The *billets* consisted of strips of paper, impressed with the royal coat of arms and

The celebrated 'Cavallini' of Sardinia, impressed on letter sheets from 1819 to 1836, denoted the payment of a tax on correspondence and cannot be regarded as postage stamps in the strict sense.

The essays by James Chalmers were printed by letterpress. Some were circular, resembling contemporary postmarks, but others consisted of upright rectangles, almost in the format eventually adopted.

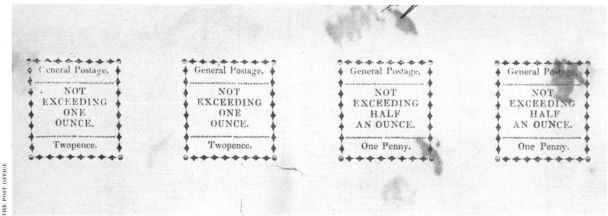

affixed to the letters by means of isinglass wafers. These labels were sold to the public for two sous (ten centimes) each. The project foundered because people tended to treat the letter boxes as litter bins, and mice had a nasty habit of eating the letters. Although de Villayer's *billets* are well documented, no actual example has yet come to light. Surprisingly, although the existence of the seventeenth-century Petit Poste was known, the practical details of its operation did not appear until the 1840s when the French Post Office was looking into the problem of postal reform and the adoption of a scheme similar to that recently introduced in Britain.

Rowland Hill's proposal for bits of paper was not as revolutionary as it might appear. Adhesive stamps were already in use in the United Kingdom, to denote the payment of taxes on patent medicines and other dutiable articles. Such labels were introduced in 1802 by the Stamping Branch of the Board of Customs and Excise at Somerset House and, by the 1830s, would be a familiar sight. Since the pre-payment of postage by means of handstruck marks had been in existence in England since the late seventeenth century it is surprising that the principle of adhesive labels adopted by Customs and Excise was not applied to postage earlier than 1840.

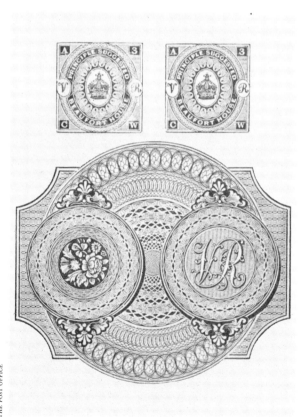

The Guildhall Medal of 1838, showing Wyon's profile of Queen Victoria. Portraits based on Wyon's medal were used on many early British Commonwealth issues.

Intricate engine-turning and corner lettering were anti-forgery devices advocated by Whiting and subsequently used in the Perkins Bacon British stamps.

Prepaid stamped wrappers and letter sheets, which Hill considered more important than labels, were also in existence before 1840. The Italian Kingdom of Sardinia introduced letter sheets with stamps in denominations of 15, 25 and 50 centesimi in 1819. These sheets, known as *Cavallini* (little horsemen) from the design on the stamps, indicated the prepayment of a government tax on correspondence rather than a postal charge, and controversy over their postal status has raged ever since. Similar sheets were proposed by Lieutenant Curry Gabriel Treffenberg of Sweden in 1823, emulating the *Carta Sigillata*, or stamped forms used in legal transactions. Stamped paper of this sort had been in use in Sweden since 1660, and though its use was not extended to letter postage as Treffenberg had envisaged, it was adopted in 1824 for newspaper stamps. Many countries, including Britain, levied a tax on newspapers and pamphlets in the eighteenth and early nineteenth centuries, primarily as a curb on the press. As a concession, however, newspapers could be transmitted free through the post, so these stamps may be regarded as quasi-postage stamps. Many other articles subject to tax had a stamp impressed directly onto them (almanacs, playing cards, hatbands, etc.) or onto their wrappers (dice, gloves), so the concept of a printed stamp was well established long before Rowland Hill's time.

The tax on legal documents in Britain was denoted by an elaborately embossed device, affixed to the vellum or parchment by means of a small lead staple. This, in turn, was secured at the back of the document by a small upright rectangle of paper bearing the royal monogram. It was this piece of backing paper, which had no fiscal or monetary validity in itself, that gave Rowland Hill the idea for the proposed adhesive postage stamps—and this format has been retained to this day in many parts of the world for the permanent series, or 'definitive stamps' as they are known to collectors.

The adhesive postage stamp was such a novel concept in 1839 that the British Treasury decided to hold a public competition for designs for the proposed stamps and stationery. Significantly the public concentrated (as did Hill himself) on the stationery and paid scant attention to the adhesive stamps. Of the 2,600 entries submitted, only 49 related to adhesive stamps. Of these, nineteen were short-listed for consideration and in the end four prizes of a hundred pounds each were awarded. Three of the winners, Charles Whiting, Henry Cole and Benjamin Cheverton, were closely associated with Hill in his campaign for postal reform. Cole (who was later knighted) is best remembered as the pioneer of the Christmas card, but Whiting alone subsequently made his mark as a designer and producer of postage stamps. Cheverton proposed that the penny stamps should be produced in a coil of 240 and sold for a pound. He suggested that the paper should bear a security watermark to defeat the forger and recommended that a portrait should be engraved on the stamp— 'the eye being educated to the perception of differences in the features of the face, the detection of any deviation in the forgery would be more easy'. Cole proposed a circular design, printed in sheets of 240. Whiting's bicoloured designs, with their intricate pattern of engine turning, were modelled on the medicine tax stamps then in use.

In the end it was Hill's own suggestion which was adopted and developed into the world's first adhesive stamps. He produced sketches of small upright rectangles, showing the profile of the young Queen Victoria, and submitted them (probably as early as July 1839) to the Anglo-American printing firm of Perkins, Bacon and Petch. This firm originated in the United States and specialized in printed calico. In 1819, however, Jacob Perkins invented a process for steel engraving and this, together with his improved rose engine which produced an intricate pattern of spiral lines, soon established him as a printer of banknotes and other security documents. The firm came to London and expanded in the 1820s and 1830s. Although their methods were copied by other printers, they were, in 1839, undoubtedly the leading exponents of security printing using the intaglio method. At Hill's behest they produced specimens for the proposed stamps, though they did not enter the Treasury competition. At the end of 1839 the task of designing and printing the stamps began. The principal motif chosen was the Queen's profile, based on the Guildhall Medal by William Wyon of 1838. Henry Corbould prepared sketches based on this profile and the work of engraving it was given to Charles Heath and his son Frederick. The finished dies and the plates from which the stamps were printed (in denominations of 1 and 2 pence) were prepared by Perkins, Bacon and Petch, security paper bearing a crown watermark was procured from Stacey Wise in March 1840 and the stamps were in production the following month. They were distributed to post offices and available to the public by 1 May, though they did not become postally valid till 6 May.

The team of men who conceived the first stamps had to consider five criteria. The stamps had to be easy to handle, they had to show their purpose clearly, they had to bear the mark of authority, they had to be easy to produce—yet difficult to forge.

Thus they were small in size, rectangular in shape, and printed in sheets which made accounting easy —a penny each, a row of twelve for a shilling, a whole sheet of 240 for a pound. The paper was gummed so that it was easy to lick the stamp and affix it to the letter. Until the advent of perforations a decade later, however, the stamps posed a problem. They had to be cut apart with scissors or a knife and the stout paper made it difficult to tear them off the sheet. The purpose of the stamps was indicated by the inscription POSTAGE ONE PENNY (or TWOPENCE) in white lettering across the top and bottom panels. Authority was conveyed by the dignified profile of the Queen, which also satisfied the fifth factor by making it difficult for the would-be forger. When the portrait had to be re-engraved in 1858 by William Humphrys the very slight differences were instantly detectable. The stamps were printed by the recess or intaglio method, which works on the principle of the ink lying in the grooves and recesses of the plate; when paper is applied to the plate under great pressure it is forced into these recesses where it picks up the ink. Stamps printed by this method have tell-tale ridges in the paper. The Perkins, Bacon and Petch method of production was not the fastest or the cheapest then available, but it was one which made forgery exceedingly difficult and that is why it was preferred. When it is remembered that, before the advent of the half-tone block, newspaper, magazine and book illustrations were all hand-engraved, it will be realized that there were plenty of skilled craftsmen in the mid-nineteenth century who could have produced a competent forgery. And though the sum involved seems small, it should be borne in mind that a penny in 1840 was the equivalent of about seventy-five new pence in earning and purchasing power. Apart from the royal profile and the intricate engine-turned background, the first postage stamps incorporated two letters in the lower corners to combat the forger and the faker. Each stamp in the sheet had a different combination of letters—AA, AB, AC and so on, from the top left-hand corner, down to TJ, TK and TL in the lower right-hand corner. Any forger would have to counterfeit a variety of letters to avoid suspicion. The corner letters appeared in the lower corners only at first. In 1864, however, they were added to the upper corners as well, but in reverse order. This was because unscrupulous individuals were cutting up the unobliterated portions of two stamps, matching them together and making an apparently unused stamp which could then be stuck on a letter and sent through the post. Oddly enough, with the exception of the stamps of the Australian state of Victoria in 1854, the device of corner lettering was confined to Great Britain, where it survived on stamps as late as 1887.

The resulting stamps, the Penny Black and Twopence Blue of 1840, possessed a classic beauty and simplicity that has seldom been equalled since. In one respect the producers of these stamps slipped up. The colours were too similar, and the black one made it difficult to detect the postmark. Accordingly, the colour of the penny stamp was changed in 1841 to red, while two horizontal white lines were added to the design of the twopenny so that it could be more readily distinguished from the penny one in poor light.

The Penny Black of 1840, the world's first adhesive postage stamp (19 × 22mm). The classic simplicity of a small upright rectangle depicting the ruler's profile has remained standard in the United Kingdom, with very few exceptions, and has also served as a model for many definitive issues throughout the world down to the present day. The Penny Black was designed by Henry Corbould, engraved by Charles and Frederick Heath and recess-printed by Perkins, Bacon and Petch. The design, in modified form, was utilized for all British 1 penny and 2 pence stamps for forty years.

1. Letterpress: Best results are obtained when a simple, functional design is used, with open lines and little shading. If too many lines converge the ink tends to clog in the recesses and the image becomes blurred.

2. Photogravure: This is a process that allows the designer wide scope, for it gives good, rich colours and interesting half-tone reproduction. Here the Queen's head has an embossed appearance.

3. Embossing: The design is in colourless relief on a flat colour background, and is usually printed and embossed in one operation.

4. Offset lithography: Stamp designs for this purpose can be very varied and can incorporate half-tone illustrations, but the overall appearance is of a rather flat colour, without the subtleties of photogravure.

5. Recess or Intaglio: Intaglio printing has a 'quality' appearance, for much finer engraving is possible than with letterpress. Stamps printed by this process are very difficult to forge.

6. Combined letterpress and lithography: The best qualities of each process are combined—the wide range of colours and tonal values add interest to the design while the inscription and denomination are clearly printed by letterpress.

1

2

3

4

5

6

2
The printing processes

ALTHOUGH there are many variations and combinations of printing processes involved in stamp production, they can be reduced to three basic methods, each with its own distinct characteristics and each producing a distinctive result. All other processes, including those used today, are merely refinements or developments of these basic methods.

The oldest method of printing· is that known variously as letterpress, typography, relief printing or surface printing. The image which is to be transferred to the paper is raised above the rest of the printing plate, ink is applied to the surface of the raised portions and the paper applied under pressure to the forme to be printed. The ink is transferred from the raised portion to the paper and the paper may be slightly indented at the points of pressure. The backs of stamps produced by this method usually show signs of ridging. Because the uninked parts of the plate have to be cut away, the resulting lines tend to be comparatively coarse. Thus this method is best suited to simple outlines, with shading in parallel lines. Cross-hatching becomes difficult since the interstices would soon become clogged with ink and the resultant image would be blurred. A notorious example of this fault is to be found in the British halfpenny and penny stamps of 1911 in which the engraver J. A. C. Harrison attempted to reproduce the fine lines in the King's beard and hair. The dies had to be re-engraved and the lines opened up in order to avoid this blurring effect.

The plates for letterpress or surface printing may be produced in several ways. The traditional method began with a die engraved in reverse on soft steel, chemically hardened, a soft steel roller rocked over it and the image transferred in positive to the roller. The roller would pick up several images in this way and then, in turn, be hardened. Subsequently it would be rocked over a polished steel plate and the images transferred in negative again to the plate the requisite number of times. The plate would then be hardened and made ready for printing. The mass production of the basic image could be effected in other ways. A variation of this was to engrave the die on a piece of hardwood, prepare a plaster matrix from it and make a cast-metal stereo or cliché from the matrix. The clichés could then be assembled in a forme and clamped to a bed. Errors of colour in the early issues of Spain, Sweden, the Cape of Good Hope and other countries arose from the insertion of a stereo of the wrong denomination in a forme of a certain value. A refinement of this process was electrotypography, patented in 1841 and used extensively for the stamps of the Italian states. The basic image was engraved in some soft material such as wax and then coated with blacklead. Copper was deposited on the surface of the wax by electrolysis. The copper shell could then be removed, backed with a soft alloy and faced with nickel or some other hard metal, again by electrolytic action. In general, electrotypes resulted in finer details than stereotypes. Although the original die would have to be engraved by hand, the process of reproducing the stereos or electros could be speeded up by making a composite stereo of six or ten subjects and then producing secondary multiples from the master set. Framework and lettering could also be produced mechanically and, of course, one profile engraving could be reproduced any number of times and rocked into the master dies of many stamps by means of transfer rollers. Thus De La Rue's chief portrait engraver, Joubert, engraved a series of eight profiles of Queen Victoria and these, with innumerable variations of frame, were used for the bulk of British and colonial stamps from 1855 until 1902.

Variations of typography (here used in its rather narrow philatelic sense and not in its true graphical meaning) include typesetting and typewriting, both of which have been used to produce stamps. Many stamps, invariably produced in emergencies or under primitive conditions, have been printed from movable type. The designs are usually quite functional, and consist merely of the lettering and numerals of value, enclosed in a simple frame or printers' rule. The stamps of the Indian states of Bamra, Soruth and Nawanagar include utilitarian examples composed entirely of lettering. Printers' ornament, however, was sometimes incorporated to give a more pleasing effect or to prevent forgery. The first stamps of Hawaii (1851) and the stamps of Reunion (1862), as well as several issues produced by the Confederacy during the American Civil War, show considerable ingenuity in the arrangement and repetition of ornament in typeset stamps. Many of the typeset stamps of British Guiana included a cut of a sailing ship, from the ornament used in newspaper shipping advertisements. The Indian state of Kishangarh, however, was one of the very few countries to use half-tone photographs as the subject of stamps. This type of illustration, used in books, magazines and newspapers, has too coarse a screen (the pattern of dots) to make it practicable for stamp printing. Typewriting has had a fairly limited application to stamps and is covered fully in the chapter on the Primitives. In addition, however, a few stamps have been reproduced from typewriting by a duplicating process. These include the telegraph stamps of Matabeleland and several of the emergency issues produced in Germany at the end of the Second World War.

Allied to typography, though distinct from it, is the process known as embossing. Though not used very often for adhesive stamps, it has been a firm favourite for postal stationery, and the majority of British stamped envelopes from 1841 to the present day have been printed by this method. Long before the advent of Uniform Penny Postage, however, embossing was used in the production of the tax stamps on legal documents, and this has continued from 1694 until today, at the Stamping Department of the Board of Inland Revenue, Somerset House in London. It is not surprising that this process should have been suggested in many of the designs submitted to the Treasury competition of 1839 and some of these, notably those entered by Charles Whiting and Robert Sievier, were extremely elegant in appearance. The individual method of production, however, made embossing too slow a process to be used extensively in the manufacture of adhesive stamps and consequently its use was confined to the 6 and 10 pence and 1 shilling stamps of Britain issued between 1847 and 1856. Embossing was relatively popular in Europe, and was used to print the stamps of many German states, Portugal, Switzerland and Sardinia. It is now used infrequently, West Germany being one of the very few countries which use embossing in adhesive stamps from time to time.

In embossing, the original die is engraved rather like a cameo, the details being achieved by variations in the depth of the sculpture. Intermediate dies

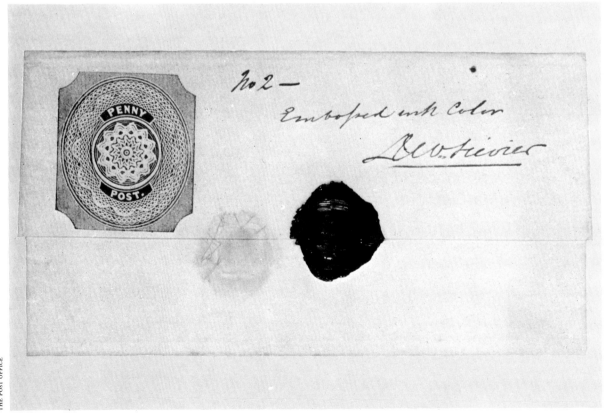

(known as punches) are struck from the master die and then working dies struck from the punches. The ink is spread on the flat portions of the die and the paper pressed onto the die with great force, either using a 'male' matrix in steel, or a pad of leather, to squeeze the paper into the recesses of the die. Simultaneously the paper takes up the ink from the unrecessed portions of the die. Thus the design is shown in colourless relief against a flat, coloured background. The British embossed stamps were struck singly and, as a result, the spacing of the stamps on the sheet was often irregular, sometimes overlapping. A modern variation of embossing is die stamping on metal foil, used extensively by the Walsall Lithographic Company in the manufacture of the free-form stamps of Tonga, Sierra Leone, Bhutan and several Arab sheikhdoms. The profile of Queen Elizabeth on many recent British commemoratives is inserted by embossing on metal foil applied from a metallic ribbon under pressure from a die, like the gilding on book bindings.

Diametrically opposed to typography or *relief* printing is intaglio or *recess* printing. In this case the ink lies in the recesses or grooves of the plate, whereas in typography the ink lies on the raised portions of the plate. In intaglio, ink is applied to the plate and carefully worked into the grooves. Then the plate is wiped clean. This, of course, does not remove the ink which lies in the recesses. The paper usually has to be dampened (though more modern machinery and paper do not require this) in order to make it more pliable, and then is laid on top of the plate and forced down under great pressure, so that the plate bites into the paper. The paper squeezed into the grooves picks up the ink; this is what gives stamps and banknotes printed in this fashion their characteristic ridged surface. This process is known as *intaglio, taille douce*, recess printing or direct plate printing. Philatelists often use the term 'line engraving', though strictly speaking it is the plate which is line-engraved and the stamps recess-printed from such plates. Intaglio was used for the low-value British stamps from 1840 to 1880 and for many colonial and foreign stamps printed by Perkins Bacon in the same period. It has also been used for the vast majority of United States and Canadian stamps up to the present time, and is also extensively used by Austria, France, Czechoslovakia, Switzerland and the Scandinavian countries. It is used nowadays for high-value stamps in many countries including Great Britain.

The advantages of intaglio are that much finer and more sensitive engraving is possible than with typography and this offers considerably more scope to the designer and engraver and a greater protection against forgery. In typography and lithography the layer of ink on the paper is of the same thickness over the whole image. In intaglio-printed and line-engraved stamps, all gradations from light to dark can be achieved in one line. Not only is the line narrower or wider in places, but the thickness of ink on the paper also varies. The back of the recess-printed image shows this variation in depth. Though largely superseded by photogravure on the grounds of expense and technical limitations, intaglio is still favoured on account of its quality appearance. Its technical limitations have largely been overcome and the Beaune-Lambert process has made it possible to print three colours by applying them to the printing plate with separate formes and rollers.

Photogravure, first used for stamps in 1914, is really only a variation of intaglio. Although an intaglio plate can be engraved by hand, the same results can be achieved by etching, a process by which lines are eaten out of a copper plate by acid. This method of reproducing drawings was discovered in the late Middle Ages and was used once or twice by Albrecht Dürer (who used iron plates), and extensively by Rembrandt and many other artists. The copper plate was first coated with wax and then the

The Treasury Competition essays submitted by the sculptor and engraver, Robert W. Sievier, advocated the use of embossing combined with intricate engine-turning as an economic method of defeating the forger. He suggested either the royal profile or the coat of arms as suitable motifs.

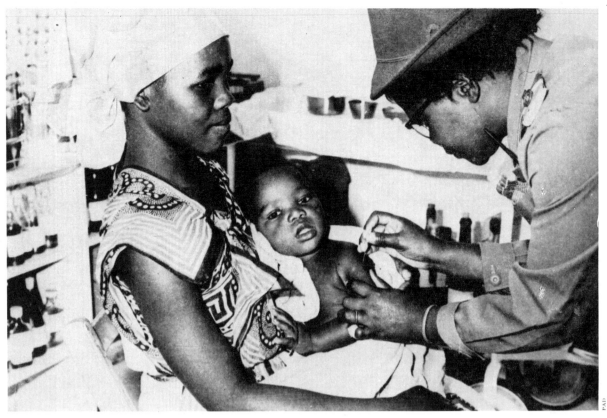

Some of the stages involved in designing a stamp: Swaziland's series marking the twenty-fifth anniversary of the World Health Organization, 1973, designed by PAD Studio and printed in multicolour offset lithography by Questa.

Above: A black and white photograph provides exact reference for the artist.

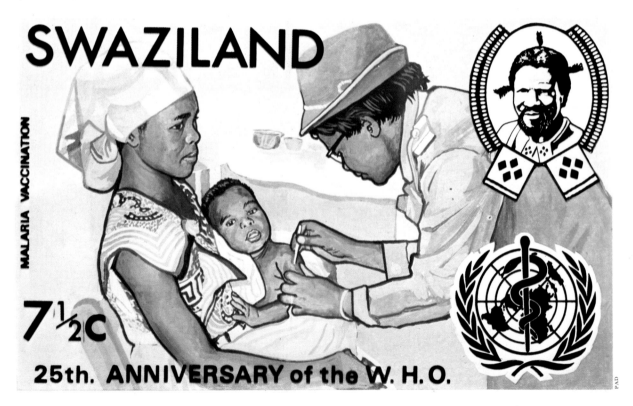

artist drew on the plate with a fine stylus which removed the wax. Acid was applied to the plate and bit into the copper where it was no longer protected by the acid-resistant wax coating. The plate was then carefully washed and the wax melted off. Impressions could then be taken from the plate by the method described above.

Photogravure, also known as heliogravure or roto-gravure, consists basically of reproducing the effects of an original on a copper cylinder by photographic means. A photographic print is made on special sensitized paper coated with gelatine, which is then affixed to a polished copper cylinder. Immersion in water removes the gelatinized paper leaving a deposit of gelatine in those areas hardened by exposure to light. The cylinder is then dipped in acid and the parts of the copper which are unprotected are eaten into. As in the preparation of half-tone plates for letterpress printing, a screen of fine squares is used during the photographic stage, this having the effect of breaking up the light and dark areas of the image into patterns of tiny dots, each of which becomes a minute pinprick on the surface of the copper. The ink lies in these tiny pits, just as it lies in the grooves of a line-engraved plate. The paper applied to the plate under great pressure picks up ink from these pits.

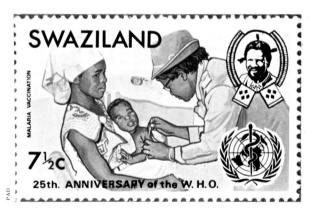

An example of the issued stamp (45 × 28mm).

Left: The colour artwork from which the stamp is produced is four times the size of the finished stamp. It is reduced photographically to its correct size so the artist does not have to work in miniature. Before this stage, a rough impression will have been submitted to the authorities for approval. The size of the rough varies, but designers usually choose a size that is large enough to look attractive but small enough to give an impression of the final effect.

Variations in light and density are achieved by the spacing of these dots; in the light areas of the design they are very sparse, while in the darkest portions they are so thickly clustered as to appear as a solid mass of colour.

The advent of a photographic process in stamp production revolutionized design in several respects. Previously the design had originated from a master die engraved by hand to the dimensions of the finished stamp. The artist who designed the stamp had to think at all times in terms of a small area. Thumbnail sketches had to be prepared in pen and ink, each stroke representing a line of the engraver's burin. The care and exactitude required by this method meant that the designer had to give great thought to the balance of the elements of the design, the style and arrangement of the lettering, and the incorporation of ornament. That so many stamp designs of the nineteenth century were excessively cluttered and their inscriptions inordinately repetitious is due to the fact that designers and engravers took a pride in their ability to cram as much detail as possible into the available space; but that does not detract from the amount of careful preparation involved in making dies for letterpress or intaglio production.

With photogravure, however, it was no longer necessary to 'think small'. The designer could prepare the original artwork in any size he wished and the result would then be reduced photographically to the required area. All that was required of the artist was that he keep the dimensions of his work in the same proportions as the finished product. Theoretically it is no longer necessary for a designer to produce any original artistry in his work. A stamp reproducing an Old Master painting, for example, may begin with a coloured photograph of the painting, and the inscriptions, value, coat of arms, royal profile or other symbol may merely be added by means of successive overlays stuck on top of the photograph. The complete 'scissors and paste' job is then re-photographed and reduced to stamp size. Lettering, portraits and emblems are taken from stock, lines of shading can be inserted mechanically or delicate toning added with an air brush. Inevitably the bulk of stamps produced in photogravure have a rather mechanical appearance and the genius of the individual artist often has little chance to express itself. From the original photograph of the design a multi-positive is made which can be built up, by the 'step and repeat' process, to make the required cylinder of a hundred or two hundred subjects, or whatever the final sheet size will be.

In addition to letterpress and intaglio, the third

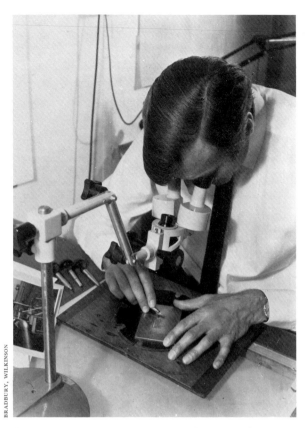

Great care is taken with the engraving of a steel die for intaglio printing, where the image area is slightly below the non-printing areas on the plate. The small recesses in the final printing plate hold the ink, which is drawn out by the paper. The different amounts of ink in the varying recesses determine the tonal colour values on the printed stamp.

After engraving, an impression of the master die is taken up onto a soft steel roll in a transfer press. The steel roll is then hardened so that the impression cannot be altered.

great traditional method of stamp printing was lithography. This process was developed by Alois Senefelder at the beginning of the nineteenth century and depended originally on the use of polished limestone from the Solenhofen quarries in Germany, but less cumbersome methods have since done away with the necessity for these stone slabs. The process depends primarily on the mutual antipathy of water and grease. A design is drawn on the polished stone surface with greasy ink. The stone is then wetted, but the water is repelled by the inked portions. Subsequently, greasy ink is applied to the plate by means of a roller. Naturally the wet parts of the plate repel the ink, but ink adheres to the areas previously inked. When a sheet of paper is laid on the plate, the wet ink is transferred to the paper. In this way the design is picked up by the paper. The multiplication of a design for the purposes of stamp production can be achieved in several ways. The basic design may be engraved and impressions made from the die, intaglio or letterpress. These impressions can then be built up on special paper, using special inks, and transferred to the stone in the way that children's transfers are treated. Distortion or creasing of these transfers during the stage of laying down the images on the plate may result in freaks such as the 1911 Newfoundland 1 cent stamp showing the spelling error NFWFOUNDLAND.

Zinc plates are now used instead of limestone, and images transferred to the plate by photographic means. This type of lithography is sometimes referred to as photozincography. Lithography was used extensively in stamp production in the nineteenth century but then went out of fashion. Its limitations were its flat appearance and unsatisfactory results unless the paper used was absolutely smooth. As it was a

The steel roll is now used as the master and the image is reproduced many times on a steel printing plate. This plate is then used to print all the sheets of stamps so that they will all be an exact replica of the master steel die.

When the ink on the printed sheets is thoroughly dry the perforation holes are added. The perforation holes are usually made by a machine which has a row of pins held at the top by a horizontal bar, under which the printed stamps are fed. A rotary method of perforating may also be used.

cheap process requiring little basic equipment it tended to be favoured by the more backward countries, to whom the quality of design mattered little anyway. Photolithography was used experimentally by Bavaria in 1913, but was rapidly superseded by photogravure.

With the advent of the offset method of lithography many of the former disadvantages of the process have been eliminated. In the offset method the image of the design is not transferred directly from the plate to the paper, but indirectly, through an intermediate rubber roller from which it is then offset onto the paper. This eliminates the problems arising from the unevenness of the paper and gives a more satisfactory result from the technical viewpoint, though lithography still lacks the depth and tonal qualities of photogravure. A variation of this is known as Delacryl, patented by De La Rue and aiming to combine the technical accuracy of modern offset lithography with the aesthetic qualities of photogravure. Like photogravure, lithography is capable of an almost infinite range of colour combinations, which is what makes it so popular with postal administrations nowadays. In recent years there have been many experiments in combining the different processes: recess or letterpress combined with photogravure or lithography. Britain's Inigo Jones series of 1973 was originally to have been printed entirely in recess, but as the result of a printer's dispute the work had to be done in letterpress and lithography— an unusual combination. The Parliamentary Conference stamps of September 1973 were produced by a combination of letterpress and intaglio. The effects of the more usual combinations of recess and lithography or photogravure are discussed more fully in chapter 12.

Cape of Good Hope, 4 pence 'Triangular', 1853 (base 44mm). The design, by Charles Bell the Surveyor General, shows the seated figure of Hope, and represents one of the rare incursions of Perkins Bacon into the allegorical field. The unusual format (retaining the height of the Penny Black but with a base of twice that dimension) is said to have been adopted to assist semi-literate sorting clerks in identifying local mail.

3
The old masters

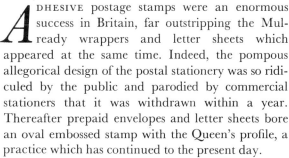

ADHESIVE postage stamps were an enormous success in Britain, far outstripping the Mulready wrappers and letter sheets which appeared at the same time. Indeed, the pompous allegorical design of the postal stationery was so ridiculed by the public and parodied by commercial stationers that it was withdrawn within a year. Thereafter prepaid envelopes and letter sheets bore an oval embossed stamp with the Queen's profile, a practice which has continued to the present day.

In other countries, however, the adhesive stamp was slow to catch on. In several countries, where postal reforms were effected, postal stationery in fact appeared before adhesives—in Finland, Poland, Russia and Württemberg. Sydney, New South Wales, actually had embossed wrappers and letter sheets in 1838—two years before the mother country—but adhesive stamps were not adopted until January 1850. In many instances it was left to private enterprise to produce stamps before the government postal administration followed suit. It should be remembered, however, that in many parts of the world communications (including the post) were still largely in private hands. Thus the first stamps to appear in the world outside Britain were produced by a private organization, the New York City Dispatch Post, in February 1842. This company, founded by an Englishman, Henry Windsor, and Alexander Greig, issued a 3 cent stamp, printed in black and bearing a portrait of George Washington, the first President of the United States. Although this was a private venture, it immediately established two traditions in the United States—the portrayal of Washington (who has graced every American definitive series ever since) and the avoidance of the portrait of a living American. Admittedly some of the other private delivery companies which flourished in the United States in the 1840s were not so punctilious in this respect (some even portrayed their promoters), but when the first Postmaster's issues appeared in 1845, and the general series appeared two years later, the penchant for past presidents was well established.

The City Dispatch Post stamp, and the 5 cent

stamp of the New York Postmaster in 1845, not only portrayed Washington, but were line-engraved by the firm of Rawdon, Wright, Hatch and Edson which subsequently adopted the neater-sounding name of the American Bank Note Company. This firm printed the first general issue of the United States in 1847 and many of the subsequent issues of that country in the nineteenth century, but it was in other parts of the American continent that they really made their mark. With the exception of the Basle 'Dove' of 1845 (printed by Krebs of Frankfurt-am-Main), all the stamps of the first decade were indigenous productions and bore, in their design, inherent national characteristics. But from 1850 on, many countries which lacked security printing facilities, or were under the political domination of a colonial power, had their stamps printed for them in other parts of the world. In this manner, a fair proportion of the classic issues (those from the period 1840 to 1870) were recess-printed either by the American Bank Note Company or by Perkins Bacon. Only the larger, independent countries, or those which were forced, through remoteness, to fall back on their own resources, printed stamps for themselves—and even they tended to be influenced by the leaders in this field and used similar designs.

By the end of 1849 postage stamps were being used in ten countries and already exhibited a wide variety of subjects and treatment. Of the ten countries using stamps, only four had followed Cheverton's principle regarding portraiture. Apart from Britain and the United States, Mauritius (1847) had issued stamps portraying Queen Victoria in a hideous parody of the contemporary British issues. These curious local makeshifts, and their even more hideous successors, are dealt with in greater detail in the next chapter. In July 1849 Belgium introduced stamps, and portrayed King Leopold I. Like the United States stamps, the Belgian issues preferred a full-face 'proper' portrait, rather than the stylized, medallic profile of Queen Victoria favoured by Britain and Mauritius. The Belgian design conveyed a more natural effect by dispensing with the usual framework, but this was short-lived and subsequent issues showed the King's portrait in an upright oval frame. France introduced stamps in January 1849, but instead of using the portrait of a living person, chose the profile of Ceres, goddess of agriculture, in a circular frame, with a rectangular border. The head of Ceres was taken from ancient Greek coins—a logical source of inspiration since coins and stamps were analogous in many respects. After the coup of 1852 which

W. MULREADY. R.A.   POSTAGE ONE PENNY.   JOHN THOMPSON

brought Louis Napoleon Bonaparte to power, his profile was substituted for that of Ceres—first as president and then as emperor (1853). In recognition of his victories in the campaign of 1859–60 a laurel wreath was added to his brow. After the collapse of the Second Empire in 1870, Ceres was brought out of the attic to replace the erstwhile Bonaparte. Thenceforward France was firmly wedded to the allegorical treatment of portraiture on definitive stamps and this has continued to the present time.

Three countries chose numeral designs, based on the figures of value. Brazil originally planned to use the youthful portrait of Dom Pedro II, but his ministers felt that it would be *lèse majesté* to deface the royal features with a postmark and therefore settled for curious circular designs (known to collectors as the 'Bull's Eyes') in which the numerals of value appeared on engine-turned backgrounds, bereft of any inscription. These stamps were superseded the following year by smaller designs with sloping numerals (*Inclinados*) and then, in 1850, by upright numerals on an engine-turned background (the 'Goat's Eyes'). When Dom Pedro eventually appeared on the stamps of Brazil (1866) he was a man of mature years. The Swiss canton of Zurich likewise used numeral design, for the 4 and 6 rappen stamps of

March 1843. In addition, these stamps had an overall pattern of red lines, as an underprint for security reasons. This is a fairly common feature in banknote and security printing but relatively rare in stamps. Outstanding examples included the early stamps of Denmark (1854–8), the high-value stamps of the North German Confederation and the German Empire (1869–72) and the French 50 franc stamp of 1936. In 1849 the first German stamp, Bavaria's celebrated *Schwarzer Einser* (the black one) appeared. In this case the numeral which was the dominant motif was given suitable ornamental treatment, though the higher denominations of the series, released later, had plain white numerals.

If we ignore the Bermuda postmasters' makeshifts (contrived by applying postmarks to pieces of paper and filling in the value in manuscript), the remaining countries provide us with the earliest examples of heraldry and pictorialism. The Swiss canton of Basle (1845) produced the first multicoloured stamp—black, red and blue—featuring the cantonal arms of a dove. Geneva (1843) also adopted the cantonal coat of arms for a curious bipartite stamp nicknamed 'the Double Geneva'. The stamp consisted, in effect, of two 5 centime stamps, each of which could be used on local mail, whereas the combined unit prepaid the

The pictorial design by William Mulready, RA, for envelopes and wrappers was intended to complement the adhesive stamps of 1840. Its pompous vignettes symbolizing the communication of Britannia with the far-flung Empire were derided by the public. Parodies of this design were immensely popular and hastened the withdrawal of the Mulready design after a few months.

An engraving by Armytage, after Mulready's painting 'The Sonnet'. Narrative paintings of this type, so popular in Victorian Britain, were Mulready's chief *forte*.

postage to other parts of Switzerland. As an incentive to the public, the combined unit was sold for 8 centimes—an example of discount postage which was not emulated anywhere else except Turkey (1905) and Belgium (1946). Along with portraiture and numerals, heraldry was to become the principal motif in nineteenth-century stamp design. Subsequently, heraldic elements were taken out of their armorial context and developed as the motif of stamps—and this led to a more pictorial approach. As early as 1847, however, a stamp had appeared with a miniature picture which was based neither on a portrait nor on a coat of arms. In April of that year a 5 cent stamp was issued for postage on mail carried by the coastal steamer *Lady McLeod*, plying between San Fernando and Port of Spain in Trinidad. The stamp was undenominated and its sole inscription consisted of the monogram L MCL. Above this appeared a handsome engraving of a ship, sails billowing, funnel belching smoke. This was the forerunner of a long line of semi-official or private postage stamps, issued by shipping companies which operated mail contracts in the nineteenth century and usually engraved with a suitably nautical motif. The 'Lady McLeod' stamp was not valid for postage in Trinidad itself, and four years elapsed before that island introduced its own stamps.

At mid-century the postage stamp surged ahead. Apart from the Swiss Confederation, which followed the lead of three cantons, the year 1850 witnessed stamps from ten countries or postal administrations. These confirmed the trends already established, with portraiture from Spain, Victoria and Prussia, heraldry from New South Wales, Switzerland, Austria, Lombardo-Venezia and Schleswig-Holstein. Hanover's 1 gutegroschen stamp which made its debut in December 1850 featured the numeral surmounted by the royal coat of arms. British Guiana's crude 'Cotton-reels' resembled the Bermuda postmasters' issues and are covered in the next chapter.

By the end of 1850, therefore, stamps were taking on a recognizable shape and there were certain clearly defined conventions which designers were beginning to follow. As yet, the appearance of the country's name on its stamps was purely optional, since the stamps were still largely confined to the country of origin. Britain, Brazil, Belgium and Spain, for instance, did not feel the need to indicate in the design the name of the country. With the 1870s and the greater volume of international mail, this was becoming necessary and one of the first regulations laid down by the Universal Postal Union in 1874 was that stamps had to bear the name of the country of origin—the United Kingdom alone being exempted from this, on account of her premier position as the

France originated the simple but effective device of the 'squared circle'—a medallic profile set in a rectangular frame, ornamented with Greek borders and giving the country name and denominations in horizontal panels. First used for the Ceres stamps of the Republic (1849) (1), it was adapted to the Napoleon III issues of the Second Empire (2). This well-tried motif was adapted for the first Greek stamps in 1861 (5), portraying Hermes, and was blatantly plagiarized by Matthew Pipet for the stamps of Corrientes (1856-80) (4). The family resemblance can also be seen in Norway's stamps of 1856 portraying Oscar I (3), and Romania's lithographed series depicting Carol I, in 1872 (6). (These stamps are enlarged to twice their original size.)

inventor of stamps. In 1850, however, there were more subtle ways of indicating the country of origin. The Australian state of Victoria, for example, chose a full-face portrait of Queen Victoria and felt that no other form of identification was necessary, while the neighbouring state of New South Wales presupposed an intimate knowledge of Latin in its citizens and rendered the name in the abbreviated form: NOV. CAMB. AUST. Switzerland, which had a language problem, had to be content with *Orts Post* or *Poste Locale*, but then settled merely for the word *Rayon* (region or radius) with Roman numerals to denote the relevant postal tariff according to the distance carried. The stamps of Schleswig-Holstein identified themselves by the letters s and H in the upper corners.

By the end of their second decade stamps had been introduced by eighty-five countries, and had penetrated to every part of the globe. A much clearer pattern was emerging, heraldry and the portraits of rulers enjoying almost equal popularity, with over thirty countries in each category. Allegorical subjects accounted for a large minority, typified by the graceful seated figure of Hope engraved on the Cape triangulars (1853) and the standardized designs of Britannia seated on sugar bags used by Barbados, Mauritius and Trinidad from 1851 onwards. Numerals

1. France, Ceres, 20c., 1849

2. France, Napoleon III, 1c., 1853

3. Norway, Oscar I, 3 skilling, 1856

4. Corrientes, 3c., 1873

5. Greece, 1 lepton, 1861

6. Romania, 10 bani, 1872

Brazil, 30 reis 'Goat's Eyes', 1845 (twice original size). The need to identify the country of origin did not arise until stamps became universal.

Schleswig-Holstein, 1 schilling, 1850 (twice original size). Designed and engraved by M. Claudius and typographed by H. W. Kobner & Lemkuhl of Altona. Here initials in the upper corners served to identify the issuing country. The coat of arms was embossed in colourless relief, anticipating many of the later German States' issues.

had declined in popularity, even in the German states where they had enjoyed their greatest vogue. Baden, Bavaria and Württemberg, the great southern states, abandoned numerals in favour of coats of arms, though Württemberg reverted to numeral designs from 1869 onwards. The converse, however, occurred in Scandinavia. Denmark and Sweden embraced heraldry or heraldic elements at first, while Norway chose a portrait of King Oscar or the lion rampant; but by the early 1870s all three northern countries had settled for numeral designs.

Although all the principal methods of printing—intaglio, embossing, lithography and surface printing (or letterpress)—were employed in stamp production during the classic period, it was the first of these that undoubtedly dominated the scene and, in the hands of the great masters, established the postage stamp as a minor art form. Although the designers and engravers employed by the American Bank Note Company and Perkins Bacon attained the peak of perfection in intaglio, their talents developed along somewhat different lines. With Perkins Bacon the emphasis was laid on portraiture which, since they had secured most of the British and colonial contracts, meant the portrait of Queen Victoria. Although the profile on the Penny Black had a serenity which has never been surpassed, the later profiles of the Queen produced by this firm were less happy. William Humphrys engraved the profile of Victoria used on the stamps of New South Wales (1854), South Australia (1855) and Ceylon (1857)—only marginally less satisfactory than the Heath original on the British stamps. A new profile by Henry Corbould was adopted in 1856 for the stamps of St. Helena and certain issues of Ceylon; the treatment of the Queen's hair was too heavy and the head was tilted too far forward. Then an almost moronic profile was engraved by C. H. Jeens from a Corbould drawing and used for Ceylon and the Ionian Islands (1859). Jeens partially redeemed himself in 1860 by engraving a neat profile of the Queen, closer to the Penny Black original, and this was used for South Australia (1860) and St. Lucia (1860), Antigua (1862), Turks Islands (1867) and, in a modified form, for St. Vincent (1881).

Perkins Bacon were more fortunate in their full-face portraiture and it is for this that they are justifiably ranked among the 'greats' of stamp production. About 1852, Humphrys made an engraving based on Edward Chalon's full-face portrait of the Queen in her coronation robes. The head alone from this engraving was subsequently used for the penny stamp of Nova Scotia (1853) and the head and shoulders for the first stamps of New Zealand (1855). A slightly larger version of the portrait was used by Perkins Bacon for the stamps of Van Diemens Land (Tasmania) in 1855–8 and a variation of it, engraved by Jeens, was the subject of the stamps of Natal (1859) and Grenada and the Bahamas (both 1861). Queensland used yet another version of the Chalon portrait in 1860.

Relatively few of Perkins Bacon's designs were allegorical, but those few were memorable. As early as 1847 the firm received their first colonial contract from the Crown Agents, to print stamps for Mauritius. A favourite motif in the firm's sample engravings was Britannia and this was adapted for a series of stamps which they printed for Mauritius but which that colony did not actually issue until 1854. From the outset Perkins Bacon were acutely aware of the costs involved, so they devised an ingenious system whereby the one master engraving of Britannia could serve for more than one territory. The design had a horizontal panel at the foot, in which the name of the colony could be inserted. No denomination was printed on these stamps, the values being denoted by using different colours. Stamps in this standard design were eventually produced for Trinidad (1851) and Barbados (1852) as well as Mauritius. The idea foundered because it was felt necessary to express a value on the stamps. Consequently, a later version of the Britannia designs was made for each colony, with the name in a curve across the top, and the value in the horizontal panel at the foot. Had Perkins Bacon's original idea been retained and expanded, the Britannia design might have become a standard colonial key type, anticipating the device pioneered by De La Rue in the late 1870s.

The seated figure of Hope on the Cape triangular stamps (incidentally the first to depart from the rectangular format) is judged to be Perkins Bacon's finest allegorical design. For the Canadian provinces of Nova Scotia, New Brunswick and Newfoundland, Perkins Bacon produced sets of stamps incorporating the heraldic flowers of the United Kingdom. The stamps of Nova Scotia and New Brunswick, with the flower motifs grouped round the imperial crown, were square in format, but orientated in such a way that the design was, in fact, diamond-shaped. The Newfoundland series followed in 1857, but the penny stamp, with a similar design, was orientated on an upright rectangular basis, while the other denominations were in new floral designs conforming to the orthodox format. The 3 pence stamp, however, retained the triangular shape introduced by the Cape of Good Hope, but the design was far less satisfactory.

Perkins Bacon did not attempt to produce pictorial stamps. The nearest they came to this was the design

Denmark, 4 rigsbank skilling, 1852 (twice original size).
Engraved by M. W. Ferslew and typographed by H. H. Thiele
of Copenhagen. Denmark's first stamps took the French concept of the 'squared circle' to its logical conclusions, adopting
an exactly square format as a frame for the laureated circular
motif enclosing the state emblems. The awkward problem of
the corners was solved by inserting tiny posthorns, while the
caduceus (winged staff of Hermes) was used to balance the
lettering of POST with the value in the horizontal panels. The
inscription KONGELIGT POST FRIMAERKE (Royal Post
Stamp) seems to overstate the obvious, while omitting the
name of the country; but it reflects the need to make the
purpose clear to the user, and at that time the country name
was superfluous. Note also the use of *burelage* (the fine
background network) as protection against forgery.

Bavaria, 1 kreuzer, 1870

Baden, 30 kreuzer, 1862

The stamps of the Thurn and Taxis postal administration were
typographed by C. Naumann of Frankfurt; initially black ink
on variously coloured papers was used but coloured ink on
white paper was adopted in 1859. The Thurn and Taxis
designs were among the most Baroque ever produced, with
florid ornament in the corners, excessive repetition of the value
and posthorns or shields to fill any unoccupied spaces. The
minuscule inscriptions at the sides refer to the German-
Austrian Postal Union and the name of the postal administration respectively. Baden's armorial series, designed by L. Kurz
and printed by W. Hasper of Karlsruhe also alluded to member-
ship of the *Postverein* in the inscription. Bavaria began with
a numeral design in 1849 and switched to an embossed arms
motif in 1867, and this, with variations, lasted until the First
World War. The Teutonic penchant for numerals, however, was
retained in this arms series, with the value expressed in each
corner. (These stamps are enlarged to twice their size.)

Thurn and Taxis, 1 kreuzer, 1866

The allegorical and portrait styles adopted by such firms as Perkins Bacon and the American Bank Note Company were originally evolved in other fields of security printing. Copperplate printing for cheques and banknotes was the precursor of the fine intaglio work used on the stamps of these 'Old Masters'.

Top: Confederate States of America, 20 dollars, 1862, recessprinted by Keatinge & Ball of Columbia, South Carolina, who also printed several stamps for the Confederacy.

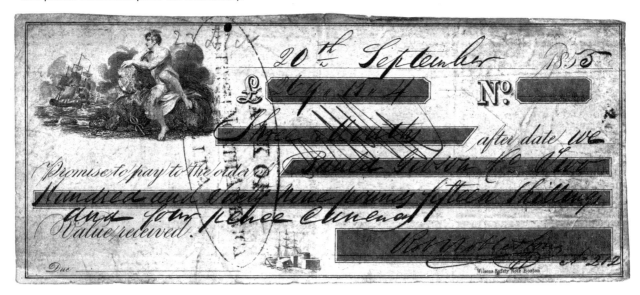

Cheque drawn on the Bank of British North America, 1853, recess-printed by Wilsons Safety Note Company, Boston. Note the vignette of Hermes and a sailing ship (symbolizing commerce and communications). Finely engraved vignettes of this type were familiar to the designers and engravers of the early stamps.

1. New South Wales, 3 pence, 1856

2. South Australia, 6 pence, 1868

3. Ionian Islands, undenominated ($\frac{1}{2}$ penny), 1859

4. Ceylon, 5 pence, 1857

5. New South Wales, 5 pence, 1863

6. St. Helena, 1 penny, 1887

7. Antigua, 1 penny, 1863

8. St. Vincent, 5 pence, 1893

9. Turks Islands, 1 penny, 1867

The early philately of the British Commonwealth was dominated by Perkins Bacon, widely acknowledged as the Old Masters of stamp production. In the majority of cases they preferred medallic profiles of Queen Victoria which, though interpreted by various engravers, were based on the original Wyon Guildhall Medal of 1838. Profiles by William Humphrys were used for the stamps of New South Wales, South Australia and probably also of Ceylon and St. Helena, while Charles Henry Jeens engraved the profiles used for the Ionian Islands, Antigua, St. Vincent and Turks Islands. The profile used for the New South Wales 3 pence stamp (1) was engraved by Frederick Heath of Penny Black fame. Many of these handsome designs, set against Perkins Bacon's inimitable engine-turning, were the work of E. H. Corbould. In the case of the New South Wales 5 pence (5) he adapted an original 'Garter' design by the Australian artist T. W. Levinge. Though they produced a quality product, Perkins Bacon were not above effecting economies wherever possible. Compare the background of the Ceylon stamp (4) with that of the Van Diemen's Land penny stamp (page 36) on which it was modified. In the smaller colonies a basic stamp might be printed in various colours and new values surcharged accordingly (6, 8) or a design might be printed without any value expressed (3) and the value denoted by the colour of the stamp.

Natal, 1 penny, 1859   Grenada, 1 penny, 1861

Van Diemen's Land
(Tasmania), 1 penny, 1864   New Zealand,
6 pence, 1862

Perkins Bacon adapted the full-face portrait of Queen Victoria in her coronation robes, by A. Edward Chalon, RA (above), for the stamps of several colonies. The portraits, showing varying amounts of neck and shoulders, were engraved by Jeens (Grenada and Natal) and Humphrys (left).

1. Mauritius,
undenominated, 1848   2. Barbados,
1 shilling, 1858

3. Trinidad,
1 penny, 1909   4. Trinidad, undenominated
(1 penny), 1859

Three colonies had a standardized allegorical design, depicting the seated figure of Britannia. Originally the value was determined by the colour but subsequently the designs were altered to include a value inscription. Trinidad continued to use the Britannia motif long after it was abandoned elsewhere; note the contrast in treatment between the Perkins Bacon 1 penny of 1859 (4) and the De La Rue typographed stamp of 1909 (3).

for Western Australia (1854) featuring a black swan, the colonial emblem, in a transverse format against the characteristic engine-turned background.

The stamps from the Perkins Bacon stable all had a recognizable family likeness, no matter what the country concerned or the subject of the design. Undoubtedly this was due to the intricate backgrounds against which the principal motifs were set, but this arose not so much out of aesthetic considerations as economy. The firm was not averse to using the same backgrounds for the stamps of different countries. Thus the background for the horizontal format stamps which they printed for the Pacific Steam Navigation Company was used for the vertical format stamps of Ceylon. In 1853 they printed the first stamps of Chile, with a sensitive profile of Christopher Columbus on a circular background, and two years later modified this background for the Chalon Heads of New Zealand. Similarities in background may be detected in the stamps of South Australia and New Zealand, and St. Vincent and Van Diemens Land. The design of the Turks Islands stamps was modified from that of Antigua, while the Chalon Head stamps of Natal, Grenada and the Bahamas, with upright ovals set in frames of vertical engine-turning, are first cousins.

In 1863 a dispute with the Crown Agents over security arrangements lost Perkins Bacon their colonial contracts. They were forced to hand over the plates to their up-and-coming rivals, De La Rue (see chapter 5)—to whom they also lost their lucrative British contracts in 1880. Thereafter Perkins Bacon were relegated to the second division of stamp producers, though they continued to print occasional fine stamps right up to the outbreak of the Second World War.

While the Canadian provinces looked to Perkins Bacon, Canada itself went to New York. The series of 1851 which the American Bank Note Company printed had all the hallmarks evident in the United States pair of 1847—full-face portraiture, open numerals, bold lettering, and a penchant for scrollwork in the surrounding frame. Though Rawdon, Wright, Hatch and Edson did the printing, the designs were produced locally, by Sir Sandford Fleming, the noted civil engineer. A lively portrait of the Queen, based loosely on the Chalon portrait, was used for the 12 pence, but Prince Albert, the Prince Consort, appeared on the 6 pence and Jacques Cartier, discoverer of Canada, on the 10 pence—this last one conforming to the American tradition of portraying dead heroes rather than living personali-

Nova Scotia, 3 pence, 1851
(22 × 22mm)

Western Australia, 1 penny, 1865-72
(23 × 20mm)

Apart from the Britannia design, relatively few of Perkins Bacon's stamps had symbolic motifs. Nova Scotia's diamond-shaped 3 pence stamp featured the heraldic flowers of the United Kingdom, with the Canadian mayflower at the foot. Western Australia's celebrated black swans provided material for the stamps from 1854.

ties. The 3 pence stamp, in a horizontal format, showed the beaver, Canada's national emblem, but in contrast with Perkins Bacon's treatment of the Western Australian emblem three years later, the beaver was depicted in its natural habitat. This modest pictorial was a hint of things to come. In 1860 the contract for the stamps of New Brunswick passed from Perkins Bacon to the American Bank Note Company and a handsome pictorial series resulted. The Postmaster-General, Charles Connell, upset the public by putting his own bearded portrait on the 5 cent stamp. He was forced to resign and the offending stamp was hastily withdrawn before the day of issue, to be replaced by one showing the Queen. The 1 cent stamp showed a wood-burning locomotive and the $12\frac{1}{2}$ cent depicted a steamship—highlighting important aspects of communications—while the 17 cent stamp portrayed the Prince of Wales (later King Edward VII) in Highland costume.

Newfoundland changed over to the American Bank Note Company six years later and extended the pictorial principle even further, with vignettes showing a codfish (2 cents), seal (5 cents) and an Atlantic brigantine (13 cents). An attractive portrait of the late Prince Consort on the 10 cent stamp showed how far the American firm had developed

Specimen five pound note of the Deal Bank, engraved by Robert Branston. It clearly shows the characteristics of intricate engine-turning and fine engraving which were later to become the hallmark of Perkins Bacon's stamps.

MARY EVANS

Chile, 10 centavos, 1853. The profile of Columbus is super-imposed on a background which Perkins Bacon subsequently adapted for the stamps of New Zealand.

1. United States, 2 cents, 1869

A less formal approach to portraiture was adopted by the American security printers. The American Bank Note Company adapted the Chalon portrait of Queen Victoria and the result is more sympathetic though the enlargement of the diadem is unfortunate. The scrollwork is in the best American tradition of that period. The National Bank Note Company's series of 1861 consolidated the American tradition for historic personalities. In most cases, however, the fine portraits were swamped by rococo scrollwork and needless repetition (in this case, of the value and the letters US).

2. Newfoundland, ½ cent, 1894

Nova Scotia, 8½ cents, 1860

3. New Brunswick, 1 cent, 1860

United States, 10 cents, 1861

The American printers were the first to inject pictorialism into stamp design. New Brunswick's series of 1860 by the American Bank Note Company included a wood-burning locomotive (3). The National Bank Note Company's issue for the United States (1869) featured the famous Pony Express (1), among other examples of communications. The British American Bank Note Company of Montreal produced numerous pictorial designs for Newfoundland, including the Landseer-type Dog of 1894 (2).

1. Mexico, 2 reales, 1864

2. Brazil, 80 reis, 1866

3. Chile, 5 centavos, 1877

4. El Salvador, ½ real, 1867

5. Costa Rica, 2 reales, 1863

6. Guatemala, 1 centavo, 1881

7. Nicaragua, 1 centavo, 1869

8. Peru, 10 centavos, 1866

in fifteen years. Two different portraits of the Queen were used, a somewhat stylized profile for the 12 cent and a full-face portrait on the 24 cent. Two years later, however, the kilted Prince of Wales was added to this portrait gallery and, at the same time, a 6 cent stamp showing the middle-aged Queen in widow's weeds. With this series Newfoundland established two traditions—of portraying a wide range of members of the royal family other than the reigning sovereign, and of using contemporary portraits of the monarch. While Britain and the majority of the colonies continued to use the profile of the Queen as she was at the time of her coronation, right down to the end of her reign, Newfoundland—and, to a lesser extent, Canada and the Australian states—chose more mature portraits.

In their own country, however, the American Bank Note Company were less fortunate. In 1851 the contract for printing American stamps passed to the Philadelphia firm of Toppan, Carpenter, Casilear and Co., who produced a set of historic personalities in a large format replete with curlicues, spirals and trellis work. Such extravagant embellishment was much loved in the latter half of the nineteenth century, and echoed the ornate fussiness in furniture and architecture throughout the same period. After the Civil War a new series was produced by the National Bank Note Company which partially broke away from the portraiture tradition by including pictorial designs, either illustrating communications or familiarizing the public with great events in American history. In the first group come the three stamps featuring a Pony Express rider (2 cents), a locomotive (3 cents) and steamship (12 cents). In the second come the two bicoloured stamps reproducing paintings by Vanderlyn and Trumbull of the landing of Columbus (15 cents) and the signing of the Declaration of Independence (24 cents). This was the first trace of that didactic element which dominated American stamps from the end of the nineteenth century onwards. The United States was the first country to appreciate the educational value of stamps, as a means of inculcating American ideas, traditions, history and culture in a population which contained a very high proportion of immigrants. The American Bank Note Company did not get back a United States printing contract until 1879, by which time unadulterated portraiture was the order of the day. Since then the United States has produced ten distinct definitive sets and in these at least 90 per cent of the designs have portrayed famous Americans. Since 1869, pictorial designs in the definitive range

In the latter half of the nineteenth century the stamps of many Latin American countries were recess-printed by the American Bank Note Company. Portraits or pictorialized versions of the national emblems were especially favoured. The treatment of 'speaking' portraits is best illustrated in the stamps of Mexico and Brazil (1, 2). Although the framework of the latter is relatively simple the designers could not resist the temptation to add a few touches of scrollwork in their usual fashion. The Chilean series of 1877 (3) shows an uneasy compromise between the numeral and portrait schools of thought with Columbus coming off second best. Mountainous scenery and native fauna adapted from heraldry enlivened the stamps of the Central American countries and Peru.

New Brunswick, 10 cents, 1860, recess-printed by the American Bank Note Company (twice original size). A relatively straightforward design, marred by excessive repetition of the value—in words, Roman and Arabic numerals. The American version of the Chalon portrait is more humanized than that engraved by Humphrys for Perkins Bacon (page 36).

have appeared only fleetingly, in 1922-38 and in 1954-65. The American Bank Note Company printed American stamps for little more than a decade, losing the contract in 1894 to the United States Bureau of Engraving and Printing which has produced them ever since.

The success of the American Bank Note Company lay in Latin America, and it is here that their finest and most characteristic work may be seen. Unlike Perkins Bacon, they did not specialize in any one medium, but demonstrated their versatility in portraiture, allegory and purely pictorial themes. In portraiture their most sensitive work included the Rivadavia and other historic portraits for Argentina (1867-74 and 1877-87), the Dom Pedro II issues of Brazil (1866-8 and 1878-9) and the Hidalgo series of Mexico (1864). Their profile of Columbus for Chile (1867) was inferior to that of Perkins Bacon, and the later Chilean stamps, with tiny portraits of Columbus balanced on large numerals of value, scarcely did this firm credit. Beautifully engraved coats of arms were produced for Bolivia (1868-90), Ecuador (1881) and Nicaragua (1882), but landscapes based on the national emblems were rendered in a more natural, pictorial form for Nicaragua (1862-71), Costa Rica (1863-75) and Salvador (1867). Likewise the quetzal,

national bird of Guatemala, appeared on attractive bicoloured stamps in a quasi-natural setting (perched on top of a Grecian column!), effecting a compromise between the heraldic and the purely pictorial. The American Bank Note Company had a penchant for fancy framework, but preferred a plain background to pictures or portraits, whereas Perkins Bacon kept ornament to a minimum and stuck rigidly to intricate (though muted) backgrounds. Perkins Bacon were sparing in their use of lettering and numerals and never believed in repeating themselves. The American Bank Note Company, on the other hand, believed that one could not have too much of a good thing. Numerals were frequently repeated in all four corners of a design, with the value expressed in words for good measure. The New Brunswick 10 cent stamp, for example, has the value expressed in words (CENTS appearing twice), in Roman numerals (four times) and Arabic numerals (twice). If Perkins Bacon were obsessed by fear of forgery, the American Bank Note Company seemed to be neurotic about leaving odd corners of the design unfilled by indications of the purpose or value of the stamp.

Although these two major companies dominated the philately of the classic period, they were by no means the only ones to produce fine intaglio engrav-

Chile, 1 centavo, 1900

British Guiana, 4 cents, 1860

ing. Excellent work in the same genre was produced for the United States by both the National and the Continental Bank Note companies, and these firms vied with the American Bank Note Company in winning occasional Latin American contracts. In Britain, De La Rue continued to print stamps from the Perkins Bacon plates but preferred their own typographical method (see chapter 5). Waterlow and Sons began printing stamps in 1852, but relied mainly on lithography, a process they used for the ship designs of British Guiana. Later they reverted to intaglio and produced an attractive Columbus series for Chile in 1900, a vast improvement over the American Bank Note issues for that country. Bradbury Wilkinson made their philatelic debut in 1869 with a stamp for the Indian state of Hyderabad. Nine years later they recess-printed sets for the Falkland Islands and Transvaal. They adopted a dignified profile, not unlike that already used by the British American Bank Note Company (an American Bank Note subsidiary) for Canada. The frames for these sets were more ornate than Perkins Bacon would have used, but less fussy and convoluted than the American style. De La Rue did not attempt to print intaglio stamps to their own design until 1879 when they produced a series for Labuan, the poor

1. Falkland Islands, 2½ pence, 1891

2. Nevis, 1 penny, 1861

Left:
Waterlow and Sons made their philatelic debut with the ship stamps of British Guiana, produced by lithography. Note the digits of the date in each corner, a peculiarity of nineteenth-century Guianese stamps. Subsequently Waterlow and Sons turned to recess-printing. Their series of 1900 for Chile, with the perennial Columbus motif, was a vast improvement over the American Bank Note version previously in use. (Both stamps are enlarged to twice their original size.)

Perkins Bacon's monopoly of intaglio-printing was assailed by other security printers. Bradbury Wilkinson began with sets for the Falkland Islands (1) and the Transvaal in 1879, using a profile similar to that current in Canada. Nissen and Parker were one of a number of small companies which made a brief incursion into this field with stamps for West Indian territories; note the frame of the Nevis stamp (2), 'borrowed' from the contemporary British stamps. With the Labuan series of 1879-92 (3) De La Rue made their first, if inauspicious, attempt at intaglio; the influence of their typographic process is clearly evident in this design.

3. Labuan, 2 cents, 1892

results showing that they were still thinking in terms of surface printing which was their forte. It was not until the 1890s that De La Rue, like Waterlow, woke up to the advantages of intaglio, especially for pictorial designs, and this aspect is discussed in chapter 6.

That such a high proportion of the classic stamps of the nineteenth century can be regarded as minor works of art is all the more remarkable when it is remembered that they were produced for a mundane purpose. Paradoxically the artistic qualities of postage stamps declined rapidly in the 1880s and 1890s, at a time when it was becoming fashionable to imbue the most utilitarian objects with artistic embellishments. The early designers of stamps were essentially practical men, concerned with the production of an article which would fulfill all its requirements. The size of stamps was kept small, colours were usually well chosen and striking, so that different values could readily be distinguished in the poor lighting of the period, motifs were relatively simple at first, though fear of forgery entailed great attention to the intricacies of backgrounds and spandrels, and at a time when output was relatively low considerable care was lavished on the printing itself. Thus it was a combination of these factors which, unconsciously, resulted in some of the finest stamps of all time.

It is virtually impossible to assess the relative merits of designs in the classic period, since designers were seldom identified. In the heyday of recess printing the engraver was the key figure in the design and production of stamps, and it can be assumed that such craftsmen as Charles Henry Jeens, Charles and Frederick Heath, William Humphrys, Henry and Edward Corbould and William Wyon were given a free hand in the interpretation of an idea rather than working to specific designs drawn up by other employees of their firms. It seems probable that the designs evolved by the American printers were even more of a team effort. The extravagant use of lettering and numerals, combined with florid embellishment, was the hallmark of the American productions, whereas straightforward portraiture on intricate backgrounds with relatively plain frames and sparse use of lettering was the Perkins Bacon hallmark. Both Bradbury Wilkinson and Waterlow revealed, in their use of elaborate frames and mannered lettering, an approach to security printing which was influenced by their experience with banknotes.

The postage stamp in the classic period had no pretensions to art, and was therefore untrammelled by the prevailing traditions of romanticism and classicism which were to be found in other branches of the applied and decorative arts in the same period. So far as the stamp may be said to have been influenced by existing art forms, coins were predominant. This affinity is strongly evident in the many fine profiles and allegorical compositions found on stamps, particularly in Europe and the British Commonwealth, from 1840 to about 1890.

Sculpted profiles from coins and medals lent themselves admirably to the two-dimensional field of postage stamps, once designers and engravers had mastered the technique of adapting the tones of light and shade to the lines of intaglio or letterpress. Significantly the coin profile treatment of portraiture has only been entirely successful since the development of photogravure in the 1930s.
Left to right: coin profiles of Queen Victoria, King Edward VII and Napoleon III of France. Jean-Jacques Barré engraved Napoleon's profile for both coins and stamps.

Right: A page of trade advertisements showing various miniature motifs and trade-marks. Line blocks of this type, combining pictorial and allegorical elements, were used extensively in bill-heads, letter-heads and newspaper advertising in the mid-nineteenth century. The locally-printed stamps of British Guiana (1856) and many of the U.S. local stamps (1842-63) used such miniature vignettes while their influence on contemporary stamp design was widespread.

WIREWORK.

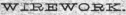

TRADE MARK

THOS. P. HAWKINS & SON,
27 DALE END, BIRMINGHAM.

WIRE GAUZE,

RIDDLES,
SIEVES,
SCREENS,
STEEL WIRE,
MOULDERS'
BRUSHES,

AND
ALL KINDS
OF
WIRE WORK.

A. A. JAMES,
45/7 Paradise Street, West Bromwich,
Near BIRMINGHAM.

MISCELLANEOUS

Articles divers.

Verschiedenartiges.

Artículos diversos.

ASBESTOS.
"PHOENIX."

THE BRITISH ASBESTOS COMPANY LONDON

TRADE MARK

**BRITISH
ASBESTOS
COMPANY,**
10 Duke Street,
Aldgate,
LONDON, E.C.

Cast Steel Hair and Knitting Pins.

BOARD SCHOOLS. TRADE MARK.

CHARLES COURT,
PLYMOUTH WORKS
REDDITCH.

Bread and Butter Knives.

STAFF OF LIFE

TRADE MARK.

F. W. DOVER
Sycamore Tree Works,
114 Rockingham Street,
SHEFFIELD.

Bread and Butter Platters.

TRADE MARK

SYCAMORE TREE.

F. W. DOVER,
Sycamore Tree Works,
114 Rockingham Street,
SHEFFIELD.

DESIGNS FOR:

FRET WORK.

TRADE MARK

H. ZILLES,
9 South Street, Finsbury, London, E.C.

Grindstones and Rubstones.

"BILSTON"

JOB HICKMAN,
BILSTON, STAFFORDSHIRE,
ENGLAND.

Sponge Cloths, Dusters, &c.

TRADE MARK

RIGBY, WAINWRIGHT & CO.,
NEPTUNE WORKS, MANCHESTER.

M⸱B⸱R

McLEAN BROS. & RIGG
LIMITED,
MELBOURNE,
SYDNEY,
ADELAIDE,
NEW YORK,
LONDON.

SKATES.

C & C

GO AHEAD.

COLQUHOUN & CADMAN,
SHEFFIELD.

Piercing Saws,
Needle Files,
Watch
Main Springs,
Clock Springs,

J. N. EBERLE & CO.,
AUGSBURG, BAVARIA.

PATENT WIRE GAUZE EYE PROTECTORS.

H. V. & S.
TRADE MARK
PROTECTORS.

HENRY VALE & SONS,
219 & 220 SUMMER LANE,
BIRMINGHAM.

SAIL CANVAS

"Eureka Brand"

F. REDDAWAY & CO.,
CHELTENHAM STREET,
PENDLETON, MANCHESTER.

YOUNG'S
PATENT CORD
HOLDFAST.

W. BURLEY
PROPRIETOR,
LONDON WALL, LONDON.

CRICKET BALLS.

ECLIPSE
TRADE MARK
REGISTERED

W. & A. BATES,
St. Mary's Mills, Leicester,

G. & H. H

Tiles,
Earthenware,
Porcelain,
Bricks.

GODWIN & HEWITT,
Victoria Tile Works,
HEREFORD.

TRADE MARK REGISTERED.

Weights, Heater Irons, Sad Irons, and Charcoal Box Irons.

HAWKINS & CO.,
CROWN FOUNDRY,
DUDLEY PORT, TIPTON.

REGISTERED

CROWN

Weights, Heater Irons, Sad Irons, and Charcoal Box Irons.

HAWKINS & CO.,
CROWN FOUNDRY,
DUDLEY PORT, TIPTON.

TRADE & H Cⁱᵒ ORION 18 89 MARK.

Weights, Heater Irons, Sad Irons, and Charcoal Box Irons.

HAWKINS & CO.,
CROWN FOUNDRY,
DUDLEY PORT, TIPTON.

Lock-Stitch Sewing Machines.

"HANDY"

HARPUR & MASON,
LOZELLS ROAD,
BIRMINGHAM.

THE

"LAST DROP"
LEMON SQUEEZER.

J. T. COLLIER & CO.
17 Devonshire Street,
LONDON, E.C.

"THE DEVONSHIRE"
BURGLAR ALARM.

J. T. COLLIER & CO.
17 Devonshire Street,
LONDON, E.C.

BUNTING & FLAGS

TRADE S MARK

ARTHUR SMART & CO. MANCHESTER.

TENNIS NETS

CRICKET NETS &c

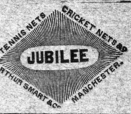

JUBILEE

ARTHUR SMART & CO. MANCHESTER.

COTTON WASTE WICKS &c

ARTHUR SMART & CO. MANCHESTER

TRADE MARK

H. DUNKLEY & SONS
FOR CLIPPER COMPO
HARNESS COMPOSITION

**HARNESS
COMPOSI-
TION.**

H. DUNKLEY & SON,
67-71 Clifton St., London, E.C.

ON METAL UMBRELLA RIBS.

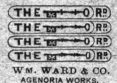

THE [ ] OR Rᴰ
THE [ ] OR Rᴰ
THE [ ] OR Rᴰ
THE [ ] OR Rᴰ

WM. WARD & CO.
AGENORIA WORKS,
BERNARD LANE, SHEFFIELD.

Flower-baskets, Cages, Garden Chairs, &c

Telegraphic Address,
"WEAVING,
BIRMINGHAM."

TRADE MARK.

GEO. BAKER,
Cecil Street,
Birmingham.

Painters' Burning-off Stoves and Sundries; Patent Cinder Sifter, and Safety Fire Shovel.

SWINGLER & AIREY,
Stanhope St., BIRMINGHAM.

The Indian princely states produced some of the most primitive designs ever used for postage stamps. The earlier issues were not trammelled unduly by European criteria in design or format, as the oval and circular stamps of Bhor and Jammu show. Jhalawar's stamps reveal the Indian penchant for mythological motifs (4). Kishengarh's early stamps, however, attempted to ape the heraldic motifs found on contemporary European stamps, but with ludicrous results (3).

1. Bhor, ½ anna, 1879 (31 × 24mm)

4. Jhalawar, ¼ anna, 1887 (21 × 25mm)

3. Kishengarh, ¼ anna, 1899 (27 × 27mm)

4
The primitives

2. Jammu and Kashmir,
1 anna, 1866 (23 × 23mm)

5. Jammu and Kashmir,
¼ anna, 1883 (20 × 25mm)

W HILE postage stamps were still in their infancy the urge to imitate the mother country was felt in several remote British colonies. Their governors had seen the new-fangled stamps, either while they were home on furlough, or on letters forwarded from Britain to their far-flung outposts of empire. In 1847 Mauritius decided to introduce adhesive stamps and, as has already been mentioned, the contract was placed, through the Crown Agents in London, with Perkins Bacon. The Governor of the island, Sir William Gomm—or rather his good lady—could not wait till supplies of the Britannias arrived. In September, Lady Gomm held a ball at Government House and she felt that it would be nice to have some stamps with which to frank the invitations. Accordingly, James Barnard, a half-blind watchmaker of Port Louis, was given the task of producing some stamps for the colony. He was given specimens of the contemporary British 1 penny red and 2 pence blue stamps as a guide and told to get on with it. He engraved one of each denomination on a small copper plate, more or less following the design of the British stamps, but inserting the words POST OFFICE and MAURITIUS in the vertical side panels. Approximately five hundred of each value were printed, laboriously by hand, and barely a dozen of each is now in existence. The following year he produced similar stamps, inscribed POST PAID in the left-hand panel. Barnard's engravings, being on soft copper plates, rapidly wore out and had to be extensively reworked—a fact which did nothing to improve their appearance. In 1858 his plates were entirely re-engraved by Sherwin, to the detriment of Queen Victoria's features. But this was as nothing compared with the lamentable performance of M. Lapirot whose 2 pence stamps have been aptly nicknamed 'Dog's Heads'. In 1859 M. Dardenne had a go, using the lithographic process to produce a slightly more faithful profile of the Queen. Surprisingly, the Britannia stamps were available all this time, but the Mauritians seem to have preferred their own home products.

The Australian states began issuing stamps in 1850 and produced designs of a higher quality and some

1. Victoria, 3 pence, 1850   2. New South Wales, 2 pence, 1853

3. Sind, ½ anna, 1852   4. India, 1 anna, 1854

Long distances and uncertain communications forced the more remote British territories on to their own resources. The Australian states produced some of the most original and competent designs among the so-called 'primitives'. India's first stamps, the Sind 'Dawks' (3), were novel in both shape (circular) and production (albino embossing). General issues of British India, released two years later, were lithographed in a more orthodox design, based on contemporary British stamps (4).

Right:
Latin America, despite the facilities and salesmanship of the American Bank Note Company and its rivals, often relied on local resources—with indifferent results. Ecuador's 1872 series (2), produced by Rivadeneira of Quito, is strongly reminiscent of the French 'squared circle' concept, complete with Greek border. Bolivia's 'Condor' design of 1866 (5) was surprisingly vigorous and effective, but it was technically unsatisfactory and the plates had to be extensively retouched due to wear and tear.

originality. Manning's laureated profile of Queen Victoria, used on the stamps of New South Wales in 1851, was actually imitated by Perkins Bacon for a consignment of stamps five years later. Similarly, Thomas Ham's full-length portrait of Queen Victoria on her throne, used by Victoria in 1852, was subsequently adapted by Perkins Bacon in 1856. The most original of the Australian designs, however, was that popularly known as the Sydney View. Robert Clayton adapted the frame of the British stamps on a larger format, with the Great Seal of the colony substituted for Victoria's profile. The vignette itself is interesting, showing the female allegory of the colony welcoming ashore a group of convicts. Numerous versions of this design were used for successive printings of 1, 2 and 3 pence stamps, but all have a naïve charm, particularly in the rendering of the central motif.

Strictly speaking, India's first stamps were the curious circular, embossed stamps issued in Sind under the authority of Sir Henry Bartle Frere in 1852, but a general issue, for use throughout British India, did not appear until two years later. The problem facing the Indian postal authorities was one of quantity and Perkins Bacon's intaglio method was too slow and expensive for the requirements of India.

The task of designing and producing stamps was therefore given to the Surveyor-General's Office in Calcutta, which had extensive experience in the use of lithography for maps. Stamps in denominations of ½ and 1 anna were designed along the same lines as the contemporary British stamps, with INDIA at the top instead of POSTAGE. Solid backgrounds replaced the intricate engine turning, and the vertical spandrels were considerably simplified in accordance with the limitations of lithography. The profiles of Queen Victoria on the ½ and 1 anna were relatively crude, but that on the 2 anna (produced at the Calcutta Mint) was much more ambitious and was a pretty good imitation of the British original.

Primitives of a sort were produced in three British colonies during temporary shortages of stamps printed in England. In each case local printers were given the task of producing stamps as close to the original as they could manage. Trinidad (1852) and Western Australia (1857) relied on lithography to manufacture passable imitations of the Britannia and Black Swan designs. The Cape of Good Hope (1861) produced the 'Woodblocks', so named on account of their rather crude appearance. They were, in fact, engraved on steel, from which stereos were made for printing by the letterpress method—diametrically opposed to

1. Buenos Aires, 1 peso, 1859

2. Ecuador, ½ real, 1872

3. Mexico, 12 centavos, 1868

4. Granadine Confederation, 2½c., 1859

5. Bolivia, 5 centavos, 1866

intaglio and, even in the hands of experts such as De La Rue, never so sensitive as intaglio. These local versions of the Old Masters, however, cannot be regarded as original contributions to the art of stamp design, since they differed from the originals only as a result of the shortcomings of the craftsmen or the processes employed.

For the true primitives we must look at those territories, like Mauritius, which decided to adopt stamps and had to rely on local resources. British Guiana began issuing stamps in 1850 and relied primarily on letterpress printing. The first stamps were circular in design, with typeset inscriptions enclosed in a circular band of printer's rule—hence the nickname 'Cottonreels'. The inscription was kept simple—just BRITISH GUIANA round the rim and the value, in upper and lower case lettering, in the centre. Subsequently, British Guiana commissioned lithographed stamps from Waterlow and Sons, showing the seal of the colony, a sailing ship. But at various times, when shipments of stamps from London were delayed, local expedients were pressed into service. It was one such emergency, in 1856, that resulted in the production of what is now the world's most valuable stamp—the 1 cent black on magenta. Baum and Dallas, proprietors of the *Royal Gazette* in George-

town, produced typeset stamps composed of movable type, printer's rule and the sailing ship ornament which they used in shipping notices. More elaborate typeset provisionals, along similar lines, appeared in 1862 and 1882.

Typesetting was also the method adopted by the Hawaiian Islands when their first stamps appeared in 1851. The so-called Missionaries, which now rank among the world's greatest rarities, made ingenious use of printer's ornaments to provide the framework for the numerals of value. As primitives go, these stamps exhibit a surprisingly high standard of workmanship. Typesetting was also used for the series of stamps intended for interisland postage (1859-65), although stamps destined for overseas mail were printed in the United States, by Holland of Boston or by the National Bank Note Company, and portrayed past and present rulers.

The French colonies were relatively slow to adopt adhesive stamps. Before the general series, produced in France, appeared in 1859, only two territories had issued stamps on their own initiative. Significantly the first of these was Reunion, an island in the Indian Ocean which may have been emulating the example of neighbouring Mauritius. Reunion's 15 and 30 centime stamps of 1852 were typeset in black on

Spain, 4 cuartos, 1855

Philippines, 5 cuartos, 1859-61

Spain's 1855 series portraying Isabella II, shows strong French influence in the design engraved by José Perez Varela. Early Filipino stamps were closely modelled on the contemporary issues of the mother country, with the same beaded medallion, bell-shaped ornament in the vertical panels and circular motif in the corners. Of all the 'primitives' these most faithfully reproduced their metropolitan counterparts.

Right:
1. Jaipur, 8 annas, 1905
2. Jaipur, $\frac{1}{2}$ anna, 1911
3. Nepal, 8 pies, 1907
4. Turkey, 20 paras, 1863
5. Tibet, $\frac{1}{3}$ trangka, 1912
6. Afghanistan, 5 afghanis, 1971

The stamps of Jaipur afford a striking contrast between the finely delineated intaglio of Perkins Bacon (1) and the crude letterpress treatment of the same subject at the local jail press (2). Primitive stamp designs lingered on in the Himalayan countries long after they had disappeared elsewhere—the Turkish 'primitive' pioneer design of 1863 (4) is nearly fifty years earlier than the other stamps shown here. Perkins Bacon produced occasional sets for Himalayan and Indian states (including this Siva Mahadeva design for Nepal (3)) but many were 'home-made'. Tibet's rubber-necked lion (5) has an affinity to the crude hammered coinage of medieval Europe, while Afghanistan's issue for Pakhtunistan Day 1971 (6) typifies the homespun quality of this country's stamps.

bluish paper. The inscriptions, 'Ile de la Reunion—Timb. Poste', were inserted, almost unobtrusively, in tiny lettering at the top and foot of the design, while the central portion of the stamps was taken up with elaborate patterns composed of printer's ornament. New Caledonia's solitary 10 centime stamp of 1860 was obviously modelled on the contemporary French stamps portraying Napoleon III. It was lithographed at Nouméa, the design being drawn on a stone by Sergeant Triquerat using the point of a pin. Attempts at individualism on the part of the French colonies were quickly stifled by the metropolitan authorities who insisted that the general colonial series was good enough.

Among the Primitives we may include certain issues of Latin America, before the angels of the American Bank Note Company descended on that continent. Three states of what is now Argentina issued stamps before the federal series appeared in 1858 and of these the stamps of Buenos Aires and Corrientes deserve mention. Pablo Cataldi produced a design for the former, showing a steamboat. The *Barquitos* of 1858 represent a praiseworthy attempt at pictorialism which Argentina itself did not repeat for more than thirty years. The stamps of Corrientes were engraved by Matthew Pipet who must have

had a specimen of a French republican stamp before him; the result was an execrable piece of plagiarism which did not flatter the original. Astonishingly, Corrientes was permitted to issue these horrors as late as 1880 before the federal government suppressed them.

Colombia, Uruguay, Mexico, Peru and Venezuela all produced their own stamps from the outset and these are reasonably well designed and executed. With the exception of Mexico, which preferred the portrait of Hidalgo, these countries favoured coats of arms or emblems, such as the sun. Bolivia adopted stamps in 1866 and, pending the arrival of armorial stamps from New York two years later, produced stamps locally bearing a crude picture of a condor, the national bird. For technical reasons the Bolivian 'Condors' produced an almost infinite range of varieties, to delight the heart of the specialist collector. For all its primitive appearance the design is vigorous and well balanced, and set in a workmanlike frame devoid of the fussiness which distinguished the later issues.

The most primitive stamps, in paper, design and manufacture, came from the countries of Asia. The Philippines, like India, managed to produce passable imitations of the stamps then current in the mother

country, before Madrid took over the design and production of Filipino stamps entirely. But the independent, and semi-independent, countries of Asia did not fall back on European originals. For that reason their stamps often exhibit features quite foreign to Occidental concepts of design. They saw no good reason, for example, for sticking rigidly to rectangular shapes and consequently a high proportion of the polygonal or circular designs ever produced came from countries such as Afghanistan and the Indian native states. Afghanistan adopted stamps about 1869 and from then until 1892 all stamps were circular. The central motif was a lion's head, and the inscriptions were grouped around it, sometimes with projecting ornaments like the rays of the sun. Jammu and Kashmir also produced circular stamps with the numeral contained in a sunburst in the centre, and inscriptions, in Arabic and Hindi, round the edge. Later issues of Kashmir were rectangular, though the inscriptions continued to appear in circular form as before. A disconcerting feature of the stamps of these countries was the tendency to release all stamps of a particular printing in the same colour, or conversely to print a denomination in several different colours. Afghanistan attained the ultimate in this respect, in 1876 producing the set of five

denominations each in five different colours—a different colour for each of the five provinces.

Religious considerations had a marked effect on Oriental stamp design. In the Moslem countries the representation of human or animal figures was taboo, so stamps were designed in which the lettering or numerals constituted the only motif. Fortunately Arabic script has decorative qualities which the Roman alphabet lacks and this led to some very pleasing results, such as the first issue of Hyderabad (1869). Turkey got round the ban on figurative work by using the crescent-and-star motif or the Sultan's *toughra* (sign manual) as a decorative feature on stamps well into the twentieth century. The Hindu states of India were no less inhibited than their Moslem counterparts in this respect, but this encouraged the use of emblems, such as daggers, or figures from Hindu mythology—such as the *apsara* or dancing nymph found on the stamps of Jhalawar. A few states, such as Kishangarh and Wadhwan, emulated the West by producing stamps with crudely drawn coats of arms. By the turn of the century, however, the ban on figures was being relaxed and eventually portraits of rulers, albeit in a crude form, began to appear. In 1904 Perkins Bacon produced a beautiful series for Jaipur, showing the chariot of the sun-god,

Surya. Seven years later a poor travesty of this design was produced at the Jail Press in Jaipur and showed, in its execution, how woefully an excellent theme could deteriorate in incompetent hands.

Many of the Indian princely states continued to issue their own stamps until 1949-50 when they were finally suppressed by the government of the Indian republic, and though many of them had attained a level of sophistication or relied on European printers, others continued to produce stamps of an other-worldly character. The states on the borders of India likewise continued with a primitive local tradition, until comparatively recently. Afghanistan's stamps were crudely designed, replete with spelling errors, and indifferently produced. Tibet used the same basic design from 1912 until 1950 when the Chinese Communists began to exert their influence over that country. The stamps were typographed in Lhasa on hand-made paper. Like the early Afghan stamps, the central motif consisted of a lion, with the inscriptions arranged around it. A later design, used from 1933 until the Chinese finally suppressed the Tibetan postal service in the early 1960s, had the lion enclosed in a square frame. The lion in this case was reduced to a few virtually meaningless lines and squiggles, reminiscent of the crude hammered coinage of mediaeval Europe. Nepal's first stamps, introduced in 1881, were in the same tradition of the Indian states, with symbols of state surrounded by inscriptions. These crude stamps survived until 1918, although Perkins Bacon recess-printed a series in 1907 showing Siva Mahadeva among the Himalayas. The same firm continued to print similar stamps for Nepal until it went out of business shortly before the Second World War, and thereafter stamps in this design were typographed at Katmandu from locally made plates.

Even highly civilized countries can be reduced to primitive stamps in times of crisis. The earliest example of this was afforded by the Confederate States of America. Pending the introduction of a general series for the Confederacy, the Union issues were invalidated in the South and local postmasters were left to their own devices. As a result, 5 or 10 cent stamps were produced in many parts of the Confederacy, ranging from the reasonably competent stamps of Memphis, typographed from an original woodcut, or the lithographed stamps of Mobile and Livingston, to the typeset issues of Fredericksburg and Danville (Virginia). Bridgeville (Alabama), Independence (Texas), Lenoir (North Carolina), New Smyrna (Florida) and other towns had hand-struck stamps, while Greenwood (Virginia) and Jetersville (Virginia) had stamps handwritten by

Confederate States of America, Memphis, 2 cents, 1861. Typographed from a woodcut, this stamp, issued in the interim period between the withdrawal of the Federal issues and the appearance of the Confederate general series, is comparatively ambitious in design and execution.

Two curiosities from the Aegean area: the stamps of the Russian post office in Rethymno were produced by a combination of typography and rubber-stamps; the abortive issue of Mount Athos was produced photographically—a method which would have been impractical for large quantities.

Rethymno, 1 metalik, 1899

Mount Athos, 1 shilling, 1916

Uganda,
5 cowries, 1896

Long Island, 2 pence, 1916

Albania, 5 grush, 1913

The earliest stamps of Uganda were produced entirely by typewriting and were relatively simple in design. Long Island's typewritten stamps were much more ambitious. The Albanian series was produced by a combination of three rubber stamps, with the value typewritten in the centre.

their respective postmasters. Postal services were organized in Polish prison camps during the Second World War and stamps were printed from woodcuts on any paper available—including the margins of newspapers, cigarette cartons and even toilet paper. The quality of the engravings and designs, however, was often surprisingly high. After the collapse of Nazi Germany, shortages of stamps in many areas, especially those overrun by the Red Army, led to a spate of local issues which reflected the exigencies of the period in their crude designs and primitive execution.

The typewriter has played an important part in the production of stamps under primitive conditions. The first stamps of Uganda, in 1895-6, were printed entirely by typewriter, by a missionary, the Reverend Ernest Miller. The first issue consisted merely of the letters UG (for Uganda Government) with the value expressed in cowrie shells. The second issue was more ambitious (as Mr. Miller's proficiency as a typist improved) and consisted of the royal monogram VR flanking the digits 96 to indicate the year, with the value in the centre and the name of the territory at the foot. The paper was foolscap sermon paper and adhesive was supplied from the resin of a local tree. Turkish fiscal stamps were overprinted in type-

writing by British forces in the First World War and an issue produced entirely by typewriting made for Long Island in the Gulf of Smyrna. Some of the earliest stamps of Albania, which won its independence of Turkey in 1912, were produced by a combination of rubber stamps, with the value inserted by typewriting.

The siege of Mafeking in 1899-1900 resulted in some unusual stamps, portraying the garrison commander, Colonel Robert Baden-Powell, and Cadet Sergeant-Major Warner Goodyear. The stamps were competently designed, but they were then photographed and reproduced by the ferroprussiate process used in the manufacture of draughtsman's plans. Photography was also used in 1916 for a projected series of stamps, produced aboard H.M.S. *Ark Royal* and intended for use in the Allied occupation of Mount Athos. The stamps, featuring the Byzantine double eagle, were inscribed in English, Russian and Greek, with values expressed in pence or shillings, lepta or drachmae and kopeks or roubles—three languages, three alphabets and three currencies forming a unique combination. The Russians, however, vetoed the invasion so the stamps were never used at Mount Athos, although a few of them passed through the British field post office at Salonika by favour.

Hejaz, 2 piastres, 1917 (38 × 22mm). The first stamps of the Hejaz (later Saudi Arabia) were designed by Agami Effendi Ali, though Lawrence of Arabia is said to have had a hand in the matter. This would explain the fact that the intricate Islamic motifs which fill every part of the surface were taken from mosques in Egypt or historic manuscripts of the Koran, for Lawrence was a classical Islamic scholar and a great admirer of Islamic art. The stamps were typographed at the office of the Survey of Egypt, Cairo in 1916-17.

5
Nineteenth-century typography

*T*O THE STAMP COLLECTOR the term 'typography' has a specialized meaning, denoting all those methods of production in which ink is transferred from the raised portions of a die or plate onto the surface of the paper. Thus it embraces typeset or letterpress printing, printing from plates engraved in relief or *en epargne*, or from stereotyped or electrotyped clichés. The terms 'surface printing', 'relief' or 'letterpress' are also encountered, but are all used to denote the same thing. Printing by these methods has several advantages over printing by the intaglio, recess or *taille douce* method; typography is relatively simple, cheaper and faster. The disadvantages are that it is more easy to forge and also gives less satisfactory results. The advantages far outweighed the disadvantages in the nineteenth century and consequently the majority of postage stamps in the second half of the century were manufactured by this process.

Typeset stamps, the most basic form of typographed issues, have already been mentioned. Apart from a certain amount of ingenuity in the arrangement of lettering and ornament, these stamps have little to commend them from the design viewpoint. They were invariably produced in exceptional circumstances and aesthetic qualities were seldom considered. In the other categories of typographed stamps, however, the quality of the design was something that mattered to a greater or lesser degree. Stereotypes, made from woodcuts, had been in use since the mid-eighteenth century for book illustration and it is not surprising therefore that this method should have been applied to stamps early on. In 1841, moreover, the process known as electrotyping was invented and this soon gained in popularity for the manufacture of high-quality printing plates from an original wood or metal die. While Britain, Brazil, Belgium and the United States chose intaglio, the other countries issuing stamps in the first decade chose typography. Although Prussia began with a recess-printed series (1850), it quickly changed to typography and eventually the Prussian State Printing Works in Berlin became one of the world's leading printers using this method, combined in many cases with embossing.

All the stamps of Bamra were produced by typesetting in black on various coloured papers. This $\frac{1}{4}$ anna belongs to the series of 1890. It is surprising that this relatively satisfactory method of production was not used more often.

Below, left:
Prussia's series portraying King William (1), designed by F. E. Eichens and engraved by H. G. Schilling, was initially recess-printed, but a later woodcut version of the design, with the king's profile reduced in size, was typographed. Typography was favoured by Spain and Sicily from the outset (2, 3). The derivation of these profile designs, with their panelled lettering, from the earliest British stamps can clearly be seen. The ornamental postmarks were designed to prevent the obliteration of the features of Queen Isabella and King Ferdinand.

Typographed heraldic designs reveal the homogeneity of stamp design and production in the Low Countries in the 1860s and 70s.

1. Prussia, 2 silbergroschen, 1850

2. Spain, 6 cuartos, 1850

3. Sicily, 2 grana, 1859

Belgium, 2 centimes, 1866

Netherlands, 1 cent, 1869

Luxembourg, 1 centime, 1870

Spain's first stamps (1850) were lithographed, but the following year typography was adopted and remained the sole method employed until the 1920s. It was the method used by the majority of the Italian and German states, by France, Austria, Russia, Portugal and the Scandinavian countries. In areas where recess printing was initially favoured it gradually extended its sway. Belgium succumbed in 1865, Holland in 1869 and Britain partially in 1855 and totally by 1880. By the end of the century recess printing survived in the United States, Switzerland, Germany (high values only) and a handful of British colonies. After 1920, typography began to decline in face of the challenge offered by photogravure and the partial recovery of intaglio. Today typography survives only in France, where it continues to be employed in the production of low-value definitives, and in a handful of British colonies where it is used for postage due labels.

Of the old German states, four—Bergedorf, Bremen, Lübeck and Oldenburg—used lithography for sets of stamps featuring the state coats of arms. Lübeck (1863) and Oldenburg (1862) subsequently placed contracts with the Prussians for typographed stamps with the state emblems embossed in colourless relief. Of the remaining states, Baden, Bavaria, Brunswick, Hanover, Saxony and Württemberg produced their own stamps so long as they continued to have separate issues, but the other states eventually relied on the Prussian state printers. There is a certain element of uniformity in the designs of these German stamps. The early issues tend to emphasize the numerals of value and were often printed in black on paper of various colours; the later issues featured, in the main, state emblems embossed albino with coloured typographed frames. Even in those stamps printed outside Berlin the Prussian influence was strong. Thus the Bavarian series of 1867, the Brunswick set of 1865 and the Saxon series of 1863, produced locally, featured embossed arms, and this idiom even extended to Austria-Hungary between 1863 and 1867. After the unification of Germany in 1871, this tradition was still maintained for many years. The imperial eagle was embossed in colourless relief with a typographed surround on stamps as late as 1889, while Bavaria (which continued to have its own stamps until 1920) used this combination of typography and embossing for an armorial series until the eve of the First World War.

This was not entirely a German idiosyncrasy. When Russia introduced adhesive stamps in 1858 they were typographed at the State Printing Works in St. Petersburg in attractive two-colour combinations, with the imperial double eagle embossed albino

in the centre. Poland adopted the same practice for its solitary stamp, the 10 kopek of 1860-67, but dispensed with the embossing, leaving the eagle completely flat, and the same applied to those stamps of the grand duchy of Finland which followed the Russian designs. The embossed and typographed stamps of Tsarist Russia survived the Romanovs and were not completely phased out until after the Revolution and subsequent civil war. Portugal was a great exponent of combined embossing and typography but substituted medallic profiles of her rulers for the coat of arms or national emblem. Embossed stamps with unusual frame shapes were current from 1853 until 1866 and embossed profiles were retained in stamps of a more conventional shape from then until 1880.

The Italian states presented an even greater degree of uniformity in production and design. With the exception of the related kingdoms of Naples and Sicily which used intaglio, and Sardinia which employed a combination of lithographed frames and embossed profiles, the remaining five states typographed their stamps. Of these, Modena, Romagna and Tuscany used electrotypes in the manufacture of the plates. Modena, Naples, Parma, the Papal States and Tuscany used the state coat of arms as the subject of their stamps. Romagna's series was the most functional in appearance, with the value in a rectangular frame surrounded on all four sides by letterpress inscriptions. Newspaper stamps issued by Parma, Tuscany and Sardinia also had a numeral motif—the latter embossed in place of the King's head. The only portraits were those of King Victor Emmanuel II on the stamps of Sardinia and King Ferdinand II on those of Sicily. So that the regal features should not be sullied by a postmark, the Sicilians devised an ornamental cancellation, designed to frame the King's profile without actually striking it. A similar device was used by Spain to avoid obliterating the homely features of Queen Isabella. The Sardinian stamps, from 1851 to 1862, were consistent in design—the King's profile in an oval, with inscriptions in four rectangular panels—but the methods of production varied. The series of 1851 was entirely lithographed, the set of 1853 was embossed on coloured paper, the issue of 1854 had lithographed frames and embossed albino profiles, while the series of 1855-63 had typographed frames and embossed profiles in the German style. The last issue of Sardinia was subsequently used throughout the newly formed Kingdom of Italy. The political upheavals which led to the unification of Italy are reflected in the stamps of the various states; the Cross of Savoy was substituted for the state coat of arms in

1. Saxony, 3 neugroschen, 1863   2. Lübeck, 2 schilling, 1859   3. Lübeck, ½ schilling, 1863   4. Brunswick, 3 groschen, 1865

5. Hamburg, 2½ schilling, 1864   6. Oldenburg, 1 groschen, 1861   7. Mecklenburg-Strelitz, 2 silbergroschen, 1864   8. Heligoland, ¼ schilling, 1873

The stamps issued by many of the smaller German states before 1867 provide a contrast in styles and treatment. Most of them preferred coats of arms or heraldic elements, but printing methods varied from state to state.

Saxony's political independence of Prussia is reflected in the stamps typographed by Giesecke and Devrient of Leipzig but the combination of coloured typography and embossed arms is Prussian in concept (1). (Giesecke and Devrient later produced stamps for Thailand and several Latin American countries and, as Deutsche Wertpapierdrückerei, continue to operate as the security printer for the German Democratic Republic to this day.) Lübeck (2, 3) originally favoured lithography, using the local printer Rathgens, but later chose typography by the Prussian state printer. Brunswick also relied on lithography, by J. H. Meyer, but the influence of the Prussian State Printing Works is clearly marked (4). Hamburg preferred local lithography by C. Adler for its lengthy series featuring the triple-tower emblem (5), while Oldenburg (6) switched from local lithography to Prussian typography. Mecklenburg-Strelitz (7) also relied on Berlin, though the dies were engraved by the local firm of Otto in Gustrow. Heligoland, though a British colony, had its stamps produced by the Prussian State Printing Works, hence the peculiarly Teutonic blend of coloured typography and the Queen's profile in colourless embossing (8).

Below:

The combination of embossing and typography was not confined to the German states. The Tsarist arms design of Russia, with minor variations, was used from 1858 until after the Revolution (1). Sardinia made prolific use of embossing, either in combination with typography, or albino on various coloured papers (2). All Portuguese stamps from 1853 to 1880 were typographed with the ruler's profile in colourless embossing; the initials at the base of the profile of King Luiz are those of the engraver, Charles Wiener (3). De La Rue, the British masters of typography, resorted to embossing in the case of only one colony, Gambia, whose 'Cameos' were produced between 1869 and 1898 (4).

3. Portugal, 5 reis, 1867

1. Russia, 35 kopeks, 1902   2. Sardinia, 40 centesimi, 1860   4. Gambia, ½ penny, 1880

Papal States,
40 centesimi, 1868

Parma, 15 centesimi, 1859

1. Serbia, 40 paras, 1869

Modena,
40 centesimi, 1859

Romagna, 8 bajocchi, 1859

2. Serbia, 2 paras, 1873

3. Great Britain,
4 pence, 1865

Coats of arms or heraldic elements formed the basis of the designs for the stamps of most Italian states, though Romagna was content with a more utilitarian design, placing emphasis on the value.

A somewhat later variant of the 'squared circle' technique was evolved by De La Rue who made their philatelic debut with the British 4 pence in 1855 (3). In the original version the corners were unadorned, but from 1862 onwards check letters were featured prominently in the corners. Inscriptions were placed in scrolls above and below the central medallion, instead of appearing in the side panels as in the original 'squared circle' designs. The comparatively intricate shading behind the profile and the engraving of the spandrels emulated the fine engine-turning used by Perkins Bacon. De La Rue's design obviously served as the model for C. V. Radonicky's series portraying Prince Milan of Serbia. The original version (1869) had a solid background to the profile (1), but this was omitted in the 1873 version (2). Note the repetition of the numerals, in the corners, a substitute for the De La Rue check letters.

the issues of Modena, Naples and Tuscany.

In design, the Italian stamps conformed largely to the convention of having the inscriptions grouped in narrow panels on all four sides of the frame. Parma diverged somewhat from this, in the series of 1857-9, with floral sprays at the sides of the coat of arms, but inscriptions continued to appear at the top and foot of the design as before. The Papal States alone showed any spark of originality, in using a different shape for every stamp of the series—ovals, rectangles, octagons and irregular forms lending variety to the principal motif of the papal tiara and crossed keys.

In Britain typography made its debut in 1855

when De La Rue produced their first 4 pence stamps. Whenever new denominations were required, the contracts went to this company, until they were producing the entire range from 3 pence to 5 pounds. Perkins Bacon, however, retained the contracts to print the four lowest denominations, from the $\frac{1}{2}$ to the 2 pence, and as these were the stamps in greatest demand the size of their operation was considerable. In 1879 they lost the remaining contracts to De La Rue and from 1880 until 1910 this company printed all British postage stamps by their typographical method. There is a depressing sameness about the De La Rue Victorian stamps of the United Kingdom.

1. Great Britain, 6 pence, 1883
2. Great Britain, 10 pence, 1887
3. Great Britain, 4 pence, 1902

De La Rue enjoyed a monopoly of British stamp contracts from 1880 to 1910 and inevitably typography was used exclusively in this period, ranging from the insipid designs of the 1883 series (1) to the rather gaudy confections of the 'Jubilee' set and their Edwardian successors (2, 3).

Right:
1. Bermuda, ½ penny, 1880
2. Barbados, 4 pence, 1882
3. St. Christopher, 1 penny, 1870
4. Tobago, 1 shilling, 1880

At first De La Rue exercised some ingenuity in devising different frames for the profiles of Queen Victoria engraved by Joubert, but as more and more colonial contracts came their way the designs gradually became standardized. Note the similarities in the designs used for St. Christopher and Tobago (3, 4) which anticipated the colonial key plates.

Like Trinidad and Western Australia, the Cape of Good Hope had De La Rue-typographed counterparts to the Perkins Bacon intaglio designs. The Cape 'Rectangulars' of 1864 were designed by Charles Bell, who had also been responsible for the Triangulars. (The stamp is twice its original size.)

Jean Ferdinand Joubert de la Ferté, their chief engraver, produced a sensitive profile of Queen Victoria which was quite a creditable imitation of the Heath profile on the penny stamps, but this profile was then used, with unswerving loyalty, on all British stamps up to 1902. This girlish profile still graced the stamps when the Queen was in her eighties; even the coinage profile had been brought up to date on several occasions, but with stamps, it seems, these things did not matter. In 1883 came the abomination known as the Unified series—an attempt to produce stamps which would serve the dual purpose of postage and revenue. All British stamps since then have had this dual function, but only the series of 1883 made it painfully obvious, by having the low values printed in dull violet and the higher values in dull green—special fugitive colours which would run if anyone attempted to wash the signature off a stamp affixed to a legal document. The dull colours were matched by atrocious designs in which the Queen's profile was forced to take second place to the numerals of value.

This dreadful series was mercifully short-lived, being replaced in 1887, the year of the Golden Jubilee, by a garish set of bicoloured stamps, in which the diminutive profiles were lost in a welter

of framework and superfluous ornament. The Jubilee designs were largely retained for the series of 1902, with the profile of King Edward VII substituted—so the late Victorians and Edwardians were seemingly well satisfied with these gaudy confections. Significantly a new design of a more restrained and dignified quality was used for the monochrome $\frac{1}{2}$, 1, $2\frac{1}{2}$ and 6 pence stamps and the trend towards less flamboyance was continued by reprinting the 4 pence stamp in one instead of two colours (1909) and introducing a 7 pence stamp the following year in sober grey-black.

Reference has already been made to the transfer of the Perkins Bacon plates and dies to De La Rue in 1862. De La Rue printed stamps for some thirteen colonies from these plates, some as late as 1883, but the majority in the 1860s. De La Rue had little enthusiasm for intaglio and as soon as was decently possible they superseded the handsome line-engraved issues of their predecessors with their own typographed stamps. Where a territory had a special preference for one sort of design, this preference was respected. The elegant Cape triangulars were replaced by rectangular stamps showing a De La Rue version of the seated Hope, and a flock of black swans in assorted frames replaced the Perkins Bacon

bird on the stamps of Western Australia. Everywhere else, however, the stolid profile of Queen Victoria, à la Joubert, became the order of the day. At first some attempt was made to vary the frames of the stamps in each series, but when ingenuity was strained to the utmost, standard frames and uniform designs —at least in each set—were introduced.

Even this began to tax the inventiveness of De La Rue's staff artists, as more and more colonial contracts fell into their lap and the graceful intaglio stamps were withdrawn from use. In 1870 the West Indian island of St. Christopher adopted adhesive stamps and De La Rue produced a series which was a foretaste of things to come. Although the stamps were printed in monochrome, the value tablets at the foot were quite clearly inserted into the plate at a later stage of the production, a precursor of the time, four years later, when stamps were produced for Lagos, with the values inscribed in a second colour. Moreover, the design of the Lagos series was suspiciously similar to that for St. Christopher. A third series in much the same design appeared in 1879 in Tobago. In the same year, De La Rue secured the contract to print stamps for Nevis and produced the first of the famous key-plate designs. The Queen's profile was enclosed in an octagon, with the name of the colony in a panel at the top and the value in a panel at the foot. This standard design, with only the names of the colonies and the values altered, was also used for stamps released by Antigua the same year and, in slightly modified forms, for stamps of Natal and Grenada in 1883. The Virgin Islands (1880), Cyprus and Turks Islands (1881) and St. Lucia (1882) also used this key-plate design.

The need for unified postage and revenue stamps in the colonies, as in the mother country, produced similar results—the reduction of the royal profile to make way for more prominent numerals of value and longer inscriptions. Ceylon (1886), Jamaica (1889) and Tasmania (1892) received stamps which attempted to vary these elements, in the same way as the British series of 1887, but by 1889 a standard design, known as Key Plate II, had been evolved. First used for the high-value stamps of the Gold Coast it gradually spread to many other colonies and remained in use, with suitable changes of portraiture, as late as 1956 (Leeward Islands). The design was fairly basic: a tiny profile of the monarch, the name of the territory at the top, a hexagonal tablet containing the numerals of value at the foot, and narrow vertical side panels inscribed POSTAGE & REVENUE. A variation of this, known as Key Plate III, had a circular medallion for the profile, and the word POSTAGE in each side panel. This design was adopted

Sierra Leone, 1½ pence, 1903

Straits Settlements,
10 cents, 1912

Mauritius, 5 cents, 1938

Leeward Islands,
$1.20, 1954

Tasmania, 2½ pence, 1892

Jamaica, 1 penny, 1889

The majority of the De La Rue colonial stamps at the turn of the century conformed to this key type which survived, with changes of portraiture, as late as 1956.

Value tablets in contrasting colours enabled De La Rue to produce an entire series of stamps for a colony, using a standard frame and portrait design. This device, used for the stamps of Tasmania and Jamaica, was an important step towards the evolution of the colonial key types.

These two key types evolved by De La Rue were comparatively little used. The second was adopted in cases where a revenue duty did not have to be indicated in the inscription.

Nevis, 6 pence, 1888

Seychelles, 3 cents, 1893

Right: Colonial key types were adopted by the other major European powers for their overseas territories. France began with the colonial general series designed by Alphée Dubois (2) but by 1892 had given each territory an individual series known as the Tablet design, in which the only difference was the territory's name printed in a second colour (3). Portugal began with the Crown design (1) and followed this with frequent changes of royal portraiture before settling for the Ceres design (5) after Portugal became a republic. Spain's colonial key types were classified according to the portrait used: Alfonso XII, Baby and Curly Head (7, 8, 9). Later issues used more mature portraits of Alfonso XIII (10). The German colonies depicted the imperial yacht *Hohenzollern* (6). Belgium and the Netherlands (11, 12) did not use key types as such, though little attempt was made to vary the designs used in their respective colonies.

1. Portuguese India, 4½ reis, 1882
2. French Colonies, 2 centimes, 1881
3. Nossi Bé, 4 centimes, 1892
4. Horta, 80 reis, 1897
5. Portuguese Guinea, 2 centavos, 1914
6. Marshall Islands, 5 pfennigs, 1900
7. Cuba, 25 centimos, 1878
8. Cuba, 1 milesima, 1896
9. Puerto Rico, 3 centavos, 1898
10. Gulf of Guinea, 40 centimos, 1914
11. Congo, 5 centimes, 1886
12. Netherlands Indies, 20 cents, 1915

1. Luxembourg, 2 centimes, 1895

2. Tunisia, 1 centime, 1888

3. Ethiopia, 8 guerches, 1894

4. Serbia, 25 paras, 1903

Luxembourg, 1 centime, 1882

France, 10 centimes, 1877

There is an uncanny similarity between France's Peace and Commerce design (J. A. Sage) and Luxembourg's Agriculture and Trade design (A. Marc) both engraved by Mouchon.

Left:
The French influence on stamp design and production was prodigious in the late nineteenth century, mainly due to Eugène Mouchon who was equally versatile as an engraver and designer. Note the 'family likeness' in his design portraying Grand Duke Adolf (1), Ethiopia's Lion series (3) and Serbia's ill-fated Alexander series (4). (The features of the murdered king were obliterated by the national coat of arms prior to issue.) Tunisia's arms series (2) was designed by Casse, but here again the formula devised by Mouchon (who engraved the series) is evident.

Right:
Dominical labels were introduced by Belgium in 1893, for use by those not wanting mail to be delivered on Sundays. The 1893-1900 series was designed by Mouchon and H. Hendrickx, and engraved by Doms. Note the tiny symbolic elements filling the corners and the cog-wheel and anchor almost hidden at the foot of the design. The same penchant for cluttering the frame with minuscule symbolism is evident in the Antwerp Fair stamps by Hendrickx, engraved by V. Lemaire.

Far right:
Persia flirted with various European printers at the turn of the century. Mouchon's hand can be discerned in the Nasr-ed-Din series of 1899, typographed by the French Government Printing Works. Enschede of Haarlem, who typographed the Lion series of 1903, went to great lengths to concoct a suitably Asiatic design replete with Persian decoration.

Belgium, 10 centimes, 1893

Belgium, 10 centimes, 1894

Persia, 1 kran, 1899

Persia, 5 chahi, 1903

in 1890 for stamps of the Seychelles which did not require a unified series. It never occurred to the authorities or De La Rue to amend the existing key plate, substituting 'POSTAGE' for '& REVENUE' in the right-hand panel; but this was fortunate since Key Plate III was in many respects a better design than Key Plate II.

The key plates at first appeared in all the colours of the rainbow, but eventually further economies were effected by printing the basic stamps in dull fugitive shades of green or purple, with only the name and value printed in contrasting colours. These dreary stamps, which dominated late Victorian and Edwardian philately and continued to flourish well into the reign of George V, marked the nadir of British colonial stamp design. To be sure, this monotonous approach was not confined to the British Empire and it was a practice adopted by all the other great colonial powers with single-minded enthusiasm. The use of key plates was particularly logical in the French colonial empire where a general series had sufficed, with very few exceptions, from 1859 onwards. From 1871 until 1881, in fact, the French colonies used the same stamps as the mother country, distinguishable only by the lack of perforations. From 1881 until 1892 an allegorical design showing the

seated figure of Commerce was used in the colonies, but as the individual territories began to issue distinctive stamps this series was overprinted or surcharged in various ways. The confusion caused by this was neatly resolved in 1893 by the introduction of the so-called Tablet key type. Allegorical figures of Commerce and Navigation sat on a prominent value tablet, beneath which was a horizontal panel for the name of the territory. The French colonial key plates were even more ruthlessly standardized than their British counterparts, in that the name of the colony was invariably printed in red on certain denominations in each series, and in blue on the other values. As a design, the Tablet type was quite artistic, being conceived by Eugene Mouchon. The pleasing appearance of individual specimens, however, does not lessen the depressing monotony of a whole galaxy of these stamps seen *en masse*. The Tablet stamps remained in use throughout the French colonies until it was replaced shortly before the First World War.

The greatest protagonist of the key-plate design was Portugal which tended to use such devices for the mother country as well. Thus the series of 1866-84 with the embossed profile of Dom Luiz was subsequently adapted for use in Angola, Cape Verde

Islands, Macao, Mozambique, Portuguese India, Timor, St. Thomé and Prince Islands, in the 1880s. But standardization had already been imposed on the various colonies, with the advent of a design in 1870 featuring the Portuguese crown. Unlike the Luiz embossed stamps, the crown series was confined to the colonies. Thenceforward the designs of certain issues in Portugal itself were modified for use in some colonies. In 1892, for example, a full-face portrait series was issued in Portugal with the word CONTINENTE (Continent—i.e., mainland), and in various island territories with the name of the colony, at the foot of the design. This practice was taken to its logical conclusion in 1895 when Mouchon designed and engraved a new series, portraying King Carlos. The Carlos design was subsequently modified for use in the numerous colonies; a new value tablet was inserted in the upper right-hand corner and the name of the colony was inscribed on the original value tablet. From then on, each change of definitive series in the motherland was the automatic signal for a similar change in the colonies. After Portugal became a republic in 1910, a design portraying Ceres was introduced and this, with variations, remained in use until the 1930s. Suitably modified for the colonies, the Ceres design survived in some instances as late as the Second World War.

Like the French, the Spaniards began with a general series, inscribed ULTRAMAR (overseas), but by the early 1870s had adopted separate issues in the more important colonies, though tending to conform to the same basic design. From 1877 on, however, colonial key-plate designs were gradually introduced, the first issues being adapted from the Spanish definitive series of 1875 bearing the profile of King Alfonso XII. In 1889 Spain issued a series portraying the baby Alfonso XIII. The stamps of the mother country were merely inscribed COMUNICACIONES, but the same design, incorporating in each instance the name of the territory, was used simultaneously for all the Spanish colonies. The 'Baby' types were followed by the 'Curly Heads' in 1896 and they, in turn, were superseded by portraits of Alfonso as a youth (1907) and in various stages of full maturity and middle age (1909-24). Since the sets were changed at almost annual intervals, either by altering the dates or the colours, the Spanish colonial key-plate stamps present a formidable array of monotonous and progressively badly designed labels. The graceful qualities of the Baby and Curly Head stamps rapidly degenerated into the diminutive and sketchy profiles lost in a maze of ornament and fussy lettering in the later Alfonso types.

Germany was the last of the major European powers to indulge in colonial adventures, joining in the 'scramble for Africa' in 1884 and carving out a sphere of influence in the Pacific soon afterwards. At first ordinary German stamps sufficed, but in the late 1890s these stamps began to appear with distinctive overprints. This paved the way for the colonial key types which were introduced in 1900. Two designs were used in each instance. The low values were in a small, upright format with a head-on view of the imperial yacht *Hohenzollern*; the higher denominations had a double-sized, horizontal design showing the same ship broadside-on. The low values were typographed, but the large-format stamps were recess-printed in attractive two-colour combinations —the only example of colonial key types produced by the more expensive process. The designs were standardized, with a scroll at the top of the design for the name of the territory. The Hohenzollern key types were used in ten colonies between 1900 and the First World War, when the colonies were seized by the Allies.

Apart from the five major colonial powers, a certain element of standardization was evident in the stamps of other countries. Austria adapted its designs from the very outset for stamps used in dependent territories. Thus the Arms series of 1850 was modified, with values expressed in Italian currency, for use in Lombardo-Venezia, and the same device was used from 1867 onwards in producing stamps for the Austrian post offices in the Turkish Empire, and for the Austrian agencies in Crete from 1907 to 1914. Belgium's definitive series of 1869–80 was adapted, with suitable changes in the inscriptions, for use in the Congo Free State in 1886, while the French post offices in China, Egypt, Turkey, Crete and Zanzibar in the early years of this century consisted of the 'Blanc', 'Mouchon' and 'Merson' designs of the mother country with the inscriptions altered accordingly. The basic designs themselves are discussed more fully in chapter 7. The situation was somewhat different in the Netherlands. In 1866 the contracts for Dutch and colonial stamps were awarded to Johann Enschede of Haarlem and from then on the stamps became increasingly standardized, though not descending to the level of the other colonial powers. Standard portraits of King William III and his daughter Wilhelmina were used from 1872, but distinctive frames were used in each territory. More or less identical designs (but not key plates) were introduced in 1902-3 in the three overseas territories of Curaçao, Netherlands Indies and Surinam, and new sets in the same idiom were in use from 1912 until the mid-thirties.

The experience gained by the leading security

Bosnia, 5 heller, 1900. The Habsburg imperial arms was the sole identifying motif possible on stamps of Bosnia-Herzegovina, a more than usually polyglot slice of the Austrian dominions.

Russia and Austria vied with each other for stamp contracts in the Balkans, reflecting their spheres of influence. The Bulgarian series, portraying Tsar Ferdinand, was typographed at the Cartographic Bureau of the Russian War Department. Albania's series portraying Prince William of Wied was designed by Gschurner and engraved by Ferdinand Schirnböck.

Bulgaria, 15 stotinki, 1901   Albania, 25 qintar, 1914

Greece, 2 lepta, 1889. The Hermes series of 1886-95 was the Belgian answer to the 'squared circle' problem. Designed by Hendrickx and engraved by Doms, these stamps were initially typographed at the Belgian Stamp Printing Works in Malines, but subsequently printed in Athens.

India, ½ anna, 1856

India, 1 rupee, 1892

De La Rue enjoyed a monopoly of Indian stamp production from 1855 till 1926. During this long period the basic elements remained the same—a profile portrait of the British monarch in a varying frame. The design of the frame, however, became progressively more elaborate in a bid to find suitably oriental settings for the royal profile. In 1926 De La Rue established a printing works at Nasik for the Indian government but formal profiles in exotic frames continued to be used on locally produced stamps until 1937 when a new approach was finally adopted.

India, 2 annas, 1911

India, 12 annas, 1902

printers in Britain, France, Belgium, Austria and the Netherlands gave them a tremendous advantage over their rivals and, as the nineteenth century wore on, many countries placed orders for stamps with the leading presses. In very few instances were the printers confronted with a design concocted in the country of origin and even when the local authorities had some ideas as to the kind of stamps they wanted, inevitably the printers left their own characteristics on the end products.

From 1849 until 1876 the contract for the production of French stamps was in the hands of the eccentric Anatole Hulot who supervised the work at the Mint in Paris. The combination of Hulot and Jean Jacques Barré (who engraved the dies) resulted in the fine, medallic profile stamps used by France in that period. Unavoidably this tried and proven concept would be extended to other countries, when they placed contracts in Paris. In 1861 Greece adopted adhesive stamps and they were closely modelled on the French designs, with a medallic profile of Hermes, messenger of the gods. The dies were engraved by Desiré Albert Barré, son of Jean Jacques, and the electrotyped plates and initial printings were made in Paris by E. Meyer. The plates were then shipped off to Athens where subsequent printings were made up to 1882. Meyer also manufactured the plates and first edition of the stamps ordered by Buenos Aires in 1859. Again a medallic profile (the head of Liberty) was used, though the transverse format and bolder framework differed radically from the contemporary French productions. Persia's first stamps (1868) were engraved by Barré and showed the lion and sun emblem in the familiar 'squared medallion'. A series for Guatemala in 1871 was prepared by Hulot, with the national coat of arms in an upright oval surrounded by the inscription, marking a breakaway from the earlier tradition; but his series of 1872 portraying Prince Carol of Romania bore an uncanny likeness to the Napoleonic stamps of France.

After 1875, Hulot's contract passed to the Bank of France, which entrusted the preparation of new French stamps to Eugene Mouchon, the engraver and designer of many fine French stamps. The new French series of 1876 was based on a design by Jules Auguste Sage, showing figures symbolizing Peace and Commerce flanking the value tablet. This design, engraved by Mouchon, was the precursor of the tablet colonial key type and also the Agriculture and Trade series engraved for Luxembourg in 1882. In 1894 Mouchon designed and engraved the first stamps of Ethiopia, bearing the portrait of Menelik II or featuring the lion of Judah, and a decade later he produced two sets for Serbia, one portraying the ill-fated King Alexander, the other celebrating the centenary of the Karageorgevich Dynasty. The Alexander series was not released without an overprint to blot out the late King's features. The Karageorgevich series, on the other hand, was believed to reveal the death mask of the assassinated ruler when the stamps were turned upside down—much to the annoyance of the new regime which had ousted the Obrenovich ruler! Poor Mouchon had to take the blame, though he protested that the appearance of the late King's ghost was quite fortuitous.

Mouchon also engraved stamps for Monaco (1885) and Tunisia (1888) and although he did not design either series, his handiwork is instantly recognizable. No doubt the designers in each instance, D. Depuis and E. Casse, were strongly influenced by prevailing French traditions. Surprisingly, Mouchon also designed quite a number of stamps for Belgium in the late nineteenth century, though these stamps were printed at Malines by the Belgian Government Printer.

The earliest Dutch stamps were recess-printed at the Mint in Utrecht and were rather nondescript profiles of King William III which owed something of their inspiration to the contemporary Belgian series. The definitive set of 1867-71, however, was clearly derived from the French 'squared circle', with bolder lettering and a more primitive form of Greek border. Although Enschede won the contract in 1866, and have held it ever since, it was many years before a distinctive Dutch style began to evolve. All that can be said of the Dutch products in the latter part of the nineteenth century is that they slavishly followed the general European fashion for fussy frames and ill-balanced lettering. The Dutch series of 1898 was largely redeemed by the sensitive composition and engraving of Mouchon. The combination of the French designer and the Dutch printer is also seen in the Persian definitive series of 1898, portraying Shah Muzaffer-ed-Din, a vast improvement over Enschede's own cluttered designs for that country four years previously.

Enschede continued to print stamps for Persia until the advent of the Pahlavi regime in 1925. The quality of these stamps is uneven, ranging from the attrctive Ahmed series of 1911 to the gilded gingerbread confections of the Muhammed Ali series of 1907. This was a period in which Enschede experimented with lithography and recess, often in combination, as well as with the more sedate typography confined to Holland and her colonies.

Before the Dutch printers got a foothold in Persia the stamps of that country were mainly produced by the Austrian State Printing Press in Vienna. The

Austrian connection lasted intermittently from 1876 until 1891 and alternated between full-face portraits of the much-moustached Shah Nasr-ed-Din, the sun emblem or the lion. The majority of these stamps were typographed, but a few were lithographed (1881) or recess-printed (1882). In design the Austrians tried to outdo the Persians, with extravagant Arabesques and Saracenic leaf patterns in the framework, the like of which was never seen in any Persian mediaeval miniature or manuscript.

Apart from the Persian excursion, Austrian stamp production tended to follow political expansion. The Balkans were Austria's particular sphere of influence and it was in that area that the Viennese stamp printers had their heyday. Apart from the armorial designs of Bosnia-Herzegovina (administered by Austria after 1878), they printed all the stamps of the independent principality of Montenegro from its inception in 1878 up to the outbreak of the First World War; in design, engraving and production the Montenegrin stamps closely parallel those of Austria during the same period. Even Serbia was forced to rely to some extent on the Austrian printers. The stamps were often designed and the plates manufactured in Vienna, though the actual printing was carried out in Belgrade. The Hungarian authorities had a separate State Printing Office in Budapest, and this is mirrored in the rather different approach to design evident in Hungarian stamps, which had a closer affinity with contemporary French issues than with those of Austria. Certain issues of Bulgaria were printed in Budapest, but they were too fleeting to establish any set pattern on the stamps of a country which made use of the printing facilities of no fewer than nine other states—from Britain to Turkey— for its issues between 1878 and 1920. The last fling in the old Viennese tradition consisted, ironically, of issues engraved by Ferdinand Schirnböck for Liechtenstein (1912) and Albania (1913), with profiles of Prince Johan II and full-face portraits of Prince William of Wied respectively. Liechtenstein seceded from its postal and customs union with Austria after the First World War and thenceforward was philatelically aligned with Switzerland. The William of Wied stamps were postponed on account of the outbreak of the war and the rapid disintegration of Albania. They were eventually released in 1920, but only after the erstwhile Prince's features were masked by the Albanian double eagle. Unoverprinted examples were looted during the war and are treasured nostalgically as mementoes of the palmy days of Kaiser Franz Josef.

Of the other state printers of the late nineteenth century, those in the Scandinavian countries and Romania were content to follow the general European fashion, but did not print stamps for other administrations. The Belgian printers at Malines, however, produced a series for Greece in 1886; their treatment of the Hermes head theme contrasts with the medallic composition of the earlier series, but is in the style which the Belgian designer Hendrickx developed for the issues of his own country. Although the Prussian printers had enjoyed a near monopoly of the stamps of the former German states, they did not print stamps for any other country before the First World War, except the Dominican Republic, for which they typographed two sets featuring the coat of arms (1901-10 and 1911-13) and lithographed a hideous series portraying Juan Pablo Duarte (1914).

Apart from their British and colonial contracts, De La Rue established an impressive record for printing stamps for many countries, using their inimitable typographic process. In the same year that they won their first British postage contract (1855) they netted an even more important one—the production of stamps for British India. All the stamps used in that subcontinent were printed by De La Rue from then until 1926 when they established a printing works at Nasik on behalf of the Indian government. For India they produced a mixture similar to that tried in Britain—a wide variety of frames with Victoria's profile as the common denominator. In 1895 they weakened slightly, to permit Baron von Angeli's august portrait of the Queen-Empress in her state robes to appear on the bicoloured rupee denominations, and this portrait was subsequently used for the 3 pies values of 1899-1900. But otherwise it was a strict diet of formal profiles in exotic frames, a legacy which Nasik did not shake off until 1937.

In 1861 De La Rue printed their first foreign stamps —1 and 5 cent stamps for the Confederate States of America. The insipid 1 cent, with its portrait of John Calhoun, was never issued because Confederate postal rates had risen before the stamps arrived; but the stern features of Jefferson Davis on the 5 cent showed that De La Rue could produce stamps in the American idiom, with a 'speaking' portrait rather than a sculptured profile. These stamps, incidentally, were the only American issue ever produced outside the territory of the United States. The collapse of the Confederacy put an end to what might have been a promising venture. Though one war balked the enterprise of this company, another proved more successful. After the *Risorgimento*, the newly united kingdom of Italy needed stamps and turned to De La Rue for help. This firm typographed the Victor Emmanuel III series of 1863 and then furnished the Italian Government Printing Works in Turin with

The official Golden Jubilee portrait of Queen Victoria, painted in 1887 by Professor Baron von Angeli, portrait painter to the Austrian, Prussian and British Courts. First used on the Indian high values in 1895, it was one of De La Rue's few concessions to 'proper' portraiture. Below: The von Angeli head used on the Indian 5 rupee issue of 1895.

Confederate States, 5 cents, 1861

Italy, 2 lire, 1862

Belgium, 20 centimes, 1865

Restraint was the keynote of De La Rue's early foreign designs. The American predilection for 'proper' portraits is evident in the Jefferson Davis stamp, based on a studio photograph. This and the 1 cent stamp showing John Calhoun were the only American stamps ever produced outside the territory of the United States, and were De La Rue's first foreign contract. They proved that De La Rue could produce more realistic portraits as well as sculptured heads; elsewhere however, De La Rue stuck to their own tradition of medallic profiles.

Right:
One basic design featuring the orange tree emblem was used by De La Rue for all the stamps of the Orange Free State from 1868 to 1900 (2). Neighbouring Transvaal (the South African Republic) was almost as conservative, but went first to Mecklenburg and subsequently to Holland for its stamps. The large arms series (1) was first printed by Otto of Gustrow, but between 1869 and 1877 was produced by no fewer than four local printers—Viljoen and the Stamp Commission (Pretoria), Borrius (Potchefstroom) and Davis (Pietermaritzburg). J. Vurtheim designed the 1885-92 series (3), typographed by Enschede; the distorted lettering of the elliptical inscriptions constrasts sadly with the panelled lettering of Otto's design.

1. Transvaal, 1 penny, 1869

2. Orange Free State, 1 penny, 1868

3. Transvaal, 5 pounds, 1892

Johore, 1 cent, 1896

Even in the more independent colonies a certain similarity was bound to creep in. The hexagonal device on the New South Wales stamp was modelled on the British 6 pence produced by De La Rue in the same year. In turn, it served as the basis for the New Zealand 6 pence (1874) and 2 pence (1882) and the Bermuda 2½ pence (1883).

Bermuda, 2½ pence, 1883

New South Wales, 6 pence, 1872

New Zealand, 2 pence, 1882

Thailand (Siam), 12 atts, 1887

De La Rue's use of dull purple or green fugitive inks, with value tablets of contrasting colours, extended beyond the British colonial key types to their South-East Asian contracts. However, in these two examples the use of full face portraits rather than the more usual De La Rue profiles gives them a slightly less formal appearance than many British colonial issues of the time.

plates and equipment. The Italian stamps of 1863-7 have the De La Rue hallmark—a wide variety of frames, with a standard profile providing the continuity. The same features can be seen clearly in the series which De La Rue typographed for Belgium in 1865, although in this instance the frames were more restrained and the profiles of King Leopold were set in uniform medallions on the French model. Variety was provided by the tiny ornaments in the spandrels and also in the lettering. De La Rue also designed a set of four stamps for Belgium in 1883 and though they were actually printed at Malines they bear a close resemblance to the British stamps produced by this firm in 1880-81. De La Rue typographed sets for Thailand (1887) and Johore (1891) which, in their combination of dull, fugitive colours and contrasting value tablets, reflect the pervasive influence of the colonial key plates of that period.

The philately of the two Boer republics in South Africa provides an interesting contrast between the work of two European printers. From 1868 until 1900, De La Rue printed the stamps of the Orange Free State in a simple rectangular design which seems oddly at variance with their usual productions, but this was due to the fact that they were supplied with rough sketches by the Bloemfontein authorities and merely interpreted the idea. The result is a pleasingly simple motif, the orange tree emblem against a background of fine horizontal shading, with inscriptions in upper and lower case lettering on all four sides. This design satisfied the burghers well enough and it continued in use until the end of the Anglo-Boer War. The neighbouring state of the Transvaal, however, had its armorial stamps designed and printed in Mecklenburg, though later printings were made locally with varying degrees of success. After the interlude of the first British occupation (1877-82) and the handsome Victorian profiles by Bradbury Wilkinson mentioned in chapter 3, the Transvaal reverted to armorial designs in 1885 and this time went to Enschede. J. Vurtheim produced an arms design in a medallion which played havoc with the lettering. The octagonal arms designs of 1894-5 were a slight improvement, but still lacked the simple dignity of De La Rue's orange tree motif.

The majority of the Australian states and New Zealand were responsible for their own stamps, and produced their own antipodean version of typography, clearly derived from De La Rue models, though New Zealand's halfpenny newspaper stamp of 1873-92 was cribbed from the British stamp of that denomination, introduced by Perkins Bacon in 1870. The greatest degree of originality in this field was exhibited by Victoria, though the quality of engraving

and printing left much to be desired. Both Victoria and New South Wales, in fact, had a significant impact on world philately, the implications of which will be found in chapters 6 and 10.

The recess-printed stamps of Perkins Bacon in the classic period had a 'substantial' appearance about them, heightened by the use of solid backgrounds which, on closer examination, turned out to be composed of intricate patterns of lines. Consciously or unconsciously, the early typographed stamps strove to emulate this solid appearance. Typography was totally unsuited to the intricate engine turning in which intaglio excelled, but the effect was simulated by close parallel lines of shading. De La Rue at first actually tried to simulate the engine turning of their competitors, and this can be seen in the early typographed issues of Britain, particularly in the 6 pence and the shilling of 1856. The 3 pence stamp of 1862 was the first of the typographed stamps which may be regarded as specifically designed to suit the limitations of the printing process, with white lettering on a solid ground, and large areas of white in the area between the central motif and the frame. From 1867 on, the British typographed stamps had increasingly open designs, a tendency which reached its zenith in the severely functional designs of the 1883 series, and in the use of white backgrounds to the profiles in the Jubilee set of 1887. Parallel developments took place in the stamps De La Rue printed for the colonies in the same period. By contrast, the colonial printers were less influenced by the Perkins Bacon intaglio tradition, and their designs were more clearly suited to typography from the outset. The first 'side-face' series of New Zealand, produced by De La Rue in 1874, belongs to the school of solid backgrounds and intricate spandrels, whereas the 2 and 5 shilling stamps engraved by Bock and Cousins of Wellington in 1878 are strikingly simple. Though the second 'side-face' series, produced by this firm between 1882 and 1897, included designs which were strongly derived from De La Rue, others—notably the $\frac{1}{2}$, $2\frac{1}{2}$ and 5 pence of 1891-5—made better use of contrasting areas of white and of more open lettering.

The most striking examples of this development are provided by Queensland, whose locally typographed stamps from 1879 to 1912 had the basic theme of Queen Victoria's profile in an upright oval; with network spandrels (1879-82), bolder lettering, but still with a solid background to the profile and ornamental spandrels (1882-95), white background to the profile (1895 onwards) and large white numerals of value replacing the earlier ornamental spandrels (after 1896).

The European countries which exploited typography seldom had any tradition of recess printing to confuse their approach to stamp design. The earliest French stamps, for example, had classical profiles on solid grounds, and though some attempt was made at shading in close parallel lines, in the stamps of 1876 to 1903, it is significant that the famous Sower design by Oscar Roty (see chapter 7) was modified three years after its inception and the lined background (which included the rising sun) replaced by a plain mass of solid colour. Solid backgrounds, throwing the motif into stark contrast, were used for many subsequent French issues, of which the most outstanding examples were the Pasteur (1923), Peace (1932), Iris (1939), Petain (1941) and Marianne (1945) series.

Hong Kong, $2, 1938

Hong Kong, 30 cents, 1862

Hong Kong, $1.30, 1960

A well-tried design, used intermittently by Hong Kong for almost a century. The restraint of frame decoration and overall simplicity contrasted radically with the usual colonial designs produced by De La Rue.

Reduction of postal rates on postcards and printed matter led to the adoption of halfpenny stamps. Both Britain (1870) and South Australia (1868) halved the area normally occupied by a penny stamp. New Zealand's halfpenny stamp was modelled on the British halfpenny and was much smaller than the contemporary Chalon portrait issues.

Not all British territories clung steadfastly to the colonial key types. British Central Africa's arms design was originally devised by the governor and explorer, Sir Harry Johnston. The Gold Coast penny of Edward VII was that country's sole exception to the key type series.

New Zealand, ½ penny, 1873

South Australia, ½ penny, 1868

Gold Coast, 1 penny, 1908

British Central Africa, 1 penny, 1897

Trinidad, 2 pence, 1898 (29 × 33mm) commemorating the quatercentenary of the discovery of the island by Columbus. Many of the countries issuing Columbus commemoratives chose paintings as their subject. Trinidad's motif, however, was based on a stained glass window. In using intaglio for this stamp De La Rue demonstrated their versatility in face of the challenge from Waterlow and Sons and Bradbury Wilkinson, who were now vigorously competing for contracts.

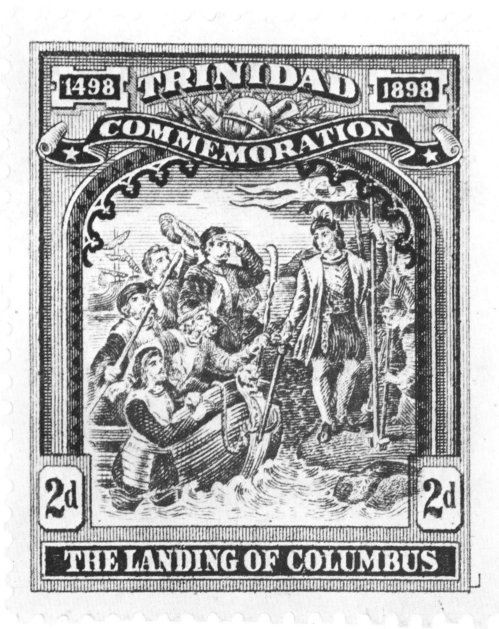

6
Fin de siècle pictorialism

U P TO NOW we have considered the postage stamp merely as a label denoting the prepayment of postage, but within two decades of its birth it had acquired another identity: it had become a collectable object. By 1860 the number of stamps available all over the world had risen to about a thousand. The first dealers (albeit part-time only) were beginning to appear, and periodicals were devoting space to the hobby of stamp collecting. The tempo increased enormously in the 1860s; the first magazines devoted entirely to the hobby were published, the first catalogues and handbooks appeared, the earliest societies were founded—and postal administrations woke up to the fact that there were people who were actually prepared to purchase stamps, not for the purpose of posting letters but to treasure in an album. In the embryo days of philately the only way one could acquire stamps from far-off lands (unless one had business or family correspondence with them) was to write direct to the Postmaster, enclosing a remittance and hoping for the best. A few of the more enterprising dealers, like Edward Stanley Gibbons in England or J. Walter Scott in New York, built up contacts in remote countries and were able to import stamps in considerable quantities to supply the demands of their customers.

Occasionally a postal administration would run short of a certain denomination, or postal rates would change, necessitating the introduction of a new stamp. In emergencies of this sort, existing stamps would often be surcharged with a new value. As soon as the stamp collectors heard of this emergency issue there would be a furore, and orders would come streaming in. Unfortunately this craze for 'provisionals' tempted some of the less scrupulous, more impecunious countries to issue such stamps with undue frequency. One of the earliest, and most blatant, offenders in this respect was the South American republic of Uruguay which produced a spate of temporary surcharges in January 1866, knowing full well that a consignment of brand-new stamps was on its way—if not actually in Montevideo harbour at the time. The surcharged series lasted nine days,

and the new series, from Maclure, Macdonald and Co., of Glasgow, appeared on 10 January. In passing it should be mentioned that the new stamps were interesting in their highly ornamental treatment of the numerals of value, with the national emblems entwined. This was to be a characteristic of Uruguayan stamps down to the end of the century, but gradually a pictorial element crept in, with allegorical figures (1889) followed by trains, ships, bulls and gauchos (1895).

As the century wore on, however, collectors became more sophisticated and were less likely to fall for such naïve subterfuges. At the same time, a number of small countries came to rely on philatelic revenue and sought ways of legitimately increasing their output of stamps and also making them more attractive to collectors.

Stamps were changed for technical reasons—a new printer, new plates or changes in postal rates —or political reasons, such as a change of ruler or government. Theoretically, changes in the postage stamps should have been relatively infrequent, so the problem was how to find some other reason which would justify more frequent issues. In 1888 New South Wales had a double celebration—the centenary of the establishment of the colony and the fiftieth anniversary of the embossed letter sheets of 1838. Special philatelic items were produced for both events. In 1876 the United States had issued embossed envelopes to celebrate the Philadelphia Centennial Exposition marking the centenary of the Declaration of Independence, but twelve years elapsed before New South Wales followed up this idea with a commemorative postcard for the postal jubilee. For the centenary of the colony, however, New South Wales produced a lengthy series of stamps inscribed ONE HUNDRED YEARS. These stamps replaced the Queen's Heads then in use and are regarded as the first commemorative issue, though this description has to be qualified for several reasons. Unlike later commemoratives, the New South Wales series remained in use for over twelve years, undergoing various changes in perforation during that period, and other denominations or changes of colour were introduced

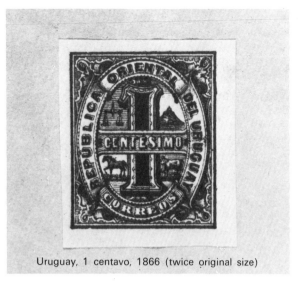

Uruguay, 1 centavo, 1866 (twice original size)

This stamp was one of the few produced by the Glasgow printers, Maclure and Macdonald. It combined Uruguay's predilection for numerals with an attempt to emulate the American Bank Note Company's practice of converting heraldic elements into tiny pictorial vignettes.

The Lake District, an illustration from a selection of William Wordsworth's poems, designed by Birket Foster and engraved by the Brothers Dalziel in 1859. Books became more illustrated in the last half of the nineteenth century, and designers of pictorial stamps may well have been influenced by the current fashion.

Pictorialism spread across the South Pacific in the late nineteenth century, at a time when it was virtually ignored everywhere else. Fiji's canoe scene (2) was obviously inspired by the Sydney view of 1888 (1). Significantly these early efforts at pictorialism were in a small format and printed by letterpress—a size and process seldom suited to a pictorial treatment.

1. New South Wales,
1 penny, 1888

2. Fiji, 1 penny, 1896

3. Cook Islands,
½ penny, 1902

4. Samoa,
half crown, 1899

from time to time, so that, to all intents and purposes, the series was a permanent definitive issue. In that respect, therefore, it seemed to differ in no wise from the first stamps of Baden and Württemberg (1851) which bore inscriptions relating to the inauguration of the German-Austrian Postal Union the previous year. The concept of special, short-term issues of stamps originated in Germany in 1887, when one of the numerous private local posts issued a set of stamps to mark the Ninth Federal Shooting Contest.

Although the claim of New South Wales to have pioneered commemorative stamps has frequently been assailed, there is no doubt that the series of 1888 marked an important breakthrough. The stamps were typographed locally, crudely engraved and overloaded with fussy floral ornament, into which the lettering was not only merged but sometimes completely lost. The appearance of the stamps might have been improved had intaglio been used, but that would have only partially redeemed the overall tastelessness of the designs. What is so outstanding about this series is the fact that, for the first time, a country had produced a set which was entirely pictorial in character: a view of Sydney, so different from the naïve rendition of Clayton in 1850 (1 penny); emu (2 pence), lyre-bird (8 pence) and kangaroo (1 shilling) representing the wildlife; portraits of Captain Cook (4 pence), Queen Victoria (6 pence), Governor Phillip and Governor Carrington (20 shillings) and a map of Australia (5 shillings).

The impact of the New South Wales series of 1888 cannot be overemphasized. It had a pronounced effect on the other Australian colonies, all of which attempted pictorial stamps to some extent during the ensuing quarter of a century that remained to them before the general issues of the Australian Commonwealth were introduced in 1913. The Diamond Jubilee of Queen Victoria was celebrated in 1897. By that time commemorative stamps, if not yet fashionable, were no longer so revolutionary and the event was marked by stamps in several colonies. New South Wales, as usual, went one better and produced a pair of stamps with postal values of 1 and 2½ pence, but sold for a shilling and 2 shillings and 6 pence respectively. The enormous premiums were given to a TB sanatorium, and this purpose was indicated in the stamps which bore the inscription 'Consumptives' Home' and allegorical designs symbolizing charity. The same idea was adopted in neighbouring Victoria which raised money for a hospital fund by issuing two stamps portraying Queen Victoria. The penny stamp was actually inscribed 'Charity'—and this is the term by which such semi-postal stamps are usually denoted. Both Victoria and Queensland later issued charity stamps with large premiums, in aid of patriotic funds during the Boer War (1900). Victoria's pair showed troops in the South African veld and, appropriately, the Victoria Cross, the highest British award for bravery. Queensland used a design showing the ghostly outline of the elderly Queen in the sky above a group of three servicemen and the Union Jack—a motif which was successfully cribbed by Virgil Reilly for a series of four stamps issued by Australia in 1940 in tribute to the men and women of the Australian Imperial Forces.

In the purely pictorial field it was left to South Australia and Tasmania to develop the idea begun by New South Wales. South Australia released a 2½ pence stamp in 1894 showing a kangaroo in the bush, alongside a profile of Queen Victoria. Four years later a halfpenny stamp depicted the General Post Office in Adelaide. This design, typographed by De La Rue, failed for three reasons: it was printed in a wishy-washy shade of yellow-green which did nothing to improve the clarity of the engraving; it was conceived in a small format which did not do justice to the subject; and the photograph on which it was based included a telegraph pole and wires—all of which were faithfully incorporated in the design, but spoiled the effect. It was left to Tasmania to produce one of the most effective pictorial sets of that period, a fitting close to the nineteenth century, but before examining this series it is necessary to consider developments elsewhere.

Despite the universal use of typography in the late nineteenth century there were, here and there, fleeting attempts to provide stamps which would catch the eye (and the money) of the collector. Bradbury Wilkinson and Waterlow & Sons were primarily concerned in the manufacture of banknotes but from time to time they also produced postage stamps, using the same process (intaglio) and techniques (elaborate scrollwork and *guilloche* patterns). In stamp design Bradbury Wilkinson clung to the more traditional approach, though the Queensland high values of 1882, with a coquettish version of the Chalon portrait and an elaborate banknote style of frame, indicated a fresh approach to an old subject. Thereafter Bradbury Wilkinson produced excellent designs for the chartered companies—British South Africa and British East Africa—featuring arms and insignia set in elaborate banknote frames. Waterlow produced handsome stamps portraying Queen Victoria for Niger Coast (1893-7), but for North Borneo came up with a lengthy series of gorgeous bicoloured pictorials (1894). This series, with its vignettes of pheasants, stags, crocodiles, palms, scenery and native chiefs, retained the elaborate frames associated

Queensland, 9 pence, 1903

Both Queensland and New South Wales had identical 9 pence stamps symbolizing the unification of the Australian states. South Australia's 2½ pence of 1894 combined royal portraiture with a pictorialized heraldic element—the kangaroo. Australia's first truly pictorial definitive stamp, however, was South Australia's halfpenny of 1898, typographed by De La Rue.

Right: The use of pictures with vignetted edges fitted into the surrounding frame, and a penchant for scrolled ornament, were typical banknote features which Waterlows successfully adapted in their pictorial stamp designs. Compare the Nyassa and North Borneo stamps (below) with this detail from a Chinese banknote of 1936, designed and engraved by Waterlow and Sons.

South Australia, 2½ pence, 1894

South Australia, ½ penny, 1898

1. British South Africa Company, 3 pence, 1896
2. British East Africa Company, 5 annas, 1894
3. Niger Coast, 2 pence, 1894
4. North Borneo, 1 cent, 1894
5. Portuguese Nyassa, 10 reis, 1901
6. North Borneo, 5 cents, 1909

The chartered companies went to the banknote printers for their stamps and, with the exception of the Niger Coast, chose designs that featured their coats of arms. Waterlows subsequently revolutionized the pictorial stamp with their handsome two-colour designs for the British and Portuguese chartered companies in North Borneo and Nyassa. The concept of a royal portrait inset in the frame, pioneered in Nyassa, was later extended to the British colonies in the 1930s.

1

2

3

4

5

6

with banknotes, but broke entirely new ground and proved that the pictorial idiom worked well, given the right printing process and a suitably large format. Waterlow went on to produce further intaglio extravaganzas for North Borneo—in 1897-1902, 1909-22, 1939 and 1961—thus spanning the three major phases of pictorialism and maintaining this tradition at times when pictorial stamps were largely unfashionable elsewhere.

De La Rue suddenly woke up to this competition and belatedly turned to intaglio to meet the challenge. In 1879 De La Rue had used this process reluctantly to print a series for Labuan with the Queen's profile in a comparatively plain frame, but this set, done on the cheap, was not a success and seventeen years elapsed before De La Rue again used this process. Significantly it was recess, rather than surface printing, that De La Rue used for the first stamps of Zanzibar, released in 1896. The Sultan's portrait was finely engraved, but the surrounding frame was in the coarse, vigorous style often associated with *en epargne*. The following year, however, De La Rue recess-printed a beautiful series of bicoloured pictorials for the South Pacific kingdom of Tonga. This handsome series, with its scenery, wildlife and portraits of native rulers, pleased the Tongans im-

mensely, for it remained in use, with variations and occasional additions, until 1953—a record for philatelic longevity. In 1899 De La Rue recess-printed a series of monochrome pictorials for Malta and in the same year executed a splendid series of large pictorials for Tasmania. Eight designs were used, each depicting landmarks and scenery of the island and obviously aiming to publicize its tourist attractions. The designs were subsequently lithographed in Melbourne, and an even later version was typographed from electrotypes. The later versions of the series lacked the clarity of the De La Rue originals and demonstrated forcibly that intaglio was the best method for pictorial designs. The De La Rue experiment in Tasmania was repeated in 1900 by Jamaica which commissioned a penny stamp, showing the Llandovery Falls, based on a photograph. Originally printed in monochrome, this stamp later appeared in two colours—slate-black vignette and red frame—but after this promising start Jamaica abandoned pictorialism and reverted to surface-printed arms and royal profiles in 1903.

In the closing years of the nineteenth century Waterlow and the American Bank Note Company vied with each other in the production of handsome pictorials. In 1898 Waterlow produced a series of

1. Tonga, half crown, 1897

2. Malta, 4½ pence, 1899

3. Tasmania, 6 pence, 1899

4. Jamaica, 1 penny, 1900–1

1. New Zealand, 5 shillings, 1898

2. New Zealand, 8 pence, 1898

3. New Zealand, 1 penny, 1901

Waterlows recess-printed pictorial stamps for New Zealand at the turn of the century. Of the 1898 series, the top value featuring Mount Cook (1) alone did justice to the subject. The remaining values were spoiled by cluttered frames, while the 8 pence stamp echoed the Uruguayan obsession for making the value clear, at the expense of the vignette.

Left: De La Rue met the Waterlow challenge with large-sized intaglio pictorials printed, for the most part, in monochrome. The Jamaican penny, showing the Llandovery Falls (4), appeared originally in red but was re-issued a year later with the vignette in black and the frame in red.

Above right: All early American commemorative stamps were linked to exhibitions and fairs. The first of these was the lengthy series marking the Columbian Exposition of 1893, the $5 stamp depicting the special Columbian commemorative coin. Elaborate frames, often incorporating tiny allegorical motifs, were the hallmark of these American stamps, the philatelic equivalent of the 'Beaux Arts' tradition in American furniture and architecture at the turn of the century.

Right: A prime example of the designer's ingenuity in cramming as much as possible into the design was Guatemala's Central American Exposition series of 1897 which includes the presidential portrait, the arms of the five Central American republics, the torch of learning and vignettes of land and sea transport. Twenty-five years later Portugal's Trans-Atlantic commemorative echoes the same cluttered style.

United States, 2 cents, 1901

United States, $5, 1893

Portugal, 40 centavos, 1923

Guatemala, 1 centavo, 1897

thirteen designs for New Zealand, with the emphasis on scenery, though three values depicted birds and the 8 pence stamp showed a native war canoe. This stamp used the numeral of value as a vehicle for the inscriptions and a frame for the tiny vignettes of crown and canoe, but this was a rare display of whimsicality which probably derived from the designs produced by this firm for Uruguay, with that country's long tradition for decorative numerals. The New Zealand pictorials were later printed in Wellington, and other designs, including the famous Penny Universal of 1901, were added to the series. Like Queensland and Victoria, New Zealand struck a patriotic note in 1900, with a 1½ pence definitive stamp showing troops in South Africa.

Curiously, pictorialism was very slow to catch on in Europe. With the exception of a few commemoratives (discussed later in this chapter), only one country produced pictorial stamps before the end of the century. On New Year's Day, 1900, Germany released a 1 mark stamp featuring the General Post Office in Berlin and later the same year produced a design symbolizing the union of north and south Germany (2 marks), and reproductions of paintings by Wilhelm Pape (3 and 5 marks). These double-sized pictorials were recess-printed, whereas the small-format lower values were typographed.

In 1900 Bradbury Wilkinson ventured into the pictorial field with a series of stamps for Crete which, since 1898, had formed an autonomous part of the Turkish Empire under the joint administration of the major European powers. The stamps for the most part reproduced Cretan coins of the classical period; designs portraying Prince George of Greece and a statue of King Minos were less successful. Bicoloured high values, introduced in 1905, established something of a pattern. Vignettes of landscapes in black were set in heavy, ornate frames of a contrasting colour. This precedent was followed in the 1 drachma stamp of 1907, which even contrived to incorporate four tiny coins in the corners of the framework. This style of recess-printed pictorial was adopted enthusiastically by Waterlow in 1926 for the Spanish Red Cross series. Gradually the formula of pictorial vignette (invariably a landscape), ornate frame containing the inscriptions, and assorted value tablets, coats of arms, heraldic devices and portraits inset in the corners, became standard for the vast majority of the pictorial stamps of the world in the thirties and forties. Bradbury Wilkinson developed this genre of pictorialism in their early work for Balkan countries, adapting designs by A. Mitov and G. Estavian for Bulgaria (1911) and by Oskan Effendi for Turkey (1913). Elsewhere in Europe pictorial definitive stamps did not appear until 1914 when Switzerland issued a set of recess-printed high values depicting mountain scenery, and it was not until the 1920s that the fashion for pictorials began to take hold.

The remaining pictorial designs of the late nineteenth century were all commemorative in origin. The New South Wales innovation of 1888 was slow to catch on elsewhere, but it was given tremendous impetus in 1892, when many countries in the Western Hemisphere began to celebrate the quatercentenary of the voyages of discovery by Christopher Columbus. Hundreds of stamps appeared in America in the closing years of the century in honour of Columbus and this explains why, for over fifty years, this Genoese seaman was the most popular figure portrayed on the world's stamps, except for Queen Victoria and King George V. For the United States the American Bank Note Company produced a set of sixteen designs, most of which were based on paintings illustrating the life and times of Columbus. The series ranged in value from 1 cent to 5 dollars, and sparked off protests from collectors who felt that this was excessive. The stamps ostensibly commemorated the Columbian Exposition at Chicago in 1893. For many years thereafter the only American commemoratives were issued in connection with world's fairs and exhibitions—Trans-Mississippi (1898), Pan-American (1901), Louisiana International Exposition (1904), Jamestown Tercentenary Exposition (1907), the Alaska-Yukon-Pacific (1909) and the Panama-Pacific (1913)—and all of them were pictorial in concept.

Although Spain and Italy let the Columbus celebrations go by without philatelic commemoration, Portugal adopted the idea in 1894 for a lengthy series celebrating the quincentenary of the birth of Prince Henry the Navigator. Paintings by J. V. Salgado were adapted for intaglio designs executed by the Leipzig printers, Giesecke and Devrient. The following year came an extensive series for the 700th anniversary of St. Anthony. Scenes from the life of Portugal's patron saint appeared on the stamps, which also had the words of his prayer printed on the reverse. Finally came a long set in 1898 to commemorate the quatercentenary of Vasco da Gama's discovery of the sea route to India, and on this occasion similar sets, suitably inscribed, were released in the colonies.

Europe's first commemorative set was issued in the obscure Balkan principality of Montenegro, which was to derive much of its revenue from the sale of stamps up to 1913. The initial series consisted of the definitive set with a Cyrillic overprint to commemorate the quatercentenary of printing, but two years later a bicoloured series was crudely lithographed to mark the bicentenary of the Petrovich Njegosh dynasty and the uniform design featured a view of the royal mausoleum near Cetinje. In the same year, Greece revived the Olympic Games, the most important sporting event in the ancient calendar, and publicized the event with a set of twelve stamps. The designer, Professor Gillieron, went back to classical art and sculpture for inspiration. The dies were sensitively engraved by Mouchon and the stamps typographed at the French Government Printing Works, proving that, in the right hands, typography could be used for pictorial stamps with satisfactory results. A decade later Greece produced a similar series for another Olympic Games. This time the production was entrusted to Perkins Bacon using intaglio and it is interesting to compare the designs and their execution.

Queen Victoria's Diamond Jubilee resulted in a spate of stamps from seven colonies, though the event was ignored in the mother country. The year 1897 also marked the quatercentenary of Cabot's discovery of Newfoundland and that colony issued fourteen stamps for the occasion. Only the 1 cent, showing Victoria in widow's weeds, mentioned her Jubilee; the other stamps served rather to advertise the colony's natural resources and scenery—and another phenomenon, the pictorial publicity stamp, was born. Both the Leeward Islands and Barbados produced eight Jubilee stamps, the former merely overprinting its

Montenegro, 7 novcics, 1893 (twice original size). The basic stamps were typographed in Vienna but overprinted at Cetinje to mark the quatercentenary of printing in Montenegro. This was Europe's first commemorative issue.

Portugal, 10 reis, 1894

Timor, 1 avo, 1898

Portugal was an early and enthusiastic exponent of the pictorial commemorative stamp. The Prince Henry the Navigator quincentenary series was lithographed by Giesecke and Devrient after paintings by J. V. Salgado. Waterlow and Sons recess-printed sets for Portugal and her colonies in uniform designs to mark the Vasco da Gama quatercentenary of 1898. Note the strong framework giving depth to the vignette, and the restrained handling of the globes, pillars and anchors in the side panels.

Below:

Several Commonwealth countries, but not the mother country, celebrated the Diamond Jubilee of Queen Victoria with stamps in 1897-8. The Barbados series used the device of a stamp within a stamp, taking the Queen and Seahorses motif from the contemporary definitive series and adding heraldic elements and a commemorative inscription (3). Canada's series by L. Pereira and F. Brownell combined the two best-known 'proper' portraits, by Chalon and von Angeli and was recess-printed by the American Bank Note Company (2). British Guiana's series of 1898, recess-printed by De La Rue, was a belated and irrelevant issue aimed at publicizing the country rather than celebrating the royal anniversary (1).

1. British Guiana, 10 cents, 1898

3. Barbados, 1 penny, 1897

2. Canada, 50 cents, 1897

A contrast in vignette and framework afforded by Waterlows and Perkins Bacon. The elaborate frame, so typical of their banknote work, was used by Waterlow and Sons for the view of the Inkissi Falls, from a diorama by R. Mols and P. van Engelen (originally shown at the Antwerp Exhibition of 1894). The simple frame and lightly engraved background to the Greek Olympic series by Perkins Bacon show how far Perkins Bacon had progressed since their early colonial contracts.

Congo, 25 centimes, 1900

Greece, 20 lepta, 1906

definitive series with the legend SEXAGENARY-1897 and the latter redrawing its definitive design in a larger format with the dates of the reign and the royal arms incorporated. Canada, in the best American tradition, issued sixteen stamps from a ½ cent to 5 dollars, featuring the two best-known 'proper' portraits of the Queen—the Chalon and the von Angeli. Mauritius belatedly produced a 36 cent stamp the following year showing the colonial coat of arms, but British Guiana had a set of six bi-coloured pictorials recess-printed by De La Rue.

Africa's first commemorative stamp appeared in 1895 when the Transvaal introduced penny postage and marked the occasion with a double-sized pictorial lithographed in Pretoria. Inevitably, the republican arms appeared in the centre, but this was flanked by pictures of communications old and new—a mail coach and a mail train. The quality of the lithography was poor and the vignettes remained indistinct. In Asia, Japan, which did not adopt postage stamps until 1871, was an early exponent of both pictorial and commemorative stamps. Wild geese, wagtails and eagles appeared on three stamps released in 1875, but after this promising start Japan sank into a morass of fussy symbolism, aping Occidental contemporaries, and did not return to pictorialism for definitive stamps until 1922. In 1894 two stamps were issued to commemorate the Emperor's silver wedding. Double-sized designs were produced, but conformed to the symbolism of the period, with the chrysanthemum emblem flanked by two cranes. Two years later, however, four small-format stamps celebrated victory in the Sino-Japanese War and portrayed the victorious commanders. Subsequently, commemorative stamps were produced for the Crown Prince's wedding (1900) and the Russo-Japanese War (1906), each set compromising between symbolism and pictorialism by using still life compositions; in the first case rice cakes and sweetmeats, and in the second a collage of cannon and flags. This quasi-symbolic approach was retained by Japan for the majority of the commemorative stamps issued up to the mid-1930s. Like Japan, China was slow to introduce stamps (1878) and clung to Oriental symbolism. In 1894 a lengthy series celebrated the sixtieth birthday of the Dowager Empress and dragon motifs were used for all but the top value (24 cents) which featured Chinese junks. New definitive sets in 1897 and 1898 maintained the symbolic dragon tradition, but featured carp and flying geese on the higher denominations. Full-blown pictorial stamps in the Western idiom, however, did not appear until 1909 when Waterlow recess-printed a set of three showing the Temple of Heaven in Peking

1. Japan, 1½ sen, 1906

2. China, 2 cents, 1909

3. Russia, 10 kopeks, 1905

Japanese pictorials of the early twentieth century tended to be symbolic in concept. The stamp of 1906 celebrating victory over Russia, shows a classic trophy of arms (1). By contrast, Russia's war charity series featured buildings and landmarks (3). China's first truly pictorial series was the trio of 1909 depicting the Temple of Heaven, Peking—in Waterlow's now well-established formula of elaborate frames with vignettes in contrasting colours (2).

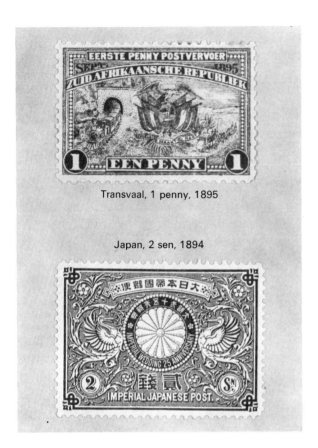

Transvaal, 1 penny, 1895

Japan, 2 sen, 1894

El Salvador, 3 centavos, 1896

El Salvador, 5 pesos, 1893

Nicaragua, 2 pesos, 1892

to mark the first year of the reign of the boy Emperor, Hsuan T'ung.

No account of late nineteenth-century pictorialism would be complete without some reference to the activities of Nicholas Seebeck in Latin America in the closing decade. Seebeck, acting on behalf of the Hamilton Bank Note Company, secured contracts from Ecuador, Honduras, Nicaragua and Salvador between 1889 and 1898, whereby he undertook to print an annual series of stamps for each country free of charge, on condition that he keep the plates and be permitted to run off additional quantities for sale to collectors. This agreement resulted in a spate of presidential portraits, allegory and a fair number of pictorials (mostly connected with the Columbus celebrations which fell conveniently into this period). The stamps were competently engraved and printed by the intaglio method, but their vignettes suffered from the usual American fault of cluttered frames and jumbled lettering. The only noteworthy designs to emerge from the Seebeck interlude were the peso values of Salvador's 1893 series, showing scenes from the life of Columbus. Fortunately the countries concerned terminated their contracts by 1898, but to this day the Seebeck issues remain a drug on the philatelic market.

Belgium, 5 centimes (27 × 38mm), advertising the Brussels Fair of 1897. Both the subject (St. Michael encountering Satan) and the lettering betray the strong influence of the Pre-Raphaelites and the neo-medievalism advocated by William Morris on the Belgian designer, G. Portieltje.

7
The influence of art nouveau

IN the nineteenth century there was little pretension to regard the stamp as a work of art in its own right. In a minority of cases, however, we do see some evidence of artistic interpretation in stamp design—if this was virtually confined, around the turn of the century, to stamps which had a symbolic motif, depicting abstract concepts such as Justice, Harmony and Liberality or the female allegory of the Republic. Here and there were also stamps in which the technique of lettering betrayed the influence of contemporary trends in art.

Towards the end of the last century many people in different countries were making a conscious effort to improve standards in the applied and decorative arts. In this, Britain took a leading (though by no means exclusive) part and it is curious to note that what in Britain is known as *Art Nouveau* (new art) is known in France as *Style Anglais* (English style) and in Italy as *Stile Liberty*—after the well-known London department store. In Germany this trend in art was known as *Jugendstil* (youth style) and in Austria as *Sezession* (since its exponents seceded from the existing tenets of art). Art Nouveau takes its name from a trendy boutique, La Maison de l'Art Nouveau, which was opened in Paris in 1895 by the Hamburg art dealer, Samuel Bing. Artists and craftsmen of many countries contributed to the development of Art Nouveau. Louis Tiffany in the United States and Emil Galle in France were the leading exponents of Art Nouveau in glass. Georg Jensen of Denmark was its interpreter in the field of silver, Charles Rennie Mackintosh in the fields of furniture and architecture.

In the two-dimensional field—which included postage stamps—there were many artists who practised Art Nouveau, from Aubrey Beardsley and Walter Crane in England to Alfons Mucha, a Czech who spent much of his career in Paris, and who later designed the first stamps and banknotes of Czechoslovakia.

If the nineteenth century witnessed a confusion of artistic styles, drawn from many sources and many past eras, Art Nouveau may be regarded as a distinctive style which could trace its ancestry to several disparate sources. It was a neo-Romantic style, which drew inspiration from the Gothic revival which was fashionable from about 1860 onwards. It also derived inspiration from the craze for anything Japanese which developed about 1875. The emphasis on curved lines may be traced back to Scandinavian and Celtic originals. Ornament went back to first principles, to nature, and was largely based on plant forms. A recurring theme, for example, is the trailing vine, ivy, tulip or lily motif. The strong element of asymmetry was borrowed from Japanese art. In the field of the applied and decorative arts Art Nouveau may be said to have been fashionable, in the strict sense, for barely a decade—from 1894 to about 1905. But in a wider context it may be said to date from the early 1880s, when William Morris founded his Arts and Crafts movement and Walter Crane founded the Art Workers' Guild. At the other end of the time scale, although it was becoming *passé* by 1905, it lingered on in certain media as late as the First World War. In the decade before the war, however, the emphasis shifted from curvilinear forms to straight lines and the cube, thus foreshadowing the emergence of the austere simplicity promoted by the Bauhaus movement in Germany after the war.

From the philatelic viewpoint, stamp design lagged noticeably behind other art forms and the heyday of the Art Nouveau stamp was from about 1905 to 1920. There were notable examples produced outside that period, particularly in the 'successor states', the emergent nations of postwar Europe.

Probably the earliest example of a stamp which exhibits the characteristics of Art Nouveau was the 5 centime value of the Brussels Exhibition set issued by Belgium in 1896. G. Portieltje's interpretation of St. Michael encountering Satan shows the influence of the pre-Raphaelite artists in its almost stained-glass treatment of the subject. The quasi-Gothic lettering and the asymmetrical ribbons complete the Art Nouveau elements of this design. A. van Nest's treatment of the same subject on the 10 centime is much more in the formal nineteenth-century tradition, though traces of Art Nouveau influence can be discerned in the scrollwork on the dominical label attached to this stamp.

A. Van Nest's treatment of the St. Michael and Satan theme for the Brussels Fair was more restrained than Portieltje's (page 86), but note the medieval parchment effect at the top of the design. Both this stamp and Portieltje's were engraved by Mouchon and typographed by the Belgian Government Printer at Malines.

Walter Crane, who produced this picture for May Day, 1894, was a disciple of William Morris. The idealized figures and ribboned treatment are closely parallel to Portieltje's stamp design (page 86). The floral excrescences in the frame were one of the hallmarks of Art Nouveau.

Above, left: Design for the title page of *Wren's City Churches* by the architect and graphic designer, A. H. Mackmurdo. He had a profound influence on graphic artists, especially in Germany, the Low Countries and Scandinavia at the turn of the century.

Mountford's elegant design for the Cape of Good Hope penny stamp of 1893 also shows a hint of Art Nouveau, not only in the delicate pose of the standing Hope, but in the *rocaille* ornament in the frame, retained for the penny denomination in the Edwardian definitive series of that country.

The series released by Germany in 1899 was strongly influenced by Art Nouveau. Paul Waldraff's sensitive profile of the actress Anna Führing epitomizing Germania has the same ethereal quality found in the young ladies painted by Mucha and Cheret, but the intertwined ribbons which adorn the frame of this design are in the pure tradition of Art Nouveau. Anton von Werner's allegorical composition symbolizing the union of north and south Germany (shown on the 2 mark value) also demonstrates the Art Nouveau style, and here again it is in the treatment of the frame ornament that the characteristic asymmetry is seen. In the original version of this design the sunrays were formed by straight lines—an idiosyncrasy favoured by exponents of Art Nouveau —but in May 1902 the vignette was redrawn with shaded sunrays which lessened the original effect.

The allegorical designs produced by Joseph Blanc and Eugene Mouchon for the French low values of 1900 betray subtle hints of Art Nouveau in the treatment of the female figures, but it is in the double-sized design by Luc-Olivier Merson for the higher denominations that the style is seen at its best. The delineation of the reclining Marianne, the curving lines of the foliage on the left, the incised lettering at the foot of the design and the asymmetrical shape of the value tablet—all are in the best traditions of *le style Anglais*. The medallist and sculptor Oscar Roty was a leading exponent of the style, as anyone acquainted with French coins at the turn of the century will testify. In so far as *La Semeuse* (the Sower) types of French stamps are derived from his magnificent coin obverse type (still in use!), Roty has left his mark on French philately, but out of its original numismatic context the two-dimensional Sower of the stamps does not reveal his Art Nouveau qualities to the same degree.

Another French artist who practised Art Nouveau forms was Eugene Grasset who designed a set of three stamps for Switzerland in 1900 to mark the twenty-fifth anniversary of the Universal Postal Union. The flowing robes of the female figure and the treatment of the inscription ribbons are the distinctive features of this design. Four years later Grasset produced another allegorical female in the Art Nouveau tradition, this time for the definitive series of Indochina.

Hungary's Turul series of 1900, the work of Joseph Böhm, has elements of Sezession in the treatment of the value and the plant ornament at the foot of the design. Apart from the floral ornamentation of the frames of the 10 and 15 forint war charity stamps designed by J. Diveky in 1916, no other Hungarian stamps showed Art Nouveau influence, though something of the style came across in the series portraying famous socialists which Ferenc Bökrös produced for the newly-founded Soviet Republic in 1919.

The purest example of Art Nouveau to be found on a stamp is G. Cellini's 1 centesimo design for Italy, issued in 1901. The irregular lettering and the ivy tendril ornament of this stamp embody two of the principal elements of *le stile Liberty*. To a lesser extent the same elements are to be found on the other denominations of the series, but in these designs they are subordinate to the eagle and portrait motifs. The qualities of Art Nouveau were strongly manifest in several Italian commemorative issues, ranging from the Kingdom Jubilee set of 1911 to the 25 centesimo value of the Mazzini series of 1922—the latter showing the imprint of Aubrey Beardsley in the treatment of the flames and the sword inscribed JVS (right). The 'Liberty style' spread to other parts of the Italian peninsula. Carpaneto's designs for the San Marino definitive series of 1903 are in the pure tradition of the Art Nouveau style in lettering and frame ornament.

In 1906 two countries produced sets of charity stamps, both of which drew on the prevailing fashion of Art Nouveau for inspiration. Professor Derkinderen's designs for the Dutch anti-TB set demonstrates how cluttered the plant forms of Art Nouveau had become by that date. It was reaction against this fussiness which led to the emergence of the straight-line motifs favoured by C. R. Mackintosh. The Netherlands remained faithful to Art Nouveau longer than most other countries; other stamps which show strong traces of this style are the curious Lion in a Garden definitive of 1923 and the Dutch Lifeboat Centenary pair of 1924.

The other country which produced charity stamps in 1906 was Romania, which got off to an ominous start with no fewer than four sets in the same year. All four designs contain elements of the style, though the most characteristic is the one which appeared first. The portrait of the Queen at her spinning wheel echoes the ethereal young ladies of Beardsley and Mucha, but as usual it is the lettering and the floral ornament which proclaim their origin most forcibly. The last of the four sets, typographed by Bradbury Wilkinson, was strongly reminiscent of the book illustrations of Rossetti and Burne-Jones, derived from

Alfons Mucha, who designed the first stamps and banknotes for Czechoslovakia, is better known in the rest of Europe for his paintings of dreamy girls with swirling tresses. This one was used on a postcard advertising cigarettes.

Far right: Mucha's exotic girls appeared on posters advertising anything from theatrical performances to the Monaco Monte Carlo railway.

Stained glass window symbolizing Spring, by Eugène Grasset. Grasset's style, a combination of Japanese and neo-gothic elements, was characterized by bold outlines which were admirably suited to stained glass. The same bold approach to line is evident in his stamp designs.

MONACO·MONTE-CARLO

CHEMINS DE FER P.L.M.
Billets d'Aller & Retour – Billets Circulaires
Billets d'Aller & Retour collectifs de famille à prix réduits.

TRAJET EN 16 HEURES PAR TRAINS DE LUXE

Reverse side of the French 50 franc banknote, designed by Luc-Olivier Merson and engraved by Romagnol. The pensive Minerva is obviously a close relation to the Marianne on Merson's stamps, even to the details of the pseudo-medieval clothing worn by both. The festoons of fruits and flowers are in the best Art Nouveau tradition.

Hungary, 50 filler, 1900

France, 40 centimes, 1900

Art Nouveau and its offshoots reigned supreme at the turn of the century (it was also known as *le stile 1900*). J. Böhm's 'Turul' design for Hungary betrays the contemporary style in floral ornament. The 'reclining Marianne' design was the work of Merson, engraved by M. Thevenin. Apart from the female figure the luxuriant foliage in the background was a characteristic decorative feature of this period.

mediaeval manuscripts, while the lettering was in the best tradition of the Gothic revival.

Although Art Nouveau was embraced enthusiastically in America, with Randolph Hearst and Theodore Roosevelt setting the trend, only one stamp of the United States shows traces of the style. In December 1908 a 10 cent Special Delivery stamp was released and enjoyed a fleeting currency. The arrangement of the hat of Mercury and the olive branch was comparable to the Art Nouveau ornament used in book illustration and book bindings at that time.

Considering the enormous contribution by British artists and craftsmen to the development of Art Nouveau, it is surprising that Britain was so late and so niggardly in applying its concepts to postage stamps. Shortly after the accession of King George V in 1910, the Postmaster-General, Herbert Samuel, asked the president of the Royal Academy for advice in the preparation of new stamp designs. As a result, three members of the Art Workers' Guild—G. W. Eve, Garth Jones and C. W. Sherborn—were commissioned to produce designs for the stamps. In the end only Eve's design was adopted and the bulk of the design work fell on the Australian sculptor and medallist, Bertram Mackennal. Mackennal's three-quarter face designs of 1911 were not well received by the public, on account of the poor quality of the portrait and the emaciated appearance of the lion on the penny denomination. The side panels of the half-penny are of interest, however, since they reveal the form which Art Nouveau took in sheet metalwork. This element, used as the background to the inscription POSTAGE & REVENUE was retained for the $\frac{1}{2}$ and $1\frac{1}{2}$ pence stamps of the definitive issues from 1912 until 1934. The best philatelic memorial to British Art Nouveau, however, was the series introduced in 1912. Mackennal was responsible for the three designs used for the lowest denominations while Eve designed the stamps from 5 pence to a shilling. The laurel and oak-leaf motifs, the plentiful use of trailing ribbons and the distinctive lettering all showed strong Art Nouveau influence. Mackennal produced the basic design and Eve the lettering for the famous Seahorse stamps of 1913. Here again, the treatment of Britannia and her team of seahorses laid emphasis on swirling lines. The rather fussy and unnecessary pendant ribbons at the top of the design were another popular feature of Art Nouveau.

Britain retained an Art Nouveau design far longer than any other country, in the Postage Due stamps which were introduced in 1914 and survived until 1971. The plant motifs used to fill the space on either side of the value tablet and the beaded border of the

Oscar Roty's figure of *La Semeuse* was first used for French coins in 1898 and subsequently adapted for stamps in 1903. The folds of her clothing and her flowing hair were popular Art Nouveau features.

Art Nouveau ribbon-work was a feature of the frame in Mountford's penny stamp of the Cape (2), but attained its peak in the Germania stamps designed by Paul Waldraff and used by Germany from 1899 to 1920 (3). This curvilinear approach to frame and inscriptions had a late flowering in the Silesian plebiscite stamps of 1920, typographed at the French Government Printing Works (1).

1. Upper Silesia, 2 marks, 1920

2. Cape of Good Hope,
1 penny, 1893

3. Germany,
80 pfennigs, 1902

Eritrea, 1 centesimo, 1903

Italy, 2 centesimi, 1901

Italy, 5 centesimi, 1901

San Marino, 1 centesimo, 1907-10

San Marino, 5 centesimi, 1903

The purest forms of philatelic Art Nouveau emanated from Italy. G. Cellini designed the low values of the Italian definitive series of 1901 (the 1c. illustrated here was subsequently overprinted for use in Eritrea). Mannered lettering based on Roman originals was Italy's main contribution to the *fin de siècle* style, but note the ubiquitous trailing ivy motif on the 1c. and the sinuous ribbons on the other values. The tiny republican enclave of San Marino reflected contemporary Italian influence in its stamps. Carpaneto's view of Mount Titano and Ortolani's allegory of Liberty have all the usual ingredients—meandering ribbons, distorted lettering and floral ornament—associated with *le stile Liberty*. All these stamps are enlarged to twice their original size.

tablet are Art Nouveau conceits. Despite the long association of British stamps with Art Nouveau, little attempt seems to have been made to extend this style to the stamps of the British Commonwealth. A possible exception would be the allegorical design by C. Dingli used on the Maltese definitive series of 1922. The figure of Melita holding a ship's rudder is obviously derived from pre-Raphaelite models. G. Vella's design, showing Britannia and Melita in a passionate embrace, falls far short of the Art Nouveau ideal and has little to distinguish it from countless other hackneyed allegorical motifs found on stamps of this period.

Art Nouveau, or *Sezession*, made enormous strides in Austria after 1902, under the leadership of Professor Koloman Moser. Moser is best remembered for his application of Art Nouveau motifs to ceramics and glassware, but he was also responsible for a number of fine stamp designs, of which the Jubilee series of 1908 was the most striking. The lettering and frame ornament of these stamps are characteristic, particularly the krone denominations of the series. The same influence was at work in the lettering of the stamps designed by R. Junk for the 1916 series, while Willi Dachauer's designs for the definitives of 1922 may be regarded as a belated outburst of Art

1. Netherlands, 10 cents, 1923

2. Romania, 5 bani, 1906

3. Romania, 10 bani, 1906

Charity or semi-postal stamps, with their tendency towards allegory, encouraged Art Nouveau motifs. Jan Toorop, better known for his ascetic posters (see page 96), adopted a similar approach in the Dutch charity set of 1923 (1). J. Pompilion's design for Romania's 25th anniversary series of 1906 (2) has features reminiscent of the Brussels Fair stamps of 1894 and betrays the prevailing influence of Art Nouveau. The charity series of the same year, with its vignette of Queen Elisabeth at her spinning wheel, has a marked Pre-Raphaelite quality (3).

Delftsche Slaolie: coloured lithograph advertising salad oil, by Jan Toorop, 1900. The best exponent of Dutch symbolism at the turn of the century, Toorop brought an ascetic quality to all his work, no matter how commercial or mundane the subject. The stylized tresses and gaunt features of his females show the influence of Frances and Margaret Macdonald of the Glasgow group. The same features survived in Toorop's stamp designs into the 1920s.

Nouveau. His design showing a gorgon-like female, for the high values of 1922-4, provoked enormous criticism in many countries and even *The Times* was moved to adverse comment.

With Austria may be bracketed Liechtenstein whose first stamps, released in 1912, were also designed by Moser and bore a close affinity to his Jubilee stamps of 1908.

In 1911 Bavaria celebrated the ninetieth birthday of Prince Regent Luitpold with a long series of stamps. The frame and side panels of the mark denominations exhibit elements of *Jugendstil* in the ornament. The stylized ploughman on the Argentinian series of the same year shows the increasing use of the straight line in Art Nouveau; in this case the sun's rays provide a parallel to the ploughed furrows.

Although Art Nouveau owed a great deal to the ancient art of Scandinavia, the countries of that region made little use of this style in their stamps. Denmark alone made use of Art Nouveau, in the circular motifs found on the 5 krone stamp of 1912 and the tendrils which decorated the vertical panels of the Northern Slesvig series of 1920. To some extent we may see the same influence at work in several stamps issued by Iceland between 1925 and 1930, particularly the Millenary sets of the latter year, but this may be regarded as a conscious twentieth-century interpretation of ancient Viking motifs.

Although Art Nouveau in general went out of fashion at the beginning of the First World War, it enjoyed an Indian summer in philately. The best examples of this emanated from Czechoslovakia whose stamps of 1918-20 were designed by Alfons Mucha, who has been described as 'the dancing dervish of the graphic line', on account of his supreme mastery of the sinuous fluidity of Art Nouveau. The lettering and frame ornament of the Hradcany definitives, the express stamps and postage due labels of the same period, furnish the best and purest examples of Art Nouveau in philately. To some extent Mucha also influenced his contemporaries, and the same treatment of background ornament is evident in the Czech Legion series of 1919 and the high values of the 1920 definitive issue, both designed by J. Obrovsky.

The three Baltic republics, Estonia, Latvia and Lithuania, embraced Art Nouveau motifs enthusiastically for their stamps in the immediate postwar period. Estonia's definitive series of 1919-20 and the Tallinn set of 1920-24 are replete with curvilinear ornament. The stylized sunrays on Latvia's series of 1918 conform to the ideals of Art Nouveau, but it is in the allegorical subjects depicted on the Independence, Courland and Latgale commemoratives of

Denmark, 20 øre, 1920

Iceland, 50 aurar, 1925

Old Norse elements were adapted for the stamps of the Scandinavian countries, especially Denmark and its dependencies. The Slesvig commemoratives of 1920, designed by V. Andersen, show the typical trailing ivy motif of Art Nouveau. H. H. Thiele's pictorial series for Iceland incorporates traditional ornaments in the frame.

The same arrangement of elements—profile, value tablet, female figure with outstretched arm and central motif—may be detected in Maura's Don Quixote design for Spain (1) and Sir Bertram Mackennal's 'Seahorses' design for Britain eight years later (2), though different techniques (letterpress and intaglio respectively) produced very different results. The same partnership of Mackennal (artist) and J. A. C. Harrison (engraver) produced the King George V three-quarter profile stamps of 1911 (3). The end-product would have been improved by using intaglio instead of letterpress, but the clogging of the fine lines in the hair and beard created a blurred effect. Both designs betray the influence of Art Nouveau in the scrollwork. C. Dingli's allegory of Melita on the Maltese stamps of 1922 (4) was a late manifestation of the pseudo-medievalism of the Pre-Raphaelites.

1. Spain, 5 centimos, 1905

2. Great Britain, 5 shillings, 1913

3. Great Britain, 1 penny, 1911

4. Malta, 1 penny, 1922

The transition from the Art Nouveau style to the later, more angular, forms was gradual and manifested itself in the subtleties of stamp design. Stylistically Bavaria's Jubilee series of 1911 (2), designed by F. A. von Kaulbach, conformed to ideas prevalent at the turn of the century, but Oscar Consée's use of photolithography was novel. J. M. Lubary's 'Ploughman' (3) is a first cousin to Roty's *La Semeuse*, complete with the same furrows and sun-ray patterns, though the rectilinear precision of this design reflects the prevailing mood in the graphic arts, abandoning curved in favour of straight lines. This design was initially recess-printed by the American Bank Note Company but subsequently typographed at the Buenos Aires Mint in a reduced format. V. Brunner's theme of a liberated Czechoslovakia (4) (typographed by the United Czech Printing Works, Prague) and Willi Dachauer's 'Gorgon' motif for Austria (1) retain elements of Art Nouveau and turn-of-the-century allegory, yet look forward to the more stylized forms associated with Art Deco. Ferdinand Schirnböck, probably the finest portrait engraver known to philately, engraved the Austrian stamps—a far cry from his sensitive and lively portraiture on the prewar stamps of Albania, Austria and Liechtenstein.

1. Austria, 25 kronen, 1922

2. Bavaria, 10 pfennigs, 1911

3. Argentina, ½ centavo, 1911

4. Czechoslovakia, 60 haleru, 1920

Right:
Art Nouveau was adopted enthusiastically by the 'Successor States' of Central and Eastern Europe. The purest example was afforded by Croatia's 1919 series (1), lithographed in Zagreb, with its Pre-Raphaelite figure, ivy leaves and stylized scrollwork. The Ukrainian damsel (5), typographed at Kiev, has close affinities with the prewar maidens of Mucha and Cheret. F. Ruszczyc's crude but vigorous designs for Central Lithuania (4) seem to have borrowed from the lithographs of Edvard Munch and the woodcuts of Gordon Craig. Bartlomiejczyk's allegory of ploughing in peacetime (3) was a popular theme in stamp design of the 1920s (see pages 107 and 108). I. Vavpotic's 'Chainbreakers' (6) and associated designs for Slovenia (7, 8, 9) (lithographed by I. Blazniks of Ljubljana) were closely identified with *Sezession* styles. Compare the ivy borders of the King Peter series with the backgrounds to Mucha's postwar Czech stamps on page 100.

1. Croatia, 3 filler, 1919   2. Central Lithuania, 2 marks, 1920   3. Poland, 2.50 korona, 1919

4. Central Lithuania, 50 fenigow, 1921   5. Ukraine, 30 shagiv, 1918   6. Slovenia, 15 vinar, 1919

7. Slovenia, 5 krona, 1919   8. Slovenia, 1 krona, 1919   9. Slovenia, 2 vinar, 1919

1. Czechoslovakia, 1 haleru, 1918

2. Czechoslovakia, 5 haleru, 1918

3. Czechoslovakia, 15 haleru, 1918

4. Czechoslovakia, 50 haleru, 1919

Under the influence of Alfons Mucha, Czechoslovakia's early stamps saw the finest flowering of Art Nouveau in philately. Mucha designed the postage, express and postage due stamps of 1918 (3 is overprinted for Eastern Silesia), and his influence can be seen in J. Obrovsky's design for the first anniversary of independence series (4).

1

2

3

4

1. Estonia, 25 penni, 1920
2. Russia, 35 kopeks, 1917
3. Russia, 1,000 roubles, 1921
4. Russia, 300 roubles, 1921

Art Nouveau made little impression on the stamps of the French colonies. A notable exception was the design by C. J. Housez for the 1909 series of St. Pierre and Miquelon, with its stylized wave motif.

Left: Post-revolutionary Russia and the Baltic states favoured Art Nouveau motifs for their stamps. The view of Tallinn (1) is virtually swamped by the curvilinear ornament in the design by E. Poland and K. Triumph. R. Zarrin's design symbolizing emancipation (2), and V. Kuprianov's allegories of agriculture and industry (3 and 4) emphasize the sun-ray motif.

Occasional examples of Art Nouveau survived as late as 1930. Its influence is seen in the Pre-Raphaelite allegory and Roman incised lettering in Tripolitania's Colonial Propaganda series designed by A. Calcagnadoro and, above all, in the distinctive lettering (showing late nineteenth century *Japonism*) of Brazil's airmail series.

Tripolitania, 60 centesimi, 1926

Brazil, 3,000 reis, 1930

1919 and 1920 that the Beardsleyesque approach to human figures is clearly evident. Lithuania's Independence stamps of 1920 have the typical sinuous lines in their frames, while the view of Gediminberg, on the air stamps of 1921 and 1922, demonstrates Art Nouveau techniques in the simplified delineation of the clouds.

The earliest stamps produced in Russia after the revolution drew on Art Nouveau for inspiration. R. Zarrin had given a foretaste of this in his treatment of the frames in several of the Romanov stamps of 1913, but this came to fruition in the 35 and 70 kopek stamps of 1917 showing a sword cutting fetters. Apart from the characteristic treatment of the sun's rays, the curved ornaments in the upper corners are quite distinctive. Similar motifs appeared on the series of 1921, particularly the designs symbolizing agriculture and industry. The higher denominations of the 1919 series produced by Poland were designed by E. Bartlomiejczyk, a leading Polish exponent of *Jugendstil*. He also designed the allegorical series of 1921 celebrating the New Constitution; the female figure and the plant motifs in the upper corners are in the characteristic style of Mucha. Certain of the stamps and postage due labels issued by Central Lithuania in 1921 betray, in their stylized treatment of clouds and sunrays, the influence of Art Nouveau. Typical plant forms were used in the frames of the Ukrainian series of 1918, though an even better example is to be found on the 20 + 20 kopek charity stamp of 1923 portraying the poet Shevchenko.

On the Adriatic, the stamps of Fiume, Slovenia and Croatia furnished numerous examples of Art Nouveau in 1919 and subsequent years. The best of these are the Freedom design of Croatia, the famous Chainbreakers of Slovenia and the designs by Gabriele d'Annunzio for the first anniversary series of Fiume. Marussig's representation of sixteenth-century Fiume, on the express stamps of 1923, not to mention the lettering and ornament in the overprints of 1923-4, provide examples of which Arthur Lazenby Liberty himself would have been proud.

The last flowering of Art Nouveau in philately took place in Latin America. Uruguay's stamp celebrating the football victory of 1924 has the typical Art Nouveau cloud formation as a background to the headless Victory of Samothrace. The last Art Nouveau design, however, came from Brazil in 1930, for a series of airmail stamps. The lettering, frame and, above all, the swirling lines of the background decoration, add up to one of the purest designs in this genre, and provide a fitting swan song to a style which had dominated the applied and decorative arts at the turn of the century.

France, 15 centimes, 1925 (23 × 40mm), from the series commemorating the Exposition Internationale des Arts Decoratifs et Industriels Modernes, designed by L. Ruet and H. Rapin. Apart from this series France made little concession to the 1920s style which later came to be known as Art Deco.

8
The influence of art deco

IN 1924 an international exhibition of modern decorative art (Exposition Internationale des Arts Décoratifs Modernes) was staged in Paris, both crystallizing the trends in modern design and stimulating its subsequent development. The term Art Deco was coined to describe the styles which were fashionable in the twenties and thirties, characterized by the prevalence of certain elements and motifs.

The frozen fountain was a popular motif in Art Deco, but there were many others. Allied to it was the pyramid, popularized by renewed interest in Egyptology following the discovery of Tutankhamun's tomb in 1922 and the discovery of the ancient civilizations of the Toltecs, Mayas and Aztecs in Central and South America. The masks and steles of those ancient peoples provided a number of motifs which recur in Art Deco. By contrast, there was a revival of the sun cult which took many forms, ranging from esoteric sun worship to the popular craze for sunbathing. The sunray motifs appear time and again in Art Deco and, derived from the sunbathing aspect, the glorification of the human body. This took sinister forms, particularly in Germany and other totalitarian countries where the image of a master race was being promoted. The ethereal quality of Mucha's young ladies, epitomizing Art Nouveau, gave way to muscular Nordic beauties with flowing hair and haughty countenance.

Above all else, Art Deco owed a great deal to Cubism and the Bauhaus movement. The Cubists, led by Picasso and Matisse, produced paintings in which human and animal form was reduced to simple geometric shapes. The Bauhaus at Weimar, under the stimulus of its founder, Walter Gropius, rebelled against the fussiness of the applied arts and substituted clean lines and stark simplicity. The flowing curvilinear patterns of Art Nouveau gave way to the austere straight lines of the Bauhaus. Geometric motifs, of rectangles, triangles and diamonds replaced the trailing vine and ivy tendrils of Art Nouveau.

The boundary between Art Deco and Art Nouveau is not hard and fast. In stamps a good example of the transition from one to the other is offered by the Austrian definitive series of 1922. Willi Dachauer's high-value design, portraying a gorgon-like figure, was pure Art Nouveau in its use of curving lines, whereas the two designs employed for the lower values were more advanced in their treatment. The stylized ear of corn and pincers and hammer motifs were in the best tradition of postwar decorative art. The geometric patterns in the side panels still have the curved line characteristic of Art Nouveau but the use of shading of varying thickness and intensity was a technique favoured by Art Deco. By 1925, however, F. Retzl and F. Zerritsch had dispensed with the wavy lines and were using straight lines for both vertical and horizontal panels of their stamps. The numerals in the low values differed radically from anything used on stamps before, but it was the trick of using fine straight lines of different thicknesses which was so characteristic of Art Deco. Note how the horizontal lines on the middle values of this series effectively balance the slanting lines of the telegraph wires in the centre of the design. For the pictorial definitives of 1929-31 R. Junk (who designed the Art Nouveau series of 1916) produced frames with geometric patterns in the vertical panels and bands of contrasting vertical straight lines in the bottom. G. Jung's costume series of 1934-6 also used fine horizontal shading behind the portraits, but the wavy line shading behind the value tablets marks a break with the Art Deco tradition. Nevertheless the lettering of this series is redolent of the thirties. Note, in particular, the shape of the s in ÖSTERREICH and GROSCHEN, and also the *moderne* style of the numerals. The same conceits are evident in the 1935 airmails, the use of photogravure heightening the *moderne* effect.

The newspaper and postage due stamps of Austria should not be overlooked, since both categories afford interesting examples of Art Deco. The 1921 Mercuries of the newspaper series were quite impressionistic, but the best examples are the 1925-34 postage dues, with diagonal bands of shading on the groschen values and horizontal bands in the schilling denominations.

The Teutonic countries seem to have been the most enthusiastic exponents of Art Deco in stamp

The Galeries Lafayette pavilion from the 1925 Paris Exhibition.
The stylized sun-ray motif, the stepped pyramid, the emphasis
on geometric lines and the impressionistic lettering were all
embodied in the Art Deco style.

Saar, 25 pfennigs, 1921, typographed at the French Government Printing Works, Paris. The elaborate framework and mannered lettering were typical of early twenties stamp design.

Obverse of the silver coinage of the Russian Soviet Federal
Socialist Republic, 1921-3, with edge inscription 'Proletariat
of all countries, Unite!' The rising sun and wheat-sheaf motifs
found parallels in Eastern European stamps of this period.

Bauhaus page design by Johannes Itten and Friedl Dicker. The graphic artists of the Bauhaus movement formulated styles of lettering which were widely used in stamps of the 1920s and 1930s.

Austria provided numerous examples of modern trends in graphic design in the interwar period. Willi Dachauer's 'Hammer and Pincers' design for the 1922 definitive series (1), and his numeral design for the corresponding postage due set (2), were more angular than his 'Gorgon' high-value design of the same year (see page 98). The predilection for geometric patterns is also discernible in J. F. Renner's newspaper stamps portraying Mercury (3) and his Parliament Building design of 1919 (4). F. Retzl's numeral design of 1925-7 (5), with its close perpendicular lines, was the very acme of geometric austerity in the twenties. Though more pictorial in composition, the 1934 costume series by G. Jung (6) still clung to modernistic lettering.

1. Austria, 1 krone, 1922
2. Austria, 4 kronen, 1922
3. Austria, 10 heller, 1920
4. Austria, 50 kronen, 1919
5. Austria, 4 groschen, 1925-7
6. Austria, 35 groschen, 1934

The *Notgeld* issued during the German hyper-inflation of 1921-1923 provided countless opportunities for experiment with new concepts of lettering and design. The female figures on D. Paderborn's design for the town of Bad-Lippspringe have the same elongated 'family likeness' found in Toorop's work, while the elliptical numerals belonged to a style fashionable in stamps of the period. The stark silhouette of Lemgo's paper money had its philatelic counterpart in contemporary stamps of Danzig.

Right:
Airmail lent itself admirably to *moderne* designs. Germany's 'plunging bird' design (3) by Professor Aufseeser, has a marked affinity with the Czech definitive design produced two years earlier by Professor Benda (4). Simple use of light and shade, facilitated by the tonal qualities of photogravure, created an effective motif for Romania's Aviation Fund stamps of 1932 (2). Germany applied modern design techniques to other kinds of stamps; for the Munich Exhibition of 1922 Professor Ehmcke produced a design incorporating stylized lettering, numerals and a version of the Munich coat of arms (1).

design. In Germany the stamps of 1919-20 which celebrated the National Assembly at Weimar were meant to symbolize the new republican order and, as such, broke away from the Wagnerian romanticism of the Germania definitives. G. A. Mathey's design, symbolizing reconstruction (25 and 30 pfennig values) is a splendid example of Art Deco, with its simplified human figure, though the effects would have been improved if the numerals of value had not been inserted in the central oval as well as in all four corners. W. Geiger's numeral design for the low-value definitives of 1921 has elements of Art Deco, but it was E. Scherff's ploughman design for the 20 mark high value which epitomizes this artistic style. Hitherto a stamp depicting ploughing would have faithfully represented a ploughman and his horse in realistic detail. Now a designer was daring to produce a picture in which the man's head was ridiculously small and his arms and legs out of all proportion to the rest of his body, while the horse conveyed the impression of a steeplechaser rather than a draught animal. As for the plough—the blade is incorrect and the harness is virtually non-existent! But the overall effect is quite pleasing, though one wonders how it appealed to stamp users in the early twenties.

For the Munich Exhibition series of 1922 Professor Ehmcke designed a set of stamps featuring a modernistic monk (the emblem of Munich). The charity pair of the same year, designed by J. V. Cissarz, depicted an allegory of Charity in the Art Deco idiom. But the best example of contemporary art was provided by the air stamps of 1922-3. Professor Aufseeser's plummeting bird is quite unlike anything that ever took to the air, with its stylized wings and tail coverts decorated with contrasting diagonal bands. A similar approach was used by J. A. R. Benda for the Czech low values of 1920-25. Thereafter Germany reverted to traditional modes of philatelic expression, though one set from the Nazi era, Sepp Semar's pair of 1936 for the International Recreational Congress in Hamburg, featured human figures in the Art Deco style.

The last of the German states to issue their own stamps also embraced the Art Deco fashion. The stylized ploughman, goddess of plenty, sower, Madonna and Child and allegorical figure of Bavaria, shown on the definitive series of 1920, were distinctly modernistic in composition, lettering and numerals. The stag conjured up by M. Korner for Württemberg's Municipal Service series of 1920 is quite impressionistic—as is Kissling's treatment of the scenery as depicted on the Official series of the same year. This series also utilized a modern style of lettering comparable to that on the Austrian series of 1934 already referred to. Danzig's stamps, particularly

1. Germany, 2 marks, 1922

2. Romania, 20 bani, 1932

3. Germany, 3 marks, 1922

4. Czechoslovakia, 5 haleru, 1920

20 marks, 1921

15 marks, 1920

40 pfennigs, 1920

Postwar German stamps reflected the contemporary experimentation in the applied and decorative arts. E. Scherff's impressionistic ploughman excited great controversy at the time: the plough-share is back to front and the anatomical detail of man and horses offended the public. The numeral designs of the 1920-2 official stamps provided an ideal opportunity for modernistic designs in which the figures were given a decorative treatment.

20 marks, 1922

2 marks, 1920

30 pfennigs, 1919

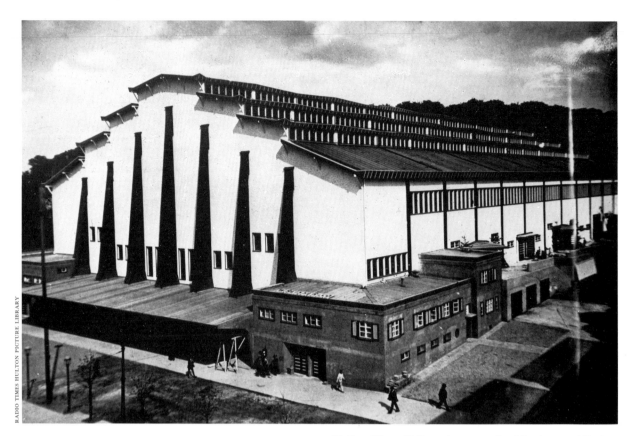

Stuttgart Town Hall, a prime example of Bauhaus architecture of the twenties. The Bauhaus movement, founded in Dessau by Walter Gropius, exerted a tremendous influence on the development of architecture in Europe after the First World War. The principle of form and function becoming an entity with individuality was extended to every branch of the applied arts, from furniture to cutlery, and was reflected in the graphic arts of the period, especially in the postage stamps of Germany, Austria, the Netherlands and Sweden in the inter-war period.

Bavaria, 5 pfennigs, 1920

Württemberg, 10 pfennigs, 1920

Only two German states continued to issue their own stamps after the formation of the Weimar Republic and both of them exhibited parallel developments in their designs. V. Zietara's ploughman and Kissling's scenic designs both relied on solid masses of colour to offset the stark simplicity of the vignettes.

the airmails from 1921 until 1925, show traces of Art Deco influence; the stylized lions, the swallow-tailed aircraft and the lettering which seems to have been a mixture of old Germanic and postwar Italic. This is seen at its best on the 1923 airmails, where a bird-like aeroplane, hybrid lettering and the sunray motif are combined.

Two issues of the early twenties are reminiscent of the woodcuts of Gordon Craig—the high values of the Saar definitive series of 1921 and the series designed by F. Ruszczyc for Central Lithuania in 1920 during the ephemeral Polish occupation of that district.

Elsewhere in Europe there were isolated examples of Art Deco. The Netherlands was a devotee of this style, especially in airmail stamps. Chris Lebeau, better known for his Art Deco glassware, designed the three air stamps of 1921 and followed this with the 'pigeon and Edam cheese' design in the same idiom. The latter series had a remarkably long life, making its debut in 1924 and surviving as late as 1946. P. A. H. Hofman's set of 1924 marking the centenary of the Dutch Lifeboat Institution, with its stylized boats and unusual double-lined lettering, is pure Art Deco. The 2 cent value of this set, incidentally, bears no name of the country. Chris Lebeau's treatment of the cockpits featured on the two air stamps of 1928 is essentially *moderne*; note the cunning use of close parallel lines and curves in the shading of the background. Both Curaçao and Surinam followed the mother country in adopting Art Deco concepts for the airmail stamps of 1930-31, both featuring a modernistic interpretation of Mercury by A. van der Vossen. This artist also produced Art Deco designs for Surinam's Green Cross charity stamps of 1928-9, but in his later work reverted to more conventional styles.

Another curiosity of Art Deco was the style of lettering in close parallel lines simulating wrought-iron work. This characteristic style is often found on book bindings of the twenties and thirties, and inevitably it appears occasionally on stamps. It is to be found on the Dutch Red Cross series of 1927 and in the low values of the series issued by France in 1930 to mark the International Colonial Exhibition. Apart from this, France made little use of Art Deco, preferring a more conservative approach to stamp design and the realistic depiction of scenery and portraits. Appropriately, however, Art Deco in its purest form was utilized on the stamps issued in 1924 in honour of the Exposition which launched the distinctive style. The rays of the torch on the 10 and 75 centime, the stylized vase on the 15 centime and the treatment of the architecture on the 25

1. Netherlands, 3 cents, 1926

2. Netherlands, 50 cents, 1923

3. Netherlands, 7½ cents, 1924

4. Netherlands, 5 guilders, 1923

The Netherlands was in the forefront of modern design in architecture and the applied arts, and postage stamps were no exception. Chris Lebeau, better known for his designs in ceramics and glassware, produced the famous 'Pigeon and Numeral' design (1) current for a quarter of a century. W. A. Konijnenburg's designs (with lettering by Jan van Krimpen) for the Jubilee series of 1923 echoed the ascetic trend pioneered by Toorop and Jan Thorn-Prikker.

centime—all produced by E. Becker—are elements which recur again and again in the art of this period.

Italy celebrated its 'new order' by issuing a series of stamps in 1923 with Fascist symbolism in a modernistic treatment. The three lowest denominations had a more traditional approach, but the eagle and fasces (1 and 2 lire) and the Roman skyline (5 lire) designed by G. Balla had the stark simplicity of outline which was to be such a strong feature of Art Deco. The majority of Italian stamps thereafter settled for conventional motifs, but an outstanding exception was the University Contests series of 1935 with its impressionistic allegorical designs and grossly distorted lettering. The same idiosyncrasy may be found on the stamps of the Italian territory of Rhodes, particularly the express and postage due issues designed by B. Bramanti in 1934-5. Although photogravure was a process admirably suited to the solid geometric patterns of Art Deco, little attempt was made to exploit this quality. Nevertheless A. Ortona's air express stamps of 1933-4 demonstrated the possibilities of this printing method. The shaded treat-

The 'wrought iron' effect was a popular device in stamps of the twenties, especially in Poland which paid close attention to sculptured lettering from 1921 onwards. Z. Kaminski was the chief exponent of this style, with stamps honouring Chopin (1927) (4) and the Poznan Exhibition (1929) (3). The geometric decoration in the side panels shows the influence of the prewar Austrian designers. The same device was used very effectively by Bulgaria in the St. Clement series of 1929 (2).

1. Poland, 4 marks, 1921

2. Bulgaria, 10 stotinki, 1929

3. Poland, 25 groszy, 1929

4. Poland, 40 groszy, 1927

1. Italy, 1 lira, 1923

2. Italy, 5 lire, 1923

3. Rhodes, 1.25 lire, 1935

4. Fiume, 20 centesimi, 1923

5. Italy, 2 lire, 1943

Art Deco took a different line in Italy, as is evident in the stamps of that country, its colonies and dependencies. The 'massy' quality of the 1923 series (1, 2) typified early Fascist art and the same approach may be seen in G. Marussig's design for the Military Post stamps of Fiume (4).

B. Bramanti specialized in distorted lettering and stylized figurative work, as shown in his designs for the stamps of Rhodes (3). A. Ortona's gradations of colour lent themselves beautifully to photogravure in the 1943 Air Express stamps (5).

Italian poster advertising anti-tuberculosis stamps. The lettering, stylized fasces and the stark symbolism of the message (today's babies, tomorrow's soldiers) had their counterpart in the commemorative stamps of the Fascist era.

Advertisement for Edgar Brandt, decorative ironwork: French, c. 1925. The stylized figures and lettering (particularly the 'lazy S') were common to every medium of graphic art in the twenties.

EDGAR BRANDT

101 BOULEVARD MURAT. PARIS

TEL. AUTEUIL   07-95 12-40

REGISTRE DU COMMERCE   DE LA SEINE N° 116570

FERRONNERIES
LUSTRERIE
OBJETS D'ART
EXPOSITION PERMANENTE

ment of the sunrays in contrasting bands reminds one of the murals favoured by Odeon cinemas in the thirties.

In 1924 Bulgaria adopted a new definitive series. The three lowest values used a lion rampant design, not unlike that of the series of 1879, but the design of the 50 stotinki value contrasted sharply, with its bold silhouette of the lion's head against a solid background. This predilection for colourless silhouettes on solid grounds was common in the Art Deco period in other artistic fields but was relatively unusual on stamps. In 1929 Bulgaria issued a set celebrating the millenary of St. Clement of Ochrid and adapted the Cyrillic lettering to the Art Deco wrought-iron effect. From Poland came two interesting sets, the first (1927) honouring Chopin and the second (1930) marking the centenary of the November Rising. The Chopin design, by Z. Kaminski, used a colourless profile on a solid ground, though realism was imparted by the addition of rudimentary lines for the hair and the features. T. Gronowski's design for the November Rising series made clever use of contrasting bands of dark and light shading on the rather surrealistic bodies of the soldiers. The previous year Kaminski designed a 25 grosz stamp for the Poznan National Exhibition and used the wrought-iron lettering technique and geometric vertical patterns of Art Deco very effectively.

Belgium flirted with Art Deco designs in the late twenties. The Orval Abbey Restoration Fund series of 1928 was traditional in design, except for the two lowest values which were photogravure and had an ultra-modern appearance, with ogives in the best traditions of the Bauhaus and lettering which was frankly futuristic. Four years later L. Buissert engraved a design featuring a reaper for the definitive low values and gave this allegorical subject a modernistic treatment.

The Scandinavian countries were wholeheartedly in the forefront of the Art Deco movement in every field of the applied arts, but produced comparatively few stamps in this genre. The best that Denmark could produce was the crowned numeral definitive design of 1933, but as this was merely the design of 1905 bereft of its Art Nouveau heart-shaped motifs, it does not really count. Sweden's sole foray into Art Deco stamp design was Ole Hjortzberg's kroner denominations of the 1924 Universal Postal Union series where a stylized carrier pigeon and wrought-iron lettering were employed. Norway ignored the style altogether, and it was left to Finland to exploit this medium more fully. The Abo commemoratives of 1929, with stylized designs, graduated shading and modernistic lettering, marked Finland's first essay in

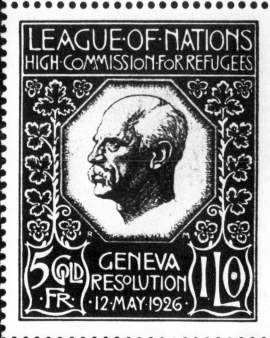

Designs for 5 gold franc stamps, portraying Fridtjof Nansen. These stamps were intended to denote prepayment of a tax levied on identity papers issued to Russian and Armenian refugees. The octagonal frame to the portrait was a popular device of the period.

Art Deco, but this was followed by A. Gallen-Kallela's cubist designs for the Kalevala series of 1935, and the stylized crusader of the Brothers-in-Arms Welfare Fund stamp of 1941—a late manifestation of the style.

Airmail was still a novelty in the twenties and thirties and the artists who designed stamps for this purpose strove to produce designs which were suitably *avant-garde*. Consequently, a large proportion of Art Deco stamps was intended for airmail. The Swiss air stamps from 1923 to 1932 faithfully reflected current trends in Art Deco, from the contrast of white on solid grounds of Bickel's 1923 series to the jazzy interpretation of 'Peace and the Air Post' produced by O. Baumberger in honour of the International Disarmament Conference of 1932. P. E. Vibert's 2

franc stamp of 1929, with a stylized pigeon against starkly outlined clouds, is another good example. Hungary's airmail series of 1933, with its symbolic design alluding to the gift of aircraft from Fascist Italy, and the allegory of the Spirit of Flight, used cloud and sunray motifs. The airmails of 1936 relied on contrasting bands of colour and the wrought-iron lettering to achieve their purpose.

An interesting blend of Art Deco with traditional art forms was provided by the stamps of the Irish Free State. The 1934 Hurling and the 1937 Constitution and St. Patrick issues combined Celtic asceticism with the simplified lines of *Art Moderne*—an experiment which was not subsequently developed. This style was well suited to typography, a process which Ireland continued to use long after it had been replaced

Art Deco made little headway in the American continent though there were some noteworthy exceptions. Compare De La Rue's treatment of the World's Fair theme (1) with the striking simplicity of the U.S. stamp for the same event showing the Trylon and Perisphere (3). Japan experimented with contrasting photogravure tones, aiming at a simple but effective motif symbolizing New Year's greetings (2). Mexico's 1934 airmail series (4) derived its inspiration from the art of the Mayas and Aztecs. Bolivia was one of the few countries to use lettering worthy of the Jazz Age, in the 1938 series lithographed by Guillermo Kraft of Buenos Aires (5).

Right: *Le Tour du Mont Blanc:* motoring poster designed by Roger Broders, 1927. Stark outlines and bold primary colours epitomized the graphic designs of the Art Deco period.

1. Ecuador, 2 centavos, 1939

2. Japan, 2 sen, 1937

3. United States, 3 cents, 1939

4. Mexico, 5 centavos, 1934

5. Bolivia, 2 bolivianos, 1938

115

1. Portugal, 1.75 escudos, 1934

2. Netherlands Indies, 5 cents, 1933

3. Switzerland, 1 franc, 1924

4. Lithuania, 5 centu, 1940

5. Switzerland, 2 francs, 1930

by other methods of printing almost everywhere else.

Nine countries in the American continent produced stamps in modernistic designs. Bolivia set the ball rolling in 1925 with an Independence Centenary set which included an excellent Archer design. The style came to maturity with the 1938 definitives whose lettering owed much to Cubism. Airmail stamps from Uruguay (1926), the Dominican Republic (1936) and Venezuela (1937) combined elements of Art Deco in their designs. The stamps issued by the revolutionaries at São Paulo in Brazil (1932) had characteristically *moderne* designs. Geometric elements were incorporated in Chile's Nitrate series of 1930 and in the San Francisco Exhibition set of Ecuador in 1937. Inevitably Mexico derived inspiration from Aztec art for the 1934 airmail series, coupled with ultra-modern lettering and frames. The sole example of Art Deco stamp design in North America was the 3 cent of 1939 commemorating the New York World's Fair. The white silhouettes of Trylon and Perisphere—themselves a product of the Art Deco period—against a solid ground, relieved only by concentric circles and horizontal lines of shading at the top and foot of the design, created a *moderne* effect. But thereafter, as everywhere else, Art Deco was abandoned in favour of traditional realism and pretty pictures in miniature.

Above, right: The Soviet pavilion, designed by K. Melnikov, at the 1925 Paris Exhibition. Note the 'wrought iron' lettering of the country name in the form of a giant hammer and sickle emblem and the emphasis on the decorative qualities of straight lines.

Right: Art Deco lettering and pictorial vignettes on a Heal's advertisement of 1929. The interwar period was one of experimentation in lettering which was often distorted or exaggerated to create special effects, or merely in search of novelty. The style of lettering in this advertisement is typical of the many ephemeral styles of the twenties. Their impact on stamp design was relatively slight except in Central Europe where they enjoyed a certain vogue.

Distorted lettering and white silhouettes were the hallmarks of *moderne* stamp design in the interwar period. Stark, white lettering against a solid background complemented the abstract designs symbolizing flight, hence the popularity of this style in airmail stamps. Lithuania's last series (before the country was absorbed into the Soviet Union) rank among the most *avant-garde* of prewar issues (4).

Ireland, 2 pence, 1934

Ireland, 3 pence, 1937

Ireland, 5 shillings, 1937

Irish stamps, after the attainment of independence in 1922, developed along lines that differed radically from British graphic design. R. J. King combined elements of Art Deco with traditional Celtic design in his Hurling (1934), New Constitution and St. Patrick (1937) stamps, typographed at the Government Printing Works in Dublin.

Sierra Leone, 3 pence, 1912 (28 × 33mm), typographed by
De La Rue. A combination of heraldry and royal portraiture,
marred by unnecessary repetition of value and duty.

9
Early twentieth-century pictorialism

THE EARLY PROMISE shown by the pictorial stamps of the closing decade of the nineteenth century was not followed by any appreciable extension of the idea after the turn of the century, and commemorative or semi-postal stamps, which gave plenty of scope for pictorial treatment, did not develop until after the First World War. During the first two decades of this century the vast majority of stamps all over the world were small upright rectangles dominated by portraits of rulers (Europe) or historic personalities (America). Allegorical subjects were also strongly favoured — Germania (Germany), La Semeuse (France), Hermes (Greece), the Ploughman (Argentina) and assorted heads of Liberty (Brazil). Whereas the European countries tended to use uniform designs for every denomination of a series, the American countries tended to go to the other extreme, with different subjects for each value; this difference in the character of European and American definitive issues has continued down to the present day. The countries in what would now be termed the Third World showed the greatest variety in the stamps of this period. It must be remembered that a large proportion of the territories in Africa, Asia and Australasia constituted colonial dependencies of European powers and most of them had to use stamps in one or other of the key-plate designs. Among the more independent countries, however, pictorialism had its beginning, and it was there that this tradition developed quite frankly with a view to balancing the budget at the expense of philatelists. Nevertheless, even in this area, pictorial stamps declined somewhat in popularity. The issues of the six Australian states, which included a fair number of pictorials, were superseded in 1913 by the Commonwealth issues and these alternated between a formal portrait of King George V and a symbolic map and kangaroo motif until 1938. New Zealand abandoned its pictorials in 1909, when a series portraying King Edward VII was introduced, and relied on royal portraits until 1935.

The reaction against pictorial stamps at the beginning of the century was two-fold: hostility of the general public towards double-sized stamps which were harder to lick and less convenient to stick on correspondence than the small format hitherto widely used; and distrust from the philatelic public who were becoming alarmed at the increasing flow of commemorative stamps and who viewed any change in definitive issues with suspicion. It is not insignificant that, in many instances, those pictorial stamps produced in the Edwardian era were designed in the standard small format, or in a size only slightly larger. Moreover, an uneasy compromise was reached either by using a pictorial subject in a formalized treatment, or by taking a heraldic element and giving it a more pictorial treatment. In the former category the prime example was afforded by Egypt whose stamps, from 1867 to 1914, featured the Sphinx and Pyramid. From 1879 on, these stamps were typographed by De La Rue with unvarying oval vignettes. The Pyramid and Sphinx motif could be regarded as a 'house symbol' which people all over the world would readily identify with Egypt, so in that sense this vignette could be regarded as symbolic rather than pictorial. Four of the Malay states—Negri Sembilan, Pahang, Perak and Selangor—had stamps typographed for them by De La Rue in uniform designs, showing a tiger leaping from the undergrowth (1891-5). Again a pictorial subject was treated in a heraldic manner. Subsequently the same states had other designs, showing a tiger's head and a group of elephants, but the treatment was formalized as before. This paved the way for the joint issues of the Federated Malay States which featured a leaping tiger (cent values) and the elephant group (dollar values) from 1900 until 1935. The stamps were typographed by De La Rue and, again, the tiger became less pictorial, more symbolic, in their hands. Bermuda had a short-lived experiment in this kind of pictorialism, between 1902 and 1910, with a formalized view of Hamilton Dock in an elaborate frame.

The Bermuda 'Docks' were superseded by a series depicting a galleon—the badge of the colony—and this typifies De La Rue's other approach to the problem. Colonial badges were given a more pictorial treatment on the stamps which this firm printed for Montserrat and St. Kitts-Nevis (both 1903), Grenada

1. Australia, 2½ pence, 1913

2. Australia, 2 pence, 1926

3. New Zealand, 8 pence, 1909

4. New Zealand, 1 shilling, 1915

1. Sungei Ujong, 3 cents, 1895

2. Federated Malay States, 10 cents, 1900

3. Bermuda, 4 pence, 1902-9

4. Cape of Good Hope, 1 penny, 1900

Australia alternated between royal portraiture and the heraldic kangaroo for many years, often depending on which government happened to be in power at the time! New Zealand stuck to portraits until 1935. Proper portraits of King Edward VII, engraved by W. R. Royle and recess-printed in New Zealand, were used for the 1909-13 series (3). The 1915 King George V series (4), designed by H. Linley Richardson and engraved by Perkins Bacon, was evidently based on that company's classic Penny Black, but merely showed how far the Old Masters had deteriorated since 1840.

In 1903 the individual presidencies of the Leeward Islands resumed their own distinctive stamps. The various islands used motifs based on their coats of arms and De La Rue adapted the heraldic motifs to a pictorial setting, foreshadowing the full-blown pictorialism of the 1930s.

St. Kitts-Nevis
2 pence, 1903

Montserrat,
2½ pence, 1903

De La Rue evolved a brand of stylized pictorialism, suited to typography in a small format. The 'Tiger's Head' of the Malay States (1), with purple fugitive ink for the frame and vignette, and titles and values in contrasting colours, was reminiscent of the colonial key types. It gave way, in 1900, to the standard 'Leaping Tiger' design of the Federated Malay States (2). For Bermuda, De La Rue treated a view of Hamilton Dockyard as though it were a heraldic emblem (3). E. Sturman's design for the Cape of Good Hope, however, managed to combine the colony's arms with a sensitively engraved view (4).

The Pyramid and Sphinx motif in stylized form served as the basis for all Egyptian stamps from 1866 to 1914. Compare the original lithographed version designed by F. Hoff of Hirschberg, Silesia and produced by Victor Penasson of Alexandria, with De La Rue's more professional letterpress version of 1888.

Egypt, 1 millième, 1888

Egypt, 10 paras, 1867

(1906) and St. Vincent (1907). At the same time, De La Rue had not lost sight of the need, in certain circumstances, for a more wholeheartedly pictorial design in a larger format. In 1903 they typographed a series for Dominica showing a view of Roseau from the sea, but this only emphasized how dismal typography could become. In the same year they produced some pictorial designs for St. Helena which were not only unsuited to typography, but were rendered all the more hideous by including King Edward's profile and an overelaborate frame. The only redeeming feature of that year's output was a neat design for the Orange River Colony (as the Orange Free State had been redesignated). The dominant motif was the King's profile in an upright oval, but the lower part of the design featured a springbok and a gnu in the African veld. This idea, of combining the monarch's profile with a pictorial element, had been initiated by South Australia in 1894, but a decade elapsed before it was repeated and it was not until the reign of King George V that it really developed.

The larger format adopted for the St. Helena stamps was also used by De La Rue for pictorial stamps, recess-printed for British New Guinea (1901), Bahamas (1901) and Brunei (1907). These designs, featuring a *lakatoi* or sailing ship, the famous Queen's Staircase and riverside dwellings respectively, enjoyed a surprisingly long life—into the early thirties in the first two and as late as 1952 in the case of Brunei. The vignettes were sensitively engraved, but the designs as a whole were marred by fussiness in the frames. De La Rue typographed a large-sized pictorial series for the Sudan in 1898, showing a camel postman. This spirited design was later reduced to standard definitive format (1921) and in this guise survived intermittently until 1951. So popular did the camel postman pictorial design become that, in the course of the years, it took on the character of a house symbol and in more recent years has even been adapted for the coinage of the Sudanese republic. Yet it had its origins in Kitchener's reconquest of the Sudan in 1898, when Captain (later Colonel) Stanton got his bearer to pose for the subject while he sketched the design.

The idea of combining royal portraiture with a heraldic element gradually developed in the reign of King George V. This was seen at its best in the double-sized Seahorses of the United Kingdom (1912-38), carried on in the high-value stamps of King George VI (1939), but these designs never lost sight of their formal heraldic character. A more pictorial approach is apparent in the rupee denominations of India (1911), with richly caparisoned elephants flanking the King's profile, and this design, with the portrait of George VI substituted, was used from 1937 until 1949. Small-format definitive sets with the profile of King George V and a pictorialized rendering of the colonial emblem appeared in Barbados, British Guiana, Antigua, Montserrat and the Virgin Islands between 1912 and 1922, and paved the way for larger designs, giving greater scope to the pictorial element, in the middle twenties. Trinidad (1922), Dominica (1923) and St. Kitts-Nevis (1924) produced stamps in this idiom, but it was seen at its best in the issues of Gambia and St. Helena, both released in 1922. The elephant and palm tree motif and the East Indiaman off St. Helena were given even more prominence in the designs produced by Bradbury Wilkinson and Waterlow respectively for the King George VI issues of 1938, the royal profile in these instances being relegated to a secondary position.

Typography was used for a number of British colonial commemorative issues, with mixed success. De La Rue printed victory sets for the Bahamas and British Honduras in 1920-21, combining the royal profile with the badges of the colonies; but the best of these typographed sets was that produced by De La Rue for New Zealand in 1920. The firm shared the contract for the design and manufacture of the plates with Perkins Bacon and Waterlow. With the exception of the 1½ pence (head of a Maori chief) and the 1 shilling (King George V), the stamps took as their subjects allegorical statues in the London area. De La Rue used the same source of inspiration for a victory series, recess-printed for Barbados the same year.

In 1923 the colony of St. Kitts (St. Christopher) celebrated its tercentenary and a lengthy series of stamps, from a halfpenny to a pound, was typographed by De La Rue. The uniform design showed a seventeenth-century sailing ship, with Old Road Bay and Mount Misery in the background. Though the design was more carefully engraved than the abysmal Dominicans of 1903, it demonstrated yet again that typography was not a suitable medium for scenic designs. Thereafter both De La Rue and their pet process lost ground to the banknote printers, Waterlow and Bradbury Wilkinson, who recess-printed handsome commemorative sets for Cyprus (1928), the Falkland Islands (1933) and St. Helena (1934). These issues, with their bolder lettering, more open engraving, subtler tones of colour and simpler framework, set the trend for the handsome, bicoloured pictorials which appeared in the British colonies in the early thirties and gradually superseded the typographed key-plate designs.

At the end of the First World War, however, typography still reigned supreme, and the first attempts

St. Helena, 1 penny, 1912

Falkland Islands, 6 pence, 1929

Bahrain, 5 rupees, 1933

A royal profile could sometimes be combined with a pictorial motif, but the results were seldom satisfactory. India's high values combined a profile of King George V and stylized elephants, the latter reduced to the status of framework ornament. The Falkland Islands (1929) proved that portraiture and pictorialism could be amalgamated even in a small format, though Perkins Bacon were criticized for the poor profile.

Dominica favoured an outright pictorial design but De La Rue's typography produced indifferent results (1). With the 'Camel Postman' design of the Sudan (4), however, De La Rue produced a vignette which has appeared on Sudanese stamps in various forms down to the present day, and has even been adopted as the national emblem on coins. When De La Rue abandoned letterpress for intaglio they produced more pleasing pictorial stamps. The 'Lakatoi' of New Guinea (2), 'River View' of Brunei (5) and the 'Queen's Staircase' of Bahamas (3) were popular for many years.

1. Dominica, half crown, 1903-21

2. British New Guinea, ½ penny, 1901

3. Bahamas, 1 penny, 1901

4. Sudan, 1 millième, 1898

5. Brunei, $5, 1908

at entirely pictorial designs were printed by this process. Jamaica embarked on a lengthy definitive series in 1919-21, the first to be entirely pictorial in character, and used typography for the halfpenny and penny values, the denominations in commonest use. Waterlow, who had begun with lithography and then specialized in recess, produced typographed sets for Malta, New Zealand and South Africa in 1926, with predominantly pictorial motifs, and as late as 1931 the Government Printing Office in Wellington was typographing quite passable airmail stamps featuring New Zealand scenery. But now that the smaller countries fully appreciated the advantages of philatelic revenue they were more inclined to favour the more expensive intaglio method for the sake of more eye-catching results. Thus the remaining denominations of Jamaica's 1919-21 series were recess-printed by De La Rue in a curious mixture of historic vignettes (from Columbus to the Great War), prominent landmarks and outright tourist publicity posters, aping the quasi-commemorative 'publicity' sets produced by Newfoundland in 1897 and 1910. In 1923 De La Rue recess-printed the first of a series of small-format tourist publicity stamps for Newfoundland, like the Tasmanian pictorials of 1899 but in a smaller size and with neater frames. Slightly larger dimensions

De La Rue compromised successfully by incorporating both portraiture and heraldry in small format designs like the Virgin Islands stamp shown here (1). A larger format permitted greater scope for pictorialism, as in the Ascension series (2), or heraldry, as in the case of Sierra Leone (see page 118). St. Kitts-Nevis gave equal prominence to the royal profile and the colonial emblems (3), and a similar approach was adopted by Trinidad (4). St. Helena adapted heraldic elements in a more naturalistic setting for pictorial designs, in which the royal portrait was relegated to a subsidiary role (5).

1. Virgin Islands, 1½ pence, 1927
2. Ascension, 3 pence, 1924
3. St. Kitts-Nevis, 1½ pence, 1920
4. Trinidad and Tobago, 4 pence, 1922
5. St. Helena, 3 pence, 1940

New Zealand, 1 penny, 1920

Barbados, 1 penny, 1920

Victory after the First World War resulted in a few celebratory stamps from the British Commonwealth. Both New Zealand and Barbados chose statues of Victory from landmarks in London for these stamps, respectively typographed and recess-printed by De La Rue.

The definitive sets of Barbados neatly combined portraiture and heraldry by featuring the reigning sovereign in a chariot drawn by seahorses; thus only the features of the monarch needed to be changed at the beginning of each new reign. This design was introduced in 1925.

Barbados, 3 pence, 1947

were used for a similar series in 1928-9, which was later printed, with slight differences in detail, by Perkins Bacon in 1929-31. Perkins Bacon also recess-printed pictorial definitives for Newfoundland between 1932 and 1938, and also adapted the vignettes for a series in 1937 celebrating the coronation of King George VI. These definitives made good use of simple frames and bold motifs on plain backgrounds, and this was carried to its logical conclusion in the airmail series of 1933, with masses of blank space contrasting with the subjects, and bold but slim frame lines and lettering. Canada itself adopted a policy similar to Newfoundland but, in the hands of the American Bank Note Company, the Canadian Bank Note Company and the British American Bank Note Company, clung to the ornate frames characteristic of the bank-note printers. The twin-oval portraiture which had been so successful in the Jubilee series of 1897 was repeated less successfully in the Quebec Tercentenary series (1908), the Confederation Jubilee set (1927), the Silver Jubilee (1935), Coronation (1937) and Royal Visit set (1939), but it was only latterly that the frames cast off their baroque quality. The trend towards simpler frames and more prominent pictorial vignettes is also evident in the other commemoratives and the definitive sets of 1928, 1930, 1935 and 1937.

From 1931 on, many of the colonies abandoned the key plates and branched out with beautiful, intaglio pictorials, often in two colours and usually incorporating a profile of King George V, discreetly tucked away into the frame to balance the value tablet. The best of these miniature scenic and wildlife posters came from Sierra Leone (1932), Gibraltar (1931), Ascension (1934) and Ceylon (1936). Having used portrait stamps in the European manner, South Africa (1927) and New Zealand (1935) went to the other extreme and adopted pictorial designs from which the royal profile was absent. Malta compromised by issuing small-format low-value stamps with the King's portrait, but large pictorials without the portrait for the higher denominations. A similar mixture was adopted by Canada in every definitive series from 1928 to 1967 and, to a lesser extent, this was a feature of the definitive issues of Jamaica (1929-32). Certain territories produced pictorial sets which included designs with and without the King's portrait inset. This was the policy in Bermuda (1936), Cyprus (1934) and British Guiana (1934-51). Trinidad and Tobago (1935) and Aden (1937) issued pictorial sets whose designs were subsequently modified or enlarged to incorporate portraits of King George VI (1938-9).

In the period up to the Second World War the British Empire—consisting of dominions, colonies and

Bermuda, 1 farthing, 1920

Bermuda, 1 shilling, 1921

Bermuda's tercentenary was the subject of two sets. The first, designed by no less a personage than the Governor himself (Sir James Willcocks), betrays the hand of the amateur in its unnecessarily verbose inscription which De La Rue handled as neatly as possible. The twin oval concept was later adopted for definitive stamps issued by Trinidad, Grenada and St. Kitts-Nevis. A second series, designed by H. J. Dale, solved the problem of the inscription ingeniously, but the heraldic and symbolic elements stuck in the corners marred the design.

The interwar years were the heyday of the lengthy (and expensive) colonial commemorative set. Mercifully such issues were comparatively infrequent. They laid the foundations for the bicoloured pictorials of the 1930s. The St. Kitts-Nevis Tercentenary series of 1923 was typographed by De La Rue, who were apparently not deterred by the indifferent results of their earlier Dominican pictorials (see page 122). Bradbury Wilkinson's handsome intaglio designs for the Falkland and St. Helena centenaries and the Cyprus jubilee of British rule established a pattern of colonial pictorial design which lasted until the 1960s.

St. Kitts-Nevis, 1 penny, 1923

Falkland Islands, 1 pound, 1933

St. Helena, 1 penny, 1934

Cyprus, 18 piastres, 1928

1. South Africa, ½ penny, 1937

2. Newfoundland, 24 cents, 1932

3. Jamaica, 2 pence, 1921

4. Newfoundland, 48 cents, 1937

1. St. Lucia, 1½ pence, 1936
2. Ceylon, 1 rupee, 1938

By the mid-thirties the intaglio pictorial definitive, with portrait of the king inset, had become established. The St. Lucia and Ceylon sets were recess-printed by De La Rue and Bradbury Wilkinson respectively.

Pictorial definitive sets made a tentative beginning with the Jamaican series of 1919-21 (3). South Africa's Springbok design (1) first appeared in 1926 and, like the contemporary Australian kangaroo design, was an attempt to pictorialize a symbolic feature. Newfoundland was the leading exponent of the pictorial 'publicity' set, an idea that originated in the Diamond Jubilee series of 1897. By and large, these sets dispensed with the necessity for a royal portrait (2), though the design could be modified in certain circumstances. Thus Newfoundland's Coronation series of 1937 adapted the current definitive designs, with the addition of the king's portrait (4).

1. Aden, 1 rupee, 1937

2. New Zealand, 2½ pence, 1935

3. Trinidad and Tobago, 6 cents, 1935   4. Bermuda, 1s 6d, 1936   5. South Africa, 1 shilling, 1927

Protectorates—accounted for about a third of the world's stamp-issuing entities, so it is not surprising that the contribution of these territories to the development of pictorial stamp design was so considerable. Of the other major colonial groups, the German had been divided among the British, French and Belgian (for all practical, philatelic purposes), the Spanish had diminished after the loss of the Pacific and Caribbean territories to the United States. The remaining Spanish colonies, and those of neighbouring Portugal, continued to use key plates into the thirties. France alone abandoned key plates relatively early and embarked on a policy of pictorial designs. The regrouping of certain territories in West and Equatorial Africa resulted in the gradual abandonment of the Tablet key plates in favour of more pictorial designs, but these were standardized so that only the names of the territories were different. Thus the West African colonies had a definitive series in 1906 using three standard designs whose principal motifs were palm trees, and portraits of General Faidherbe and Dr. Eugene Balay, while the Equatorial African territories had stamps featuring a leopard stalking through the jungle. By 1912 the Tablet stamps had been superseded by pictorial stamps in every part of the French colonial empire.

Some countries did not attempt to combine portraiture with pictorialism but alternated the two. After a series portraying King George V South Africa switched to pictorials in 1926-1927 (5). New Zealand used royal portraits till 1935, then introduced a pictorial series recess-printed by De La Rue (2). Royal portraits were re-introduced three years later, though the pictorial series was not entirely phased out. Bermuda had a mixture of pictorials, some with and others without the royal portrait included (4). Both Aden and Trinidad (1, 3) issued pictorials without the royal portrait, but subsequently redrew the designs to incorporate portraits of George VI.

1. French Guinea, 5 centimes, 1913
2. Upper Senegal and Niger, 1 centime, 1914
3. French Somali Coast, 2 centimes, 1915
4. Martinique, 20 centimes, 1908
5. Togo, 40 centimes, 1924
6. Reunion, 1 centime, 1907
7. Mauritania, 2 centimes, 1913
8. Gabon, 20 centimes, 1910
9. Ivory Coast, 10 centimes, 1915
10. Cameroun, 2 centimes, 1925
11. French Guyana, 15 centimes, 1929
12. Middle Congo, 15 centimes, 1929
13. Niger, 2 centimes, 1927
14. Guadeloupe, 10 centimes, 1928

Djibouti (French Somali Coast Protectorate), 5 centimes, 1894. Djibouti and Obock on the Red Sea were the first French territories to have entirely pictorial stamps. They were typographed in Paris and issued imperforate, despite the simulated denticulation round the frame. The arrangement of horizontal and vertical vignettes featuring the seaport and tribesmen, together with the elaborate frame (incorporating tribal drums and textile patterns), provided some of the most unusual designs ever produced.

A gallery of gaudy pictorials, designed and manufactured in Paris for French colonial consumption. Some attempt at political grouping may be seen in the stamps of Guinea and Upper Senegal (French West Africa) (1, 2) and the horizontal designs of Mauritania and Ivory Coast (7, 9), which formed part of the same group of territories. Different frames, incorporating tribal patterns and artifacts, were used for each territory. These and many later French colonial issues resulted from the partnership of J. de la Nezière (designer) and J. Puyplat (engraver). The stamps were typographed at the French Government Printing Works, invariably in two-colour combinations which became progressively more garish. As a rule vignettes concentrated on native types and occupations with, less frequently, wildlife and scenery. Considerable ingenuity (and occasionally some artistry) was lavished on frames which ranged from the severely practical (5, 13) to the pastoral scene on the Somali Coast series (3).

The French colonial pictorials present a sad contrast to their British counterparts. They were all printed in typography at the French Government Printing Works, by the same team of designers and engravers in every instance, and followed the same pattern of bicoloured frames and vignettes—often in garish combinations. Considerable ingenuity was often displayed in cramming tiny figures, fauna and flora into the framework and the lettering was often bizarre and whimsical. Each territory was allowed three designs per series, for low, middle and high values respectively, and the sets were changed every decade or so, though the inflation that overtook the franc in the interwar years meant numerous additional denominations, provisional surcharges and changes of colour combination. Shortly before the Second World War a few of the more fortunate colonies (such as Cameroun, Dahomey, Guinea, Somali Coast and Ivory Coast) got new pictorials recess-printed in monochrome and this pattern would no doubt have been extended to all the colonies, had not the war intervened. The typographed pictorials have nothing to commend them aesthetically and they are invariably held up as examples of the very worst faults ever exhibited in stamp design.

Among the French colonial pictorials of the typographed era one group stands out from the common herd—the stamps designed by J. de la Neziere for Dahomey, Senegal, Mauritania and other West African territories. Although the vignettes themselves were poorly engraved, and the colours either drab or garish without achieving a happy medium, the frames incorporated strong geometric patterns, often with symbolism or patterns which captured the spirit of the territory concerned. This penchant for heavy borders extended to the stamps which de la Neziere also designed for French Morocco (1917-31), Lebanon and Syria (1925) and the Saar (1926-32).

Although the stamps of the French colonies in the interwar period form such a deplorable group, the same cannot be said of the stamps used in the mother country. Oscar Roty's figure of La Semeuse, in several typographed variations, ruled the scene from 1903 until 1932 and was followed, so far as the low

1

2

3

4

5

6

7

8

9

10

11

12

13

14

Morocco, 1 centime, 1923

Syria, 20 centimes, 1930

1. France, 25 centimes, 1927

2. France, 75 + 50 centimes, 1936

3. France, 1 franc, 1937

4. France, 80 centimes, 1955

5. France, 20 francs, 1954

6. France, 25 centimes, 1959

7. France, 35 + 10 centimes, 1938

8. France, 8 francs, 1955

Left:
Vaugirard of Paris dented the monopoly of the Government Printing Works by printing pictorials for several territories using 'heliogravure' (another term for photogravure). J. de la Nezière, who designed both Moroccan and Syrian sets, showed his passion for heavy, ornate frames—a relic of his earlier colonial designs.

German medal commemorating the tenth anniversary of the First World War, symbolizing 'the living spirit of our dead'. Its stark motif echoes the impressionism found in German stamps of the 1920s.

Below, left:
French definitive and commemorative stamps. The Sower (*La Semeuse*) designed by Oscar Roty, was introduced in 1903 and survived into the 1930s. Originally the figure was shown against a ploughed field with sun-rays on the horizon, but subsequently a plain, solid background was adopted (1). The Roty legacy is discernible in French low-value definitive stamps down to the present day, the Sower herself having been re-introduced in 1958. She was the prototype for the allegorical figure of Peace, designed by P. A. Laurens for the series of 1936-7 (3). Marianne, female allegory of the republic, has appeared in several issues; A. Regagnon's version of 1959 shows her in the Ship of State (6). Small-format Arms designs have been in use since 1944 for the lowest denominations; the 80 centimes of 1955, showing the arms of Roussillon, was designed by R. Louis and engraved by J. Piel (4). Apart from the typographed low values France issues intaglio pictorials at frequent intervals. Scenery and landmarks have provided the subject matter for these double-sized stamps since 1929. Typical examples are the 8 francs (Marseille) designed by H. Cheffer (8), and the 20 francs (Ajaccio) designed by Lemagny (5). Multi-colour intaglio has been used increasingly since 1954. Prewar charity issues included the Refugee pair of 1936 (2) and the annual Unemployed Intellectuals sets (7).

values were concerned, by several other allegorical designs. To this day France uses typographed allegories for the lower denominations, augmenting this (since 1944) by small-format designs featuring provincial, departmental and civic coats of arms in full colour. In 1929, however, typography gave way to intaglio for the higher denominations, produced in a larger size and featuring landmarks and scenery. This policy began with 10 and 20 franc stamps depicting the port of La Rochelle and the Pont du Gard, and since then several hundred stamps have played an enormous part in boosting the French tourist industry. The designs are changed at random from time to time; one cannot speak of definitive sets in the usual sense, since it is rather a case of one long definitive series which is for ever changing its components. At the same time, France stepped up its output of commemorative and other special issues. At first the small format was used, for stamps portraying Pasteur, Ronsard, Victor Hugo and others (1923-35), but latterly the double-sized format of the definitive pictorials was adopted for all special issues and this remained constant until the 1960s. With the advent of the Giori press in 1939, multicolour combinations with accurate registration became possible in intaglio and France has used this technique to good effect ever since.

Germany lagged behind France in adopting pictorial designs. Oddly enough, the first pictorial designs to appear in Germany were the official stamps of the 'people's state' of Württemberg (1920). The Weimar Republic, especially during the period of the hyperinflation (1923), preferred a succession of numeral designs and allegorical compositions. The only recess-printed pictorials on prewar lines were the high values of 1923-30 featuring castles and cathedrals in a heavy Teutonic manner. Unlike the Americans, the Germans had no qualms about portraying living presidents; from Ebert and Hindenburg in the twenties they stretched in an unbroken line, down to Heinemann and Ulbricht, on the respective issues of the Federal and Democratic republics. This pattern has been varied occasionally, by portraits of famous Germans (1926 and 1961-4), numeral motifs (1945-6 and 1951) and historic buildings (1948 and 1964-7), but the size of the stamps has always been kept within limits. The special issues up to 1945 were also smaller on average than those issued elsewhere. While the art of stamp design progressed in other countries, it more or less stood still in Germany, with stark Gothic lettering and historic scenes and personalities tending to glorify the past. During the Third Reich (1933-45), stamps were used blatantly to promote the image of Nazi Germany.

The Low Countries and Scandinavia adopted a policy of using numeral designs for the lowest denominations of the definitive series and portraits of the reigning monarch for the higher values, and this has continued to the present time. A slight pictorial element was introduced with the small-format, stylized pictures on the series of 1954 (Sweden) and 1963-9 (Norway). Like France, Sweden has begun augmenting her portrait definitives with handsome recess-printed pictorials—beginning with the 10 kroner stamp of 1961 and, in more recent years, gradually extending to the lower denominations. Runic motifs are a recurring theme in these issues. In Iberia, Portugal has clung to allegorical designs— Camoëns's poem *Lusiad* (1931-8), caravel (1943) and mediaeval knight (since 1953), either lithographed or typographed. Spain, on the other hand, has favoured portraiture—first Alfonso XIII (up to 1931), famous Spaniards during the republic, and aspects of Franco since 1936. Italy in the Fascist era used a mixture of royal portraiture with Roman allegory, followed by a further dose of symbolism (1945-8) and latterly (since 1953) a uniform design of Italia based loosely on the obverse of the Syracusan dekadrachms of 410 B.C. There were, however, short pictorial interludes—a series devoted to provincial occupations (1950) and reproductions of works by Michelangelo (1961).

Provincial occupations and costumes have provided Austria with material for pictorial definitives on two occasions (1934 and 1948), but scenery and landmarks have found greater favour, ranging from the high values of 1925, through Chmielkowski's attractive vignettes of 1945-7, to the present series introduced in 1957. Switzerland preferred finely engraved mountain scenery for the high-value stamps from 1914 onwards, but stuck to typographed allegories for the low values—the figure of Helvetia or William Tell and his son. In 1934 small-format stamps were introduced with scenery designed by Karl Bickel in rather coarse typography. Two years later the series was redrawn and printed in recess with far more satisfactory results. Subsequently Bickel produced a series in 1941 featuring historic personalities, notable for its use of white space as a background to the figures. Bickel's series of 1949-50 reverted to scenery, stylized as before, but sensitively engraved in a somewhat larger format. Since 1960, however, Switzerland has adopted definitive stamps recess-printed with lettering and motifs picked out against relatively solid backgrounds. The stamps feature postal history (low values), famous buildings (middle values) and the four Evangelists (high values). Soviet Russia continued to use the Tsarist arms stamps until 1923 when

RICKARDS

Rraft durch Freude

Auch Du kannst jetzt reisen!

Kraft durch Freude (Strength through Joy): poster advertising holidays through a Nazi Party savings scheme. Both the lettering and pictorial treatment had their parallels in German stamp design. Von Axster-Heudtlass, who produced this poster, designed many of the stamps of the Third Reich.

Scenery and landmarks, allegorical designs of workers and peasants, numeral designs and portraits of heads of state have been the German formulae for definitive stamps since the First World War. P. Neu's reaper design (1) was one of several in the same *genre* which replaced the Germania series; a similar theme was adopted in the immediate aftermath of the Second World War. Several high-value definitives of the interwar period featured well-known castles and were recess-printed (2). The majority of definitive stamps, however, continued to be typographed. The Ebert series of 1928 (3) was followed by the Hindenburg 'medallion' series, designed by Karl Goetz (4). With R. Klein's 'Hitler Heads' of 1941 the concept of a profile on a solid ground was resumed (5). Note the simple positioning of numerals of value in these three designs. Postwar Germany's Buildings Series (*Bautenserie*) took famous landmarks such as Cologne Cathedral (7); the same solid background, minimal lettering and numbering as Neu's designs of 1921 are evident. Numerals and posthorns, likewise used in the early twenties, made a come-back with the series of 1951-1952 (8). More recent issues of both Federal and Democratic Republics have returned to political portraiture: President Heuss (1954), President Heinemann (1972) and Walter Ulbricht (1961).

1. Germany, 160 pfennigs, 1921

2. Germany, 5,000 marks, 1923

3. Germany, 3 pfennigs, 1928

4. Germany, 4 pfennigs, 1932

5. Germany, 3 pfennigs, 1941

7. Germany, 5 pfennigs, 1948

8. Germany, 8 pfennigs, 1951

6. Germany, 12 + 18 pfennigs, 1943

9. Germany, 90 pfennigs, 1954

10. Germany, 60 pfennigs, 1972-3

11. East Germany, 15 pfennigs, 1961

The Ostberg Town Hall, Stockholm, an example of modern Scandinavian architecture incorporating traditional design elements. The same qualities of strength and functionalism pervaded Swedish stamp design in the 1920s.

1. Netherlands, 15 cents, 1924

2. Netherlands, 12 cents, 1949

3. Netherlands, 5 cents, 1947

4. Belgium, 10 centimes, 1919

5. Belgium, 3.50 francs, 1959

Dutch definitives have invariably portrayed the reigning queen, though numeral designs are favoured for the lowest denominations. A contrast in styles and treatments is provided by the typographed Wilhelmina series of 1924 (1), designed by J. Veth, the photogravure Wilhelmina series of 1947 (3), designed by S. L. Hartz with lettering by Jan van Krimpen (the overall concept and faint background pattern are reminiscent of the Penny Black), and the Juliana full-face series of 1949 (2). Subsequent Juliana issues have used profiles of the queen. Belgian definitives have alternated between profiles and full-face portraits of rulers: Henri Cheffer's celebrated 'Tin Hat' series of 1919, recess-printed by Enschede, portrayed King Albert in military uniform (4). The Baudouin series (5), in photogravure by the Belgian State Printing Works, was introduced in 1953.

1. Sweden, 10 öre, 1951   2. Sweden, 50 öre, 1962   3. Sweden, 30 öre, 1921   4. Norway, 2 øre, 1892

5. Denmark, 10 øre, 1913   6. Denmark, 30 øre, 1967

Numerals and portraits provide the subjects for Scandinavian definitives, often for the lower and higher denominations respectively. Boldly sculpted lettering on relatively plain backgrounds is the hallmark of Scandinavian stamp design, assisted by a preference for letterpress and intaglio. Denmark's crown and numeral design was introduced in 1933, though this denomination (6) was added in 1967. The world record for philatelic longevity is held by Norway's posthorn and numeral design (4), introduced in 1872 and still going strong though now printed in photogravure. Note the continuous line device in the tail of the letter 'g' in 'Sverige' (1)—a medieval calligraphic flourish seldom found in stamp design.

1. Portugal, 25 centavos, 1931   2. Portugal, 1.40 escudos, 1953   3. Spain, 15 centimos, 1901   4. Spain, 35 centimos, 1951

5. Italy, 35 lire, 1953   6. Italy, 25 centesimi, 1946

Allegory and portraiture are used respectively by Portugal and Spain. P. Guedes designed and A. Fragoso engraved the *Lusiad* design of 1931 (1), alluding to an epic poem by Camoens; the unusual overlapping of the allegorical figure and the lettering was intended to create a three-dimensional effect. Martins Barata designed the medieval knight stamps (2), lithographed at the Lisbon Mint since 1953. Like the colonies Spain preferred portraits of Alfonso XIII throughout his forty-year reign; this version (3) dates from 1901 and parallels the 'Curly Head' profile of the colonial key type. General Franco's portraits have been used since 1939 when Sanchez-Toda produced this design (4), lithographed at the State Printing Works, Madrid. Postwar Italy began with republican allegories, such as P. Paschetto's 'torch of enlightenment' (6), but has used V. Grassi's version of 'La Siracusa' (5) since 1953.

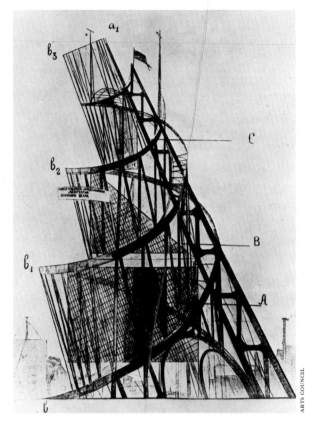

A Soviet sculpture at the Exhibition of Cultural and Economic Achievement typifies the 'socialist art' of the Stalinist era.

1. Switzerland,
30 centimes, 1925

2. Switzerland,
35 centimes, 1935

3. Switzerland,
50 centimes, 1882

4. Switzerland,
1.20 francs, 1941-58

Tatlin's monument to the Third International, 1919-20, symbolized the Utopian ideals of the Constructivists—romantic but impractical. Something of this romanticism and impracticality may be seen in Soviet stamps of the same period, especially in the 1921 definitive series by Kuprianov and Ksidias.

Left:
Swiss definitive issues have ranged from allegorial to pictorial designs. The allegorical figures of Helvetia (3) (sitting, standing or with sword) spanned the period from 1862 to 1934, latterly alternating with portraits of William Tell and his son. R. Kissling's Tell design (1) was introduced in 1914. Small scenic vignettes were adopted in 1934, but switched from letterpress to intaglio a year later, with more satisfactory results (2). A larger format was adopted in 1941 for the historic personalities series (4), designed and engraved by Karl Bickel, and this format has been retained ever since.

Right:
Russian definitives have retained the same basic formula of workers, soldiers and peasants, with occasional views of the Kremlin, since the Revolution. Neither the process (letterpress) nor the lettering have varied much over the years. Even after the fall of the Habsburg monarchy in 1918 Hungary's definitive designs continued the same traditions. The Harvesters design (7), introduced in 1916, survived a turbulent decade reflected in the various changes in inscription denoting the prevailing form of government. The King Karolyi portrait design of 1918 (6) set the pattern for portraiture on solid grounds, and restrained lettering, particularly effective after Hungary adopted photogravure in 1932. After the inflationary period, when values were expressed in millions of pengö (5), Hungary settled down to small-format pictorials (3).

1. Russia,
10 roubles, 1923

2. Russia, 6 kopeks, 1961

3. Hungary, 8 filler, 1951

4. Hungary, 30 filler, 1932

5. Hungary, 1946

6. Hungary, 20 filler, 1918

7. Hungary, 10 filler, 1919

8. Hungary, 2 filler, 1926

9. Hungary, 50 filler, 1944

a series portraying workers, peasants and soldiers was adopted. With variations these symbolic themes have continued to the present day. After his death, Lenin's portrait was included in every definitive series, while the composition of the sets was expanded to include other professions and occasional views of the Kremlin. By and large the Soviet practice of featuring the working classes on the definitive stamps has not been adopted by the other countries of the Communist bloc. Allegory and royal portraiture were standard features of the definitive sets of Bulgaria and Romania in the interwar period. Hungary had its long-lived Harvesters design for the low values and a view of the parliament buildings indifferently typographed for the high values. Stylized representations of the crown of St. Stephen and St. Matthias Church appeared fleetingly in 1926 before giving way to small designs portraying famous Magyars (1932 and 1943). The immediate postwar period was marked by more allegory (Peace, Reconstruction), posthorns and coats of arms, but since 1951 small, transverse rectangles have featured public buildings. Greece continued with its tradition of classical profiles and statuary until 1927, but then embarked on an attractive pictorial series featuring ancient landmarks and provincial costumes. These stamps were recess-printed by an astonishing range of printers— first Thomas Macdonald, then De La Rue, Perkins Bacon, Aspiotis Brothers of Corfu and even the Polish Government Printer. All subsequent definitive issues have been pictorial, purveying a strange medley of classical artifacts and modern scenery.

The 'successor states' of Central and Eastern Europe abandoned their experiments with Art Nouveau and Art Deco in the thirties, both Poland and Czechoslovakia settling for recess-printed views in conventional frames. Both countries, however, experimented in 1935-6 with a more modernist approach using white lettering on a band of solid colour with a thin frame line (Czechoslovakia) or dispensing with the frame altogether (Poland). This device was characteristic of many Polish commemoratives in the immediate prewar period. Allegory or presidential portraits provided the material for the definitives in Finland and the Baltic states, though three intaglio pictorial designs were used for the higher denominations of the Finnish series of 1930-43 and the other countries made enthusiastic use of pictorial themes for their numerous airmail issues. The definitive issues of Yugoslavia and neighbouring Albania, with their heavy frame patterns, betray Austrian influence. Both of them preferred portraits of their respective rulers, though Albania had a pictorial series (1923) reminiscent of the pre-First

1. Bulgaria, 3 stotinki, 1913

2. Bulgaria,
10 stotinki, 1941

3. Bulgaria, 3 stotinki, 1920

Plaster model by Waino Aaltonen as a preliminary study for the Aleksis Kivi Memorial, 1929-30: a typical example of the Finnish approach to Cubism in the applied and fine arts.

Above, left:
After using pictorial stamps recess-printed by Bradbury Wilkinson, Bulgaria settled down to home-produced letter-press portraiture. 'Still life', in the form of agricultural products, was a favourite topic for both letterpress and photogravure definitives.

Left:
Before the Communist republic, Romania's definitives clung to royal portraiture. Typographed profiles with ornate frames and lettering masquerading as medieval Cyrillic script were popular until the mid-twenties. Proper portraiture and simple settings heralded the first reign of the 'boy king' Michael (2); the original letterpress soon gave way to photogravure. The styles of lettering and solid backgrounds seen in L. Basarab's 1940 series (1) set the pattern for postwar Romanian definitives.

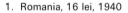

2. Romania,
30 bani, 1929

1. Romania, 16 lei, 1940

3. Romania, 1 ban, 1920

Right:
With few exceptions Greece has relied heavily on her past for inspiration in definitive design, whether it be pictorial representations of the Acropolis (1927) or Patmos Monastery (1947), bas-reliefs of mythological figures or the statue of the Venus de Milo. For the most part frames are simple with occasional concessions to classical ornament.

Greece, 2 drachmae, 1927

1. Finland, 3 markkaa, 1917-21

Greece, 1 lepton, 1911

2. Albania, 1 qindar, 1925

Greece, 100 drachmae, 1947

3. Albania, 5 qindar, 1925

Greece, 80 lepta, 1937

Definitive issues of the countries which emerged at the end of the First World War soon settled down to conventional forms, after an early period of Art Deco experiment. Finland's first definitives were designed by the Finnish-American architect, Eero Saarinen (1). Albania's pictorial series (3) of 1923 (overprinted in 1925) was typographed by the Austrian Government Printer with the characteristically elaborate framework found on earlier issues of Austria, but the Zog portrait series, typographed by Aspiotis Brothers of Corfu, struck a modern note (2).

Obverse of the 100 bolivianos note of the Central Bank of
Bolivia, 1945; engraved and recess-printed by De La Rue.
Since the twenties De La Rue has captured a large slice of
the market for security printing in Latin America and now has
a subsidiary in Bogota, Colombia.

World War stamps of the Austrian dependency of
Bosnia. Both countries experimented with stamps
printed abroad: Albania's stamps were produced in
Vienna or Rome (reflecting the transfer from one
sphere of influence to another) and even Aspiotis
Brothers of Corfu and Athens had a hand in their
production (1925), while Yugoslavia flirted with the
American Bank Note Company and De La Rue in
the twenties before becoming resigned to the local
brand of typography from 1929 onwards.

In the Third World, the few countries not under
colonial administration relied mainly on the leading
American and European printers. In the first four
decades of the century companies such as American
Bank Note, Continental Bank Note, E. A. Wright of
Philadelphia, Waterlow and De La Rue carved up
the Latin American market among themselves.
Sometimes, as in the case of Guatemala, they re-
engraved each other's dies, but more often they vied
with each other in producing heraldry and portraiture,
scenery, fauna and flora in an unending variety
designed to whet the collector's appetite rather than
satisfy any real requirement of the countries concerned. In this context the stamps of Liberia and
Ethiopia (then the only independent states in Africa)
may be considered. Both espoused pictorialism enthusiastically, but whereas Ethiopia remained faithful
to the French, and got a succession of stamps in the
same garish typography as the French colonies,
Liberia scattered contracts all over the place, with

gaudy miniature posters by most of the British and
American firms and even the Government Printing
Works in Berlin for good measure (1915-23). China's
definitives from 1913 until 1933 utilized three pictorial designs showing a junk, rice cutter and the
gateway of the Imperial Academy in Peking, but in
1931 De La Rue recess-printed a series portraying
Dr. Sun Yat-sen which was to be the first of many
such issues. No fewer than thirteen different Sun
Yat-sen series appeared between 1931 and the collapse of the Nationalist regime on the Chinese mainland in 1949. Japan's symbolic designs of the Chrysanthemum and Taisho sets (1899-1931) began to yield
ground in the twenties when a handful of stamps
depicting Fujiyama appeared. In 1926 Yomei Gate
and Nagoya Castle were featured on small-format
stamps and from then onwards there was a greater
pictorial emphasis. Historical subjects, scenery, floral
motifs and portraits of famous Japanese were introduced in 1937 and have been used ever since. During
the Second World War (1942-5) the subjects included
a girl munitions worker, shipbuilding and a fighter
pilot, but since then the emphasis has been on flowers
and shrines.

This chapter has concentrated on the gradual
development of pictorialism in the permanent or
definitive issues. Inevitably pictorialism made greater
headway in this period in the commemorative and
other special issues. The trends that emerged in this
field are discussed in chapter 11.

3. Liberia, 1 cent, 1937

1. Ethiopia, 10 centimes, 1942   2. Ethiopia, 2 guerches, 1919

The only independent African countries of the early twentieth century were eclectic in their choice of stamp printers. Ethiopia's 1919 series (2) was designed by W. Plattner and typographed by Busag of Switzerland in a passable imitation of contemporary French colonial typography. The 1942 series (1) was printed at Nasik in India, and the values added by letterpress at Khartoum. Liberia's numerous pictorials were often designed and recess-printed by De La Rue.

2. Japan, 20 sen, 1940

1. Japan, 10 sen, 1926-37

3. Japan, 1 sen, 1943   4. Japan, 20 sen, 1922

Pictorialism in a small space has been the keynote of Japanese definitives since 1922. Japan was one of the first countries to dispense with a formal frame, in the Fuji and Cherry-blossom design of 1940 by K. Noma (4).

1. Panama, 5 centesimos, 1924

2. Yugoslavia, 2 paras, 1921   3. Serbia, 15 paras, 1911-14

Serbia switched from simple portraiture typographed in Paris (3) to the more elaborate intaglio of the American Bank Note Company (2). The Panamanian series of 1924 (1) was also by the American Bank Note Company. The heavy, sculpted lettering and scrollwork were typical of their brand of florid design.

Australia, 10 shillings, 1938 (26 × 36mm), designed by R. A. Harrison, engraved by F. D. Manley and printed by John Ash. Although Australia neglected to issue any stamps in honour of the Coronation of King George VI in 1937, the definitive series released the following year amply compensated for this, by using Coronation portraits of the King and Queen on the top values.

10

Twentieth-century phenomena

MENTION has already been made of the Vasco da Gama issues of Portugal and her colonies in 1894. This idea was a logical extension of the key-plate policy and it was fortunate that commemorative stamps were still in their infancy or else this idea might have been applied more widely. As it was, the release of commemorative stamps simultaneously in the mother country and colonies was not repeated until 1931, when France herself issued five stamps to mark the International Colonial Exhibition in Paris and permitted twenty-six colonies to issue a set of four stamps apiece in standard designs. In this way the multiple commemorative or omnibus issue was born. In 1935 the three French West Indian territories issued six stamps each in standard designs to mark the tercentenary of French settlement, but in 1937 some twenty-one colonies issued sets of six each in honour of the International Exposition in Paris. What was worse was the release, in 1939, of two stamps in each of twenty-four colonies to mark an event which was not directly related to France—the New York World's Fair. Again standard designs were used. These prewar French colonial omnibus sets were beautifully recess-printed, but had a peculiar sameness about them, on account of the choice of native racial types as the subject in every instance. The same territories, however, had uniform sets later in 1939 to celebrate the 150th anniversary of the French Revolution. In this case one design sufficed for all five stamps in each series and it was done on the cheap, with a vignette in photogravure by Vaugirard of Paris, and typographed frames. Nonetheless the spirited rendering of the storming of the Bastille was a refreshing change after years of tribesmen in local costume. Between 1931 and 1956 the French colonies issued no fewer than twenty-one omnibus series, and though the countries of the French Community have by now a much greater degree of independence, a further thirty issues appeared between 1958 and 1970. While the latter issues had greater divergence in subject matter, they included in some instances territories which had left the Community but still retained philatelic ties with the former motherland.

Britain lagged behind France in the matter of omnibus issues. The Silver Jubilee of King George V was celebrated in 1935 by stamps in Britain, most of the dominions and all of the colonies and protectorates. Each of the colonies used a standard design, featuring Windsor Castle and a profile of the King in his state robes. The stamps were recess-printed in contrasting frame and vignette colours following the pattern by now established for the pictorial definitive stamps. Two years later a similar omnibus issue marked the coronation of King George VI. Full-face portraits of the King and Queen were used for single stamps in Britain (photogravure) and Canada (intaglio) and for sets of three in New Zealand and the colonial ensemble, and it is interesting to compare the treatment of the subject in each case. South Africa and the Australian dependencies chose profiles of the King alone. Australia overlooked the occasion, but made up for this by featuring the King and Queen in their coronation robes on the high values of the 1938 definitive series.

The Silver Jubilee stamps had risen dramatically in value and when the Coronation series appeared it was subject to heavy speculation with the inevitable slump. Thereafter the British Empire refrained from issuing omnibus sets until the Victory series of 1945-6. Standard designs throughout the colonies were used for seventeen sets between 1948 (Silver Wedding) and 1966 (UNESCO). Seven omnibus sets appeared between May 1965 and December 1966 and provoked such an outcry in philatelic circles that the Crown Agents (who formulated colonial stamp policy) were forced to abandon this method of raising revenue for their principals. The law of diminishing returns was beginning to apply; sales of the World Health Organization and UNESCO sets of September and December 1966 were well below the forecast and, more significantly, the number of territories wishing to avail themselves of this means of making money from collectors was also in decline. Since then the only omnibus series has marked the silver wedding of Queen Elizabeth (November 1972) and though the same portrait was used in each case, different frames and background pictorial vignettes were used to add

1. Antigua, 1 penny, 1935

2. Bechuanaland Protectorate, 3 pence, 1937

3. Great Britain, 1½ pence, 1937

Though it was pioneered by Portugal and France, Britain established the colonial omnibus issue, with the Silver Jubilee and Coronation sets of 1935-7. The colonial standard design for the Silver Jubilee, designed by H. Fleury and recess-printed by De La Rue, conformed to contemporary colonial definitive designs, with a vignetted picture and the royal profile incorporated in the frame (1). Full-face portraits were used for the Coronation sets, the colonies having recess-printed stamps designed by De La Rue staff artists (2). Britain's design, by Edmund Dulac, paralleled the styles of lettering and framework adopted in the 1938-52 definitive series (3).

Portuguese colonial issues have different designs for each territory participating in an omnibus series and greater use is made of multicolour lithography.

Timor, 10 avos, 1953

Macau, 20 avos, 1964

variety. Thus the principal merit in issuing omnibus sets—economy in design and production—has been lost.

Portugal, which, in a sense, began this insidious practice, has not been entirely blameless in its continuance, although her omnibus issues have been less frequent and usually confined to one or two stamps at a time. Single stamps honouring the statue of Our Lady of Fatima appeared in the overseas territories in 1948 and since then about a score of issues have been made, but in most cases with quite distinctive designs. Portugal also deserves the credit (or blame) for issuing sets of six stamps depicting various sports and pastimes in each colony in 1962. The stamps were in a large diamond format and different subjects appeared on every stamp, resulting in tremendous variety and some unlikely topics (cricket from the Cape Verde Islands!). No event was commemorated so these stamps can best be described as a thematic omnibus. In 1965-6 many of the Portuguese colonies issued stamps depicting historic military uniforms. In 1958-9 many of the French colonies issued one stamp each showing typical flowers of the designated territory, but it remains to be seen whether this concept of the thematic omnibus issue will be extended, either in the French or Portuguese empires or in the remaining colonies of the British Commonwealth.

Another phenomenon by which postal administrations make money is the hardy annual. This has the advantages of stimulating collectors' interest, producing a steady source of revenue, yet not (as a rule) putting the collector to a great flurry of expense. Switzerland was responsible for this idea, introducing stamps in 1913 with small premiums in aid of child welfare. Since then the annual *Pro Juventute* stamps (from the Latin inscription 'on behalf of youth' which identifies the issues) have provided a gallery of popular themes ranging from cantonal coats of arms and costumes to flowers, birds and butterflies. Since 1938 Switzerland has also issued annual charity stamps, initially for the *Fête Nationale* but latterly for a number of national funds, hence the inscription *Pro Patria* (for the homeland). Like the children's stamps, the Pro Patria series are strongly thematic, with fossils, coins and stained-glass windows among the more recent subjects, sometimes extending over several years before changing to another topic.

Child Welfare provided the *raison d'être* for most of the hardy annuals which had their inception before the Second World War and are still going strong. These stamps have been appearing each year since the twenties in Belgium, Luxembourg, the Netherlands and the Dutch overseas territories. Many of these stamps have in more recent years been designed by the children themselves, though in the main they follow the same thematic pattern as Switzerland. New Zealand has issued stamps since 1929 to raise funds for children's health camps and TB sanatoriums. These Health stamps featured aspects of children at work or play in the earlier years but in more recent times have also adopted a simple thematic approach, with pictures of birds a strong favourite in the 1950s and 1960s. Portraits of royal children have been a New Zealand favourite since 1943 and lately there has also been a return to the prewar practice of depicting children's sports and pastimes. Many other countries have charity issues of a more general nature. Winter Relief stamps were a popular feature of German philately, especially during the Weimar Republic and the Third Reich, an identical theme but different designs being used for each value in the series. Buildings and coats of arms were popular in the twenties and early thirties, but gave way, under Hitler, to scenes from Wagnerian opera (1933) and landmarks in the conquered territories (1939-40). Since the war, West Germany and West Berlin have issued *Wohlfahrtsmarken* (welfare stamps). Up to 1958 they portrayed famous humanitarians, but fairy tale scenes, costume dolls and subjects of interest to

Identical designs, with the names of the territories transposed to indicate the issuing country, were used by the Netherlands, Antilles, Surinam and New Guinea for the Statute of the Kingdom commemoratives, designed by S. L. Hartz and printed by Enschede in 1954.

children have since been used. With the exception of the New Zealand Health stamps, charity or semi-postal issues have made little headway in the British Commonwealth. Jamaica experimented with child welfare stamps in 1923-7 and Fiji emulated New Zealand by issuing Health stamps in 1951 and 1954, while South Africa produced a few sets in 1933-9 for the Voortrekker Memorial Fund. At the time of writing (1974), Britain is contemplating the introduction of annual charity stamps but it is not yet known what form these will take.

France and Finland issue stamps each December with premiums in aid of the Red Cross or TB charity. Apart from the red cross motif, the designs of these stamps vary considerably. The Finnish stamps conform to the Swiss thematic policy, but the French issues have consistently reproduced details from well-known works of art. Stamp Day is a widely used pretext for an annual issue, often bearing a small premium used to subsidize philatelic exhibitions— the only instance in which the ever charitable philatelist is actually helping to promote his own hobby. Such stamps are, or have been, issued by France, Germany, the Saar, Italy, Belgium and the Netherlands and are popular with collectors on account of their use of historic postal themes or reproductions of classic stamps.

Not all hardy annuals are intended to raise funds for charity. The best-known and now most widely used annual issue is that celebrating Christmas and primarily intended for use on greetings cards at the festive season. Apart from Canada's Imperial Penny Postage map stamp of 1898 which bore the legend XMAS because it was issued at that time of year, Christmas stamps began in Austria in 1937—an inauspicious beginning since they were, in fact, the last stamps of that unhappy country before the Nazis invaded it in March 1938. The two stamps featured a nosegay of roses, and people, wise after the event, pointed out the passable likeness of Adolf Hitler in the principal rose. Like Mouchon's death-mask stamps of Serbia, however, such a 'ghost picture' was purely accidental. Incidentally the portrait of the

1. Luxembourg, 1¾ francs, 1929
2. Switzerland, 10 centimes, 1921
3. Belgium, 15 + 5 centimes, 1925
4. Switzerland, 5 + 5 centimes, 1963
5. Belgium, 2.50 + 1 francs, 1962

Anti-tuberculosis and child welfare semi-postal issues developed in Europe, beginning with the Swiss 'Pro Juventute' stamps released annually since 1913. Heraldry, allegorical subjects and, most of all, aspects of childhood or portraits of children, have formed the basis of most designs over the years.

2. New Zealand, 2 + 1 pence, 1945

1. Germany, 20 + 10 pfennigs, 1959

3. Jamaica, 2½ pence, 1923

Charity or semi-postal stamps originated in Australia in 1897 but have since spread to all parts of the globe. Jamaica sponsored children's charity stamps in the twenties, with vignettes from photographs by Miss V. F. Taylor and frames by Frank Cundall (3). New Zealand's Health stamps have been released each year since 1929; subjects associated with childhood, such as James Berry's interpretation of the statue of Peter Pan in London, furnish most of the designs (2). Grimm's Fairy Tales have inspired many of the *Wohlfahrtsmarken* of Germany in recent years; the stylized silhouette treatment of 'Bounty from Heaven' by E. Sporer is typical of many West German charity and commemorative stamps (1). Fiji, emulating New Zealand, has produced Health stamps on a few occasions; the 1954 pair was recess-printed by Bradbury Wilkinson (4). South Africa's charity stamps (5) raised funds for the Voortrekker and Huguenot memorials. Note the bi-lingual pair (English and Afrikaans on alternate stamps).

4. Fiji, 2½ + ½ pence, 1954

5. South West Africa, ½ + ½ penny, 1939

late, unlamented Führer also appeared in the foliage of the tree shown on the West German 50 pfennig stamp of 1964. The idea of issuing Christmas stamps lapsed (with the exception of a set from Hungary in 1943) until it was resurrected by Cuba in 1954. Subsequently it spread to Australia (1957), New Zealand (1960), the United States (1963), Great Britain (1966) and many territories of the British Commonwealth. In recent years it has even extended to Germany, France and Greece. Since independence in 1948, Israel has issued annual Jewish New Year stamps and several countries (mainly in the Communist bloc) have released New Year stamps with festive motifs. Mother's Day produced a sprinkling of stamps from such countries as the United States, the Dominican Republic, Indonesia, Austria and Kuwait but, despite its obvious appeal, this theme has never caught the imagination like the Christmas stamps. Many countries, especially among the emergent nations, have issues to celebrate independence anniversaries, and for many years Afghanistan produced stamps each year for Pakhtunistan Day, promoting the country's claim to a portion of neighbouring Pakistan, but in general these annual issues are of little interest to anyone beyond the frontiers and they lack the universal appeal of Christmas or child welfare.

One other twentieth-century phenomenon has had an important effect on the philatelic market and also, to a large extent, on the development of design. In 1923 Luxembourg released a stamp in small sheets containing a solitary specimen, in honour of a philatelic exhibition. In this unobtrusive manner the miniature sheet was born, but within a decade its use had spread to most other countries. Stamps printed in this form were usually sold well above face value and dealers and collectors alike protested against this racket. For years Stanley Gibbons refused to list miniature sheets in their catalogues but bowed to demand in the mid-1960s and ended their boycott. Nowadays there are even catalogues devoted solely to miniature sheets. Sometimes they consisted of a single stamp, with or without some form of decoration in the sheet margins. Other sheets included a group of stamps, often ordinary definitives but sometimes printed in new colours for the occasion, and this was a popular method of producing a souvenir of international philatelic exhibitions without having to go to the trouble and expense of printing entirely new stamps. The souvenir element is still present, but has been swamped by the general desire of many postal administrations to mulct the collector as much as possible. Thus many of the thematic short sets issued by certain Commonwealth countries (Malawi is a notorious offender in this respect) are automatically

France, 30 + 10 centimes, Red Cross stamp, 1971 (twice original size). Many of the annual French Red Cross charity issues of recent years have reproduced famous paintings, interpreted here by the artist-engraver, Pierre Gandon who has been responsible for many French designs since the Second World War.

supported by the miniature sheets containing one of each denomination. In many cases the sheets are issued without perforations, so that imperforate varieties are deliberately created.

In the 1950s considerable ingenuity was shown in the production of sheets containing a single stamp, whose design was projected into the sheet margins. Czechoslovakia, Hungary, Israel, Romania and even West Germany have all produced outstanding examples of these pictorial sheets in recent years. From this it was but a short step to producing small sheets in which the entire 'block' constitutes the stamp. This practice seems to be particularly popular in Yemen and the sheikhdoms of the Persian Gulf where postage stamps have become a major hard currency earner. These souvenir sheets have little or no resemblance to postage stamps in the orthodox sense. Measuring anything up to six inches across, they often contain a haphazard jumble of elements and motifs. Their size alone militates against what should be their principal purpose—the prepayment of postage. It is a sad fact that these monstrosities have not contributed anything to the art of stamp design, since they liberate the designer from the traditional requirement of producing a balanced composition within the confines of small dimensions.

Christmas stamps, pioneered by Austria in 1937, have now been adopted by more than fifty countries throughout the world. Austria's pair of 1937 (1), designed by Willi Dachauer, are said to conceal a portrait of Hitler in the rose. Reproductions of Old Master paintings of the Nativity supply the bulk of the subject matter in modern Christmas issues, pandering to the twin passions for religion and fine art on stamps. America's Christmas stamps tried to be non-controversial and non-sectarian, hence the innocuous wreath and candles motif of the 1962 stamps (3). In recent years Australia has shown greater inclination to experiment with design with progressively more off-beat interpretations of traditional themes (4). Gyula Toth's bas-relief of the Adoration of the Magi (5) accorded with the style and photogravure treatment of wartime Hungarian stamps.

1. Austria, 12 groschen, 1937

2. Christmas Island, 5 cents, 1970

3. United States, 4 cents, 1962   4. Australia, 5 cents, 1969   5. Hungary, 30 filler, 1943

United States of America, 3 cents (40 × 25mm), marking the
Sesquicentennial of Tennessee Statehood, 1946. Anniversaries
of the admission of the various states to the Union have provided an abundant supply of commemorative stamps. The
formula of vignette flanked by inset oval portraits was especially popular in American commemoratives between 1936 and
1939, calling for little effort from the designer and the minimum
of understanding on the part of the user

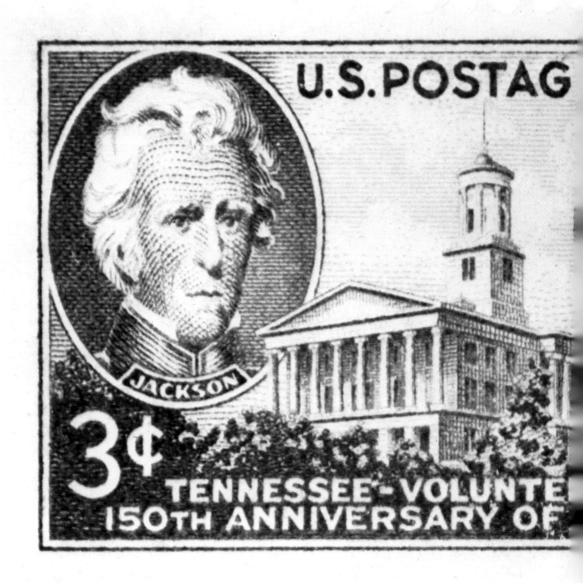

11
Pictorialism today

*I*F pictorialism made relatively little headway with definitive stamps it was inevitable that its greatest application should be in commemorative and other special issues. Although such stamps were established in the closing decade of the nineteenth century, they were surprisingly slow to catch on. Both Bavaria and Württemberg issued commemorative stamps before the First World War but Germany herself did not do so until 1919. France's first pictorial issue appeared in 1917 and consisted of charity stamps in aid of the war orphans' fund. Denmark's first commemoratives appeared in 1920 and Britain's not until 1924. Early German commemoratives were strongly symbolic in design and pictorial realism did not become established until well into the Nazi era. In Britain, however, commemorative stamps remained primarily symbolic until the 1960s. Even now, both Britain and Switzerland share with the United Nations a more abstract approach to the design of commemorative stamps than any other part of the world. The meaning of this symbolism may not always be too clear to the public in general, and for many years British stamps were strongly criticized by people who envied the pretty-pretties of France and the United States, but it must be said that British stamps, both commemorative and definitive, were characterized by well-cut lettering, the careful juxtaposition of the elements of the design and high artistic standards. The basic problem inherent in all British stamps is the inclusion of the portrait of the reigning monarch in lieu of an inscription as in every other country. This practice was not merely royalist sentiment but a downright necessity, since British stamps were used in many places where a short inscription would not have conveyed the essential validity of these stamps.

If one considers all the possible variants in inscription, this problem becomes apparent. 'British Posts' would offend the Irish; 'UK Posts' would be better, but the stamps were used in certain territories, such as the Isle of Man and the Channel Islands, which are crown dependencies and not actually parts of the United Kingdom. Objections to the royal profile, on the grounds that this hampers the designers' choice

DEWAR'S
THE SPIRIT IRRESISTIBLE

The call of the sea may not be denied, and so with the charm of Dewar's Whisky. As invigorating as the winds that blow from out of space, DEWAR'S, like a well-found ship, brings content; **boundless** and satisfying

HAROLD NELSON

Advertisement for Dewar's Whisky, by Harold Nelson. Clean lines and careful attention to shading of waves and sky—almost to the point of stylization—were characteristic of Nelson's graphics and had their counterpart in his Wembley and Postal Union Congress stamp designs of 1924-9.

of subject, are countered by the fact that there is no acceptable alternative. A coat of arms could not be devised which would be acceptable in Scotland as well as England; even the crowns used on government documents in the two countries are not identical. Ultimately one is forced back on the only solution: to retain the royal portrait as a kind of 'house symbol' by which British stamps may be instantly recognized everywhere in the world. A proper portrait (in the heraldic sense) was used exclusively on British stamps until 1966 but since then all special issues have incorporated a small, discreet silhouette, often die-stamped in gold ink so that it may stand apart from the predominant feature of the stamps. At the same time, the few half-hearted attempts to introduce pictorialism into the definitive range have now been resolutely abandoned. The high values of the 1951 and 1953-68 sets had pictorial vignettes but in later years the recess-printed high values have merely echoed the design of the photogravure lower denominations.

Pictorial commemorative stamps gained ground after the First World War mainly in such countries as the United States and the Soviet Union, both of which concentrated on low-value stamps (prepaying the inland letter rates). The object of these stamps was not so much to project an image to the world at large as to educate a large and heterogeneous population in the history, culture, traditions and 'way of life' of the country concerned. This didactic policy has remained until now the watchword in American and Russian philately. As a result, design has always tended towards banal subjects in realistic techniques which even the least sophisticated members of the community could understand. Thus the idea of the postage stamp as a work of art in its own right flies out of the window. More than any other country the Soviet Union uses postage stamps prolifically as a means of disseminating information or bringing to the attention of the public noteworthy events and personalities. The United States has shown greater restraint in this respect, although in 1948 it came perilously close to Russian prodigality by releasing commemoratives on no fewer than thirty occasions, and paid tribute to such diverse events as the fire brigade tercentenary and the centenary of the American poultry industry. A more symbolic, poster approach was evident by the early 1960s, and the Freedom from Hunger (1963), Emancipation Centenary (1963) and Bill of Rights (1966) stamps are the best examples. But all too often commemorative stamps are treated merely as miniature versions of *Saturday Evening Post* covers, typified by the stamps marking the centenary of City Mail Delivery (1963),

1. Great Britain, 1½ pence, 1924

2. Great Britain, 1s 3d, 1953

3. Great Britain, 6 pence, 1964

4. Great Britain, 6 pence, 1960

Law and Order (1968), Family Planning (1972) and the Mail Order Centenary (1973). A more adventurous trend is now emerging, with a greater willingness to experiment with lettering, such as the Love stamp of 1972 and the bowling commemorative of the same year. Since the Famous Americans marathon series of 1940 the treatment of portraiture has been hackneyed, but refreshing indications of a more impressionistic style are shown in such recent issues as those commemorating Willa Cather and George Gershwin. This liberalization of American stamp design is coupled with the abandonment of the traditional intaglio process and the adoption of combined recess and lithography since 1968.

Photogravure, more than any other single process, has revolutionized stamp design. It was used sparingly, as an alternative to the half-tone letterpress process, for book and magazine illustration around the turn of the century but it was not until 1914 that its use was extended to postage stamps. The firm of Bruckmann in Munich printed the Bavarian definitive series portraying King Ludwig III and though the quality of the process was not very good, some attempt was made to evolve designs which showed the qualities of photogravure to best advantage. The stamps were designed by Professor Schirnböck of

Following page: Poster by Vladimir Lebedev advertising children's books by Samuel Marshak (for whom Lebedev also did the illustrations). By the early thirties, when this poster was designed, a blend of impressionism and whimsicality began to appear fleetingly in Soviet stamp design, reflecting contemporary trends in graphic art. This element is seen at its best in the Graf Zeppelin stamps of 1930 and the Anti-War propaganda series of 1935.

British commemorative issues originated in 1924 and have always shown a marked preference for symbolism or stylized pictorialism. This approach was pioneered by Harold Nelson with his famous Wembley Lions of 1924-5, recess-printed by Waterlow and Sons (1). Compare Edmund Dulac's full-face formalized portrait of Queen Elizabeth, on the Coronation stamp of 1953 (2) with his work for the Coronation stamp of 1937 (page 144) and note the same style of lettering and ornament. For the Forth Road Bridge stamps of 1964 (3) Andrew Restall chose an impressionistic view of the bridge. Reynolds Stone, noted for his 'ribboned lettering' adapted the standard Europa design of Pentti Rahikainen for the CEPT stamps of 1960 (4). Note the methods of overcoming the problem of placing a 'proper' portrait of the queen (from a photograph by Dorothy Wilding) in the overall layout of a commemorative design—either the traditional inset oval or against a panel of contrasting colour.

154

1. Russia, 15 kopeks, 1941

3. Russia, 30 kopeks, 1938

2. Russia, 40 kopeks, 1957

4. Russia, 6 kopeks, 1924

5. Russia, 10 roubles, 1922

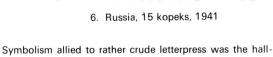

6. Russia, 15 kopeks, 1941

7. Russia, 15 kopeks, 1937

Symbolism allied to rather crude letterpress was the hallmark of early Soviet stamps, though in some, like Dubasov's Lenin mourning series (4) the stark outlines compensate for technical shortcomings. Photogravure was adopted comparatively early, to give a more realistic effect to pictorial stamps, but poor lettering and the juxtaposition of disparate elements continued to characterize many pre-war stamps. Some outside influences are evident: Dubasov's Papanin Expedition series of 1940 (3) echoed contemporary American stamp design, and Borov's series marking the First Soviet Architectural Congress (7) struck a *moderne* note at variance with the ponderous traditionalism of the buildings depicted. Since the Second World War, Soviet stamps have concentrated increasingly on 'safe' thematic subjects, such as the Handicrafts series of 1957 (2).

Austria, best known for his designs and engravings in typography and intaglio for Austria, Albania and Liechtenstein, but he deserves credit for adapting the King's portraits so that the tonal qualities of the process were given some scope. No attempt was made to improve on photogravure as applied to stamp production and for many years thereafter it was regarded merely as a cheap substitute for typography or intaglio, to be used when all else failed or was too expensive. In the event, the earliest examples of photogravure came from Czechoslovakia (1919) and Bulgaria (1920). The first country to make consistent use of this process was Romania which commissioned Bruckmann to print the Coronation series of 1922 and the King's Jubilee set of 1926. Romania subsequently went to Vaugirard of Paris for a handsome portrait series of 1927 marking the fiftieth anniversary of independence and then, beginning in 1928, used the photogravure plant installed at the Government Printing Works in Bucharest.

From 1922 on, Vaugirard printed stamps for French Morocco, Lebanon, Syria and the Saar by this process, which they preferred to call heliogravure. The South African Government Printing Works in Pretoria introduced photogravure equipment in 1930 and, like Vaugirard, began printing stamps which had previously been designed for typography or intaglio. Consequently, the majority of the photogravure pictorials of the interwar period did not do justice to the process, but continued the cluttered frames and coarse vignettes of their predecessors.

Harrison and Sons, who had wrested the British contract from De La Rue in 1910, maintained the typographical tradition but came into photogravure almost by accident. In 1923 they sent proofs of a series portraying King Fuad to Egypt. The stamps were to have been recess-printed from plates manufactured by Perkins Bacon but to save time the proofs were run off in photogravure. The Egyptian authorities were pleased with the result and insisted that this process should be used for the actual stamps. One wonders what the stamps would have looked like

1. United States, 2 cents, 1920

2. United States, 5 cents, 1940   3. United States, 8 cents, 1960

4. United States, 5 cents, 1967

5. United States, 5 cents, 1963   6. United States, 5 cents, 1965

American commemorative stamps invariably took a fairly simple, realistic view of the subject, with brief, clear captions to vignettes. The earlier stamps permitted some subtlety in the frames—the 1920 Pilgrim stamps depict American and English mayflowers in the side panels (1). The City Mail Delivery centenary stamp (5) belongs to the *Saturday Evening Post* school of narrative stamp design. Many modern American stamps have a didactic or propaganda flavour, publicizing such worthy causes as the anti-cancer campaign (6), and the tendency is now towards more abstract designs.

1. Egypt,
5 millièmes, 1923

2. Gold Coast,
2 shillings, 1928

3. Great Britain,
1 penny, 1912

4. Great Britain,
1 penny, 1934

Harrison and Sons became the leading British exponent of photogravure almost by accident, with the Fuad definitive series of Egypt (1). The Gold Coast definitive set of 1928 tried unsuccessfully to combine portraiture with pictorialism (2). For Britain Harrisons adapted the typographed Mackennal designs of 1912.

Right:

The Silver Jubilee series of 1935 (1), designed by Barnett Freedman, demonstrated the ability of photogravure to give a 'watered silk' effect to lettering. The Edward VIII series of 1936 (2) was the first serious attempt to produce a design which gave free rein to the tonal qualities of photogravure, though an actual photographic profile was not ideal for the purpose. The George VI (3) combined the talents of Edmund Dulac (profile) and Eric Gill (lettering). Michael Farrar-Bell used a 'proper' portrait of Queen Elizabeth (by Dorothy Wilding) for the series of 1952-4 (4). Abram Games' design for the Olympic 3 pence of 1948 (5) typifies the symbolic approach to commemorative design. J. R. R. Stobie's penny stamp for the third anniversary of the liberation of the Channel Islands was pictorial in concept but utterly irrelevant to the subject commemorated (6).

1. Great Britain, 1 penny, 1935

2. Great Britain,
1½ pence, 1936

3. Great Britain,
1½ pence, 1938

4. Great Britain, 2½ pence, 1952

5. Great Britain, 3 pence, 1948

6. Channel Islands, 1 penny, 1948

2. Czechoslovakia, 120 haleru, 1919

1. Bavaria, 15 pfennigs, 1914

3. Romania, 3 lei, 1922

4. Romania, 25 bani, 1935

5. Bulgaria, 50 stotinki, 1920

6. Norway, 30 + 5 öre, 1939

Photogravure was pioneered by Bavaria, with the Ludwig III series of 1914 (1), but did not spread to other countries till after the First World War. With the exception of Bavaria itself, the countries using this process were slow to appreciate its special qualities—and limitations. Thus the Czech and Bulgarian issues of 1919-20 (2, 5) used designs which were unsuited to the tonal qualities of photogravure. Romania and Norway (3, 4, 6), however, produced designs which were ideal for interpretation in this medium.

Below:
The particular advantages of photogravure in printing pictorial stamps were slow to develop. Among early countries to realize its potential were Morocco (1923) and Persia (1930), though the effect was marred by frames which were more suited to typography or intaglio.

Morocco, 2 centimes, 1923

Persia, 8 chahi, 1930

had they been recess-printed, but they were certainly as well suited to photogravure as anything else up to that date. Two years later the Egyptian Survey Department in Cairo installed its own photogravure plant and from then on the vast majority of Egyptian stamps were produced by this process. At first the designs still retained the heavy frames which were a legacy from typography, but the Agricultural Exhibition series of 1936 had no frames at all and the designs were printed against an overall toned background bled off into the perforations. The following year a similar technique was used effectively for the young Farouk definitive series. Solid colour bled off into the perforations has been a characteristic feature of Egyptian stamps up to the present day.

Harrison and Sons first applied photogravure to a British colony in 1928, when they printed a small-format series for the Gold Coast. These stamps, with their medallion profile of King George V surmounting tiny vignettes of Christiansborg Castle, were reminiscent of De La Rue's typographed pictorials for the Cape of Good Hope and the Orange River Colony at the turn of the century and were obviously conceived in the typographic rather than photogravure manner. In 1934 Harrisons recaptured the British contract which they had lost to Waterlow in 1924 and towards the end of that year they began printing the George V profile designs in photogravure instead of typography. Sir Bertram Mackennal's medallion profile of the King (originally sculpted as a clay maquette) was well suited to the new process, but the frames were too fussy. Something of the virtuosity of the process was revealed in the delicate tones of the British Silver Jubilee series of 1935. The four stamps which form a memento to the short reign of King Edward VIII (1936) were designed specifically for photogravure, and relied on plain, solid backgrounds with the minimum of ornament and lettering to set off the King's profile. The design failed only because a profile of the King, based on an actual photograph, was used. The George VI series rectified this fault by using a coinage profile whose subtle tones were beautifully suited to photogravure. These stamps, designed by Edmund Dulac with lettering by Eric Gill, were the product of a remarkable partnership. Gill's bold lettering was his main legacy to British philately and its influence may be seen in the Elizabeth II designs by Lynton Lamb and Reynolds Stone. At the beginning of the present reign (1952) a proper portrait, based on a photograph by Dorothy Wilding, was adopted for British definitive and commemorative stamps. It disappeared from the commemoratives in 1966 and was replaced on the definitive range the following year when a plaster

RADIO TIMES HULTON PICTURE LIBRARY

The versatility and genius of Eric Gill had a profound influence in different media of the fine and applied arts in the interwar period. His three-dimensional work included the statue on the facade of the BBC headquarters in London (above). In graphic design his pre-eminence in lettering overshadowed other considerations, as in this label celebrating the coming-of-age of the League of Nations Union, 1939 (below).

VICTORIA AND ALBERT MUSEUM

159

Grenada, 1 farthing, 1937

Seychelles, 5 rupees, 1938

Very few of the George VI colonial definitives were printed in photogravure; notable exceptions were the farthing stamps of Grenada and Dominica and the sets of the Seychelles and Virgin Islands.

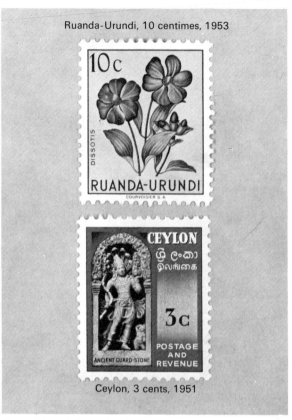

Ruanda-Urundi, 10 centimes, 1953

Ceylon, 3 cents, 1951

Courvoisier of Switzerland established a high reputation for fine quality multicolour photogravure, often expressed in delicate and subtle colours.

maquette by Arnold Machin was commissioned specifically for the purpose. At long last the promise shown by the Edward VIII series was fulfilled. All extraneous detail, such as inscriptions, crowns and heraldic flora shown on previous issues, was eliminated and the value alone picked out in white against the toned background.

Photogravure was well suited to Britain's particular brand of pictorialism and may be seen at its best in the gradations of colour on the Victory 2½ pence (1946) and the Silver Wedding and Olympic Games issues of 1948. When it came to pictorialism in the sense of reproducing actual scenes, British design was less happy. Two stamps of 1948 celebrated the third anniversary of the liberation of the Channel Islands, but all they could come up with were sketches by Messrs. Stobie and Blampied of islanders gathering seaweed for manure! These stamps, bereft of any inscription or captions, puzzled the public far more

than many of the symbolic designs of the period.

Photogravure was slow to catch on in the British colonies. In 1938 almost forty territories got new pictorial definitive sets, but the only contribution from photogravure were the farthing stamps of Dominica and Grenada, a set of heraldic stamps for the Virgin Islands (which would have looked better in recess) and a pictorial series for the Seychelles. It was not until 1950 that Mauritius and North Borneo emulated the prewar Seychelles experiment and issued stamps depicting scenery in a more naturalistic way than could ever be achieved by intaglio. Nevertheless photogravure made little headway during the ensuing six years and many colonies clung to the more aesthetically satisfying two-colour recess process. The Virgin Islands, in fact, reverted to intaglio in 1952 and North Borneo in 1961.

In the immediate postwar period the Swiss firm of Courvoisier began to emerge as the leading exponent of high-quality photogravure. The state printing works in Madrid and Rome were also turning out excellent photogravure, using designs which took note of the advantages and disadvantages of the process, but the Swiss firm was the first to break through the colour barrier and print stamps with excellent registration and lifelike tones. Harrisons began modernizing their equipment to meet this challenge, but that they fell behind the Swiss in this respect is painfully demonstrated in the Ceylon commemoratives of 1954-5 and the Australian Olympic Games issue of 1956 whose contracts were divided between Harrisons and Courvoisier. In the ensuing four years, however, Harrisons made enormous progress and by 1960 had caught up with their rivals. In that year they printed their first bicoloured stamps for Britain and then, in 1962, produced a glorious multicoloured series for the Seychelles. Five, seven and nine colour combinations were perfected, so that ultimately it was possible to reproduce accurately every subtlety of shade and colour imaginable. Regrettably such technical perfection, which Harrisons and Courvoisier now share with Enschede of Holland and Heraclio Fournier of Vitoria, is seldom matched by outstanding quality in design. The very nature of photogravure has introduced a mechanical quality into stamp design which was absent in the past. Nowadays it is sufficient for an artist to produce an enlarged design, which can then be reduced photographically to the required dimensions. Lettering and ornament is now a matter of applying successive overlays from stock to the original artwork and, as a result, many stamps have the appearance of having been slapped together by the 'scissors and paste' technique. Sometimes a device which seems unusually effective in the original artwork is lost when the design is reduced to stamp size and put into production. A good example of this is provided by the 1961 definitive series of St. Helena. The artist, Victor Whiteley, used intricate spiral motifs based on traditional island lace patterns as the background to the floral, bird and animal motifs, but when the designs were reduced to stamp size the lace patterns seemed like a latter-day attempt to simulate the fine engine turning so beloved of Perkins Bacon. In many cases actual scenic photographs, without any adaptation, are used as the basis for stamp designs. The resulting stamps look like what they are—colour transparencies with a few bits of lettering and ornament, perhaps the ruler's profile, thrown in.

Photogravure has made the business of stamp designing perilously easy. Significantly the best-designed stamps today are those printed in more traditional processes. While Austria and France strive

Hong Kong, 20 dollars, 1962

Czechoslovakia, 40 haleru, 1969

Netherlands, 7 cents, 1965

The portrait of Queen Elizabeth by Pietro Annigoni was used by several Commonwealth countries, though Hong Kong alone featured it in full colour. Various media of the fine arts have been explored for unusual treatment of subjects. Czechoslovakia used cartoons for the Celebrity series of 1969, while the Netherlands featured sculpture and an unusual perspective to create a three-dimensional effect in the Resistance commemoratives of 1965.

for perfection in naturalistic motifs produced by intaglio, Czechoslovakia has allowed her engravers and designers freedom to interpret pictorial subjects in their own, individualistic manner. This approach is not impossible using photogravure, but the temptation to rely on a photographic original is very great. Britain and the Netherlands have both achieved fine results with artistic and highly original designs in photogravure in recent years. Japan has used photogravure to a large extent since 1936, but managed to produce many masterpieces of design which probably owe much of their success to the centuries-old tradition of achieving the maximum in a small and exacting medium. Here again, the secret lies in producing designs which exploit to the full the special qualities of the photogravure process.

Lithography, used fleetingly in the nineteenth century as a cheap substitute for intaglio or letterpress, has been adapted in recent years to become a formidable rival to photogravure. Multicolour offset lithography is now used by Aspiotis, Enschede, Fournier and Bradbury Wilkinson. From the technical viewpoint it is capable of greater accuracy than photogravure, but aesthetically it is not so satisfactory, since it has a flat quality. Nevertheless this very flatness can be used to advantage and can give tremendous impact to the modern poster style of design. In the colonial omnibus design for the World Health Organization (1966), Michael Goaman used blocks of contrasting colours most effectively and this was interpreted with striking results by Harrisons in lithography, a process which was novel for that company at the time. A. Robledo's designs for the Gandhi Centenary series of Grenada (1969) were even more dramatic, lithographed in bold primary colours by Bradbury Wilkinson. De La Rue have also experimented with lithography and have patented their own brand under the name of Delacryl, characterized by sharper colours and better definition than normal lithography.

Elsewhere there have been interesting experiments combining two different processes. During the past decade Austria, Belgium and Czechoslovakia have combined photogravure backgrounds with recess-printed motifs, with attractive results. The superb quality inherent in line engraving is thus married to the infinitive colour range of photogravure. Both Czechoslovakia and the United States have also combined recess with lithography.

We live in an age of colour, in which coloured pictures in books and magazines are now taken for granted and colour television is commonplace. The technical developments of the past twenty years have made this possible, and it was to be expected that

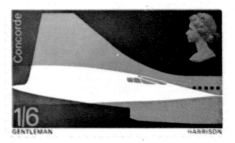

Great Britain, 1s 6d, 1969

Ireland, 4 pence, 1972

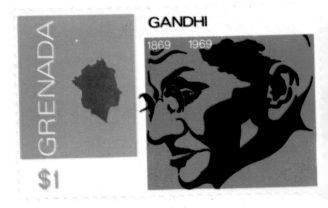

Grenada, 1 dollar, 1969

Yugoslavia, 30 paras, 1964

Czechoslovakia, 2 koruny, 1966

Yugoslavia has often used gold metallic ink to good effect in translating medieval miniatures to the medium of the postage stamp: Miroslav's Gospel, designed by D. Kazic and S. Fileki. Czechoslovakia has developed an almost abstract approach to many commemorative subjects which are handled more conventionally elsewhere: Figure-skating, Bratislava, designed by K. Pekarek and engraved by Bedrich Housa.

Simple masses of colour, often overlapped, have been used in recent years to heighten dramatic impact. David Gentleman used this treatment in his designs for Concorde's maiden flight. P. Scott's dove superimposed on the sun symbolized Ireland's Patriot Dead to commemorate the 50th anniversary of 'The Troubles'. A. Robledo's treatment of Gandhi's features and contrasting masses of primary colours were ideally suited to lithography, by Bradbury Wilkinson.

colour should also be applied to postage stamps as a matter of course. The fact that has largely been lost sight of is that a subject may be just as satisfactory, or even better, in monochrome. Colour should be no substitute for good design, though it is often regarded as such. Perhaps this modern fetish for colour, allied to bigger formats in stamp production, may be seen most forcibly in the craze for stamps reproducing works of art. This began in 1961, in France, which issued a series of four jumbo-sized stamps reproducing in multicoloured intaglio paintings by Braque, Cezanne, Matisse and de la Fresnaye. The series was an immediate success and was heavily oversubscribed by collectors. France followed this with similar stamps at annual intervals, building up an impressive art gallery which included sculpture, stained glass, lithographs and tapestry as well as oil paintings. The idea was borrowed by Czechoslovakia which produced such masterpieces as *Lady at her Toilet*, after Titian (1965) and Picasso's *Guernica* (1966). In the latter year the first series devoted to Czechoslovak art appeared and has since become a regular feature. Other countries soon jumped on the bandwagon. Even staid Britain has issued several sets featuring paintings as such, and also used Old Masters as the basis of the designs for a number of Christmas stamps. The United States began issuing a single art stamp each year, using the centenary of the birth of Frederick Remington (1961) as the pretext for a multicoloured intaglio stamp reproducing *The Smoke Signal*. In subsequent years the paintings were not tied to any particular anniversary. After an unfortunate experiment with photogravure in 1967, when Thomas Eakins's *The Biglin Brothers Racing* was produced by the Photogravure and Color Co. of Moonachie, New Jersey, the United States reverted to recess printing, but used it in combination with lithography, and this has been extended to cover the majority of recent American commemorative and thematic issues. Perhaps the trend in American design can best be demonstrated by comparing the treatment of a subject over the past forty years. In 1934 a 5 cent stamp depicted the geyser Old Faithful in the Yellowstone National Park. In 1972 a stamp with an almost identical motif was issued to mark the fiftieth anniversary of the National Parks Service. The original version was recess-printed in monochrome with sculpted lettering which was then fashionable. The recent version was printed in combined intaglio and offset lithography in five colours, and the new jumbo format, popular with American commemoratives since 1969, was used. Increasing colour and size are the twin criteria which distinguish present-day pictorials the world over from their prewar counterparts.

Netherlands, Cultural, Health and Social Welfare Fund series, 1970. Designed by R. Oxenaar on the basis of patterns devised by a computer. These stamps, the first to be 'computer-designed', consisted of spirals, concentric circles in transition, parallel planes in cube and overlapping scales. They were printed by Enschede in intaglio against a lithographed background and have a silvery, metallic look. (25 × 36mm).

12
The age of the gimmick

T HE POSTAGE STAMP has come a long way from the simple label denoting the prepayment of postage. Aside from such specialized functions as airmail, registration, late fee and postage due, the postage stamp can commemorate events and personalities, publicize tourism or promote political viewpoints. The charity or semi-postal stamp is today the most effective fund raiser. At the same time other, more efficient methods of prepaying postage have been evolved in the past century. Meter franking, introduced by New Zealand and Norway as long ago as 1904, has now spread all over the world and is widely used by commerce, while the mailomat variant, or coin-operated franking, has extended this boon to the private individual in many countries. Permit mailing, business reply envelopes and cards, rebate posting and now freepost have all eroded the need for an adhesive stamp. Although there will always be some residual necessity for adhesive stamps, especially in underdeveloped countries, it must be admitted that adhesive stamps probably account for no more than 40 per cent of all mail handled throughout the world today, and that percentage is steadily falling each year. On the other hand, the output of new stamps continues to rise. About a quarter of a million different stamps have appeared since 1840, but the present annual output is somewhere in the region of six thousand. Postage stamps are big business, supporting a multimillion pound industry in such major centres as London, Paris and New York. The British Post Office has a philatelic revenue in excess of 2·5 million pounds each year and many other countries have sales which far exceed that figure.

If stamps are used less and less on mail, who buys them in such vast quantities? The answer is the collectors, whose numbers are now astronomical. It is impossible to assess the philatelic population of the world accurately, but with an estimated three million in the United Kingdom, sixteen million in the United States and almost twenty million in the Soviet Union alone, a world figure of sixty to eighty million would not be unreasonable. It is axiomatic that philatelists are primarily concerned with the stamps of their own country, but interest would soon flag if they were not attracted towards the stamps of other countries. In the past, interest in 'foreign' stamps was politically motivated; British collectors automatically interested themselves in the stamps of the British Empire, while Americans were more likely to collect the stamps of Canada and Mexico. As the British colonies became independent in the 1950s and 1960s, the loyalty of British collectors to such countries as Ghana (the former Gold Coast) and Malawi (formerly Nyasaland) waned. The same thing happened in France, where philatelists were no longer so ready to collect anything emanating from Togo, Cameroun or Mali. Conversely the emergent nations—and the United Nations itself—enjoyed a certain vogue in the United States, but as the number of emergent nations grew, American collectors were forced to be more selective. We have now reached a point where no country can be sure of its philatelic market (other than its own indigenous collectors) and must seek ways of increasing its stamp sales abroad.

The days when collectors would fall over themselves to secure the latest provisional surcharge or minor change in perforation or watermark are gone for good. Stamps have become a hard sell, with more and more countries competing for a decreasing slice of the cake. As the output of new issues is stepped up collectors are forced to narrow their interests down to a few countries. As a result, most countries have now established philatelic agencies or bureaus to promote the sales of their stamps to collectors. Advertising and promotional campaigns now account for a large part of the overheads of postal administrations. Many countries have spent large sums on detailed market research; others have established advisory councils to assist with such problems as subject and design. The demand for more colourful stamps, coupled with advances in the techniques of production, stimulated the development of the craze for Art stamps. Old Masters and Post-Impressionists alike have been fully explored in the medium of the Art stamp in the past decade, and now postal administrations are casting the net even wider, to include stained glass, mosaics and even lace patterns. A comparatively recent development has been the use of children's designs for

United Nations, 60 cents, 1971

Malawi, 3 shillings, 1967

Bahamas, 1 dollar, 1966

Czechoslovakia, 60 haleru, 1966

1. Singapore, 30 cents, 1971

2. West Germany, 20 pfennigs, 1970

In recent years there has been a significant increase in the number of stamps which may be regarded as works of art in their own right. This is particularly true of many United Nations stamps where non-figurative designs avoid offending the political susceptibilities of member-countries.

Left:
Unusual treatments of hackneyed subjects: W. Lee showed great ingenuity in devising ways of working the flags of the 31 Commonwealth countries into a single motif (1); West Germany's Voluntary Relief Services series of 1970 (2) applied contemporary poster techniques to achieve an unusual rounded effect.

Right:
The quest for more and more unusual subjects or treatments has greatly enriched the variety of modern stamp design. Papua New Guinea's native artifacts series of 1969, designed by the Rev. H. A. Brown, was produced by Enschede in bipartite units, each half being usable as a separate stamp (1). Ireland's definitive issues of 1968 and 1971 drew on medieval Celtic art, though the stamps themselves were designed by a West German artist, Heinrich Gerl (2). Dominica's 1969 definitive series used an ornamental capital D, in the style of a medieval illuminated manuscript, as the frame to the pictorial vignettes (3). The Cook Islands have borrowed heavily on the art of Paul Gauguin and the Old Masters (4). Both British Honduras and the New Hebrides have used timber graining as a background to designs featuring trees (5).

1. Netherlands Antilles, 6 + 3 cents, 1963 2. Czechoslovakia, 30 haleru, 1968

3. Netherlands, 10 + 6 cents, 1965

A novel approach is the stamp designed by children—or, more accurately, the stamp whose motif is based on children's art. The Netherlands Antilles Child Welfare series of 1963 (1) and 1965 (3) were based on prize-winning entries in a children's art competition. West Germany's Child Welfare series of 1971 (4) also used children's drawings and paintings. The Czechoslovakian 30 haleru of 1968 featured a painting by Jiri Beutler aged ten (an inmate of Teresin concentration camp).

4. West Germany, 10 + 5 pfennigs, 1971

1. Papua New Guinea, 10 + 10 cents, 1969

2. Ireland, 9 pence, 1971

4. Cook Islands, 22 cents, 1967

3. Dominica, 3 cents, 1969

5. British Honduras, 22 cents, 1

postage stamps. Czechoslovakia pioneered this with a set of three in 1958. Monaco used paintings by schoolchildren for a series of stamps in 1962 honouring the United Nations Children's Charter. The following year the Netherlands Antilles held a painting competition and used the five winning entries for a series of child welfare stamps. Children's designs were used for child welfare stamps by the Netherlands in 1965 and have been adapted for the annual Children's Day stamps of Yugoslavia since 1964. Christmas stamps designed by children have been issued by Britain, Canada and Sweden, while Greece, Poland, Luxembourg, Japan and Argentina are among the other countries which have recently produced stamps of this sort.

The prevalence of stamps featuring paintings, or deriving in some way from an original work of art, has perhaps compensated for the fact that few stamps of the present day are works of art in themselves. Czechoslovak stamps provide one of the refreshing exceptions. There have been many excellent designs in which even mundane subjects have been given an artistic treatment, aided by the retention of intaglio which gives the artist and engraver greater scope for personal interpretation of a subject. The designs range from the whimsical, like Karel Svolinsky's head of a singer on the 30 haleru of 1963, to the vorticist, exemplified by J. Paukert's 'Victorious February' commemorative of 1968. Other Czech artists whose distinctive style may be recognized on their country's stamps are Max Svabinsky, Jiri Svengsbir and Ladislav Jirka. Outside Czechoslovakia few artists are permitted to express their personality in stamp design. Among the notable exceptions may be mentioned Hatem Elmekki whose numerous designs for Tunisia often have a surrealist quality. Among these may be cited 'Unsettled Forecast' used for the World Meteorological Day stamps of 1963, 'Joined Hooks' shown on the International Co-operation Year stamp of 1966, and 'Electronic Man' for Post Office Electronics in 1968. Nearly all the stamps of Malta since 1955 have been designed by Chevalier Emmanuel Cremona. His versatility is immense, ranging from straightforward portraiture (Dante, Churchill, Kennedy), through his impressionist treatment of the Christmas theme to the cubism of his Trade series of 1966 and the Osaka World Fair set of 1970. Cremona's monopoly of Maltese stamp design was breached in 1970 by J. Casha whose 'Peace and Justice' design for the twenty-fifth anniversary of the United Nations is very much in the Cremona idiom.

Scandinavia was in the forefront of modern design in architecture and the applied arts of this century, and the postage stamp is one of the media in which a

Tunisia, 20 millièmes, 1967

Malta, 3 pence, 1958

The most unusual and original designs in recent years have come from Tunisia and Malta where Hatem Elmekki and Emmanuel Cremona have respectively been given a free hand. Elmekki's designs range from the pure abstract to whimsical surrealism. Cremona's art is eclectic, borrowing from many diverse styles, both medieval and ultra-modern.

distinctive Scandinavian style has been evolved. Much of the credit for this should go to the Finnish-American architect and designer Eero Saarinen whose designs for the first issues of the Finnish republic in 1917 set the pace for subsequent designers, notably Miss Hammarsten Jansson who enjoyed a near monopoly of Finnish stamp design from 1929 to 1960. Together with her pupils and colleagues, A. Gallen-Kallela and A. Lauren, she developed a style of design which dispensed with the traditional frame lines and used bold, white lettering on a solid ground. The tradition of well-balanced elements and dramatic impact in

1. Sweden, 2 kronor, 1972

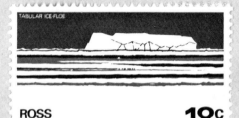

2. Ross Dependency, 18 cents, 1972

3. St. Helena, 1 pound, 1968

4. Pitcairn Islands, 20 cents, 1969

The traditional framework of a design has been dispensed with in many cases, allowing the designer greater freedom to concentrate on the vignette. Sweden's China Palace stamp (1) used tinted paper bled off into the perforations—a technique perfected by Jennifer Toombs in the Pitcairn series of 1969 (4). St. Helena's definitive series of 1968 (3) designed by Sylvia Goaman used an unusual 'pen and wash' treatment for lithography. Mark Cleverley, who has designed recent stamps for Ross Dependency and New Zealand, has spurned the conventional use of frame lines to create quite startling effects (2).

Right:
Cremona's 1958 stamp design (opposite) may have been inspired by this construction (in aluminium baked black, plastic, gold wire, bronze mesh and steel) by Naum Gabo.

the principal motifs has been continued by Olavi Vepsalainen and Pentti Rahikainen who, between them, have designed the majority of Finnish stamps since 1959. Some credit for the uniformly high standard of execution must also go to Bengt Ekholm who has engraved the dies for many Finnish stamps since 1946.

Although Finland has turned in recent years to multicolour offset lithography, a high proportion of her stamps are still produced by recess printing, a process which also finds continuing favour in Denmark and Sweden. Curiously, Denmark only turned

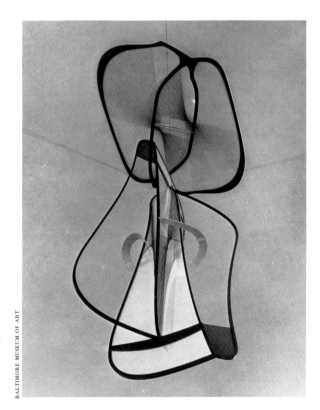

Stamps for propaganda

1. Communist China, 8 fen, 1968
2. Nationalist China, 2.50 yuan, 1971
3. Cuba, 3 centavos, 1966
4. United States, 5 cents, 1963
5. Italy, 25 lire, 1954
6. New Zealand, 1½ pence, 1900

All the stamps on these two pages have a 'message', whether it is a political viewpoint (1) or simply an encouragement to pay taxes promptly. (Italy's 25 lire stamp (5) is inscribed 'everyone must contribute to the public expense'.) An early example is J. Nairn's patriotic design for New Zealand (6), issued in 1900 during the Boer War and, appropriately, printed in khaki. Cuba and the United States provide more modern examples, with two views of the Bay of Pigs abortive invasion of Cuba (3, 4).

1
2

1. Czechoslovakia, 2 haleru, 1938
2. Germany, 3 pfennigs, 1935

The prewar territorial aggrandisement of Nazi Germany was well documented in stamps of the period. E. Glimtzer's design entitled 'The Saar comes Home' was one of several allegorical compositions which signposted German territorial gains. Czech stamps were overprinted 'Wir Sind Frei' (we are free) with the swastika emblem, after the Sudetenland was overrun in 1938.

1. North Korea, 10 chon, 1960
2. Revolutionary Committee of South Vietnam, 3 dong, 1972

Communist opposition to American foreign policy has been mute—so far as the stamps of the European satellites are concerned, but North Korea and Vietnam do not pull their punches, and produce stamps whose designs have been crude and effective. North Korea's stamp of 1960, for an international journalists' conference, shows pens as bayonets attacking the American imperialist hyena. Vietnam's stamps marking the tenth anniversary of the war show lightning shattering an American helmet. North Vietnamese stamps have even caricatured President Nixon.

1. Venezuela, 10 centavos, 1896
2. Bulgaria, 10 stotinki, 1921
3. Jordan, 80 fils, 1964

Stamps featuring maps are frequently used to promote a particular political viewpoint. Venezuela used the Miranda commemoratives of 1896 to advance a claim to British Guiana's territory west of the Essequibo river (1). Bulgaria prepared a set showing a map of Macedonia, seized from Serbia in 1915 (2). The stamps, designed by D. Gudjenov and typographed in Berlin, were not released till 1921. They were withdrawn after three days, following protests from Yugoslavia which had recaptured Macedonia at the end of the First World War. Jordan's Arab Summit Conference stamps of 1964 completely ignored the existence of Israel on their map (3).

Stamps are now widely used to back up government campaigns, such as road safety. One of a series issued by Cuba in 1970, for Transport Week.

to intaglio in 1933, at a time when other countries were turning to photogravure. Previously Danish stamps had been typographed in a rather heavy style reminiscent of German stamps of the same period. The outstanding designer over the past thirty years has been Viggo Bang. With Mads Stage (since 1962) he has produced most of the pictorial designs in the more orthodox style. In the past decade, however, there have been a few indications of a more experimental approach to design, of which P. von Schantz's allegory of Jet Flight (1961), Frederiksen's Refugee 66 motif (1966) and R. Mortensen's non-figurative stamp (1969) are typical. It is interesting to compare the intaglio symbolism of modern Danish stamps with the photogravure symbolism of their British contemporaries.

Like Denmark, Sweden abandoned typography in favour of intaglio. Somewhat stylized portraiture and figurative work, against coarse unframed, quadrille backgrounds, combined the characteristics of Danish and Finnish design in the interwar period. Sweden, more than any other country, developed the art of the pictorial design in the small format usually reserved elsewhere for definitive stamps, and the discipline entailed in 'thinking small' resulted in some of the finest examples of balanced composition and restrained lettering. In recent years, however, the design and appearance of Swedish stamps have been greatly enlivened. Although the solid, typically Scandinavian background is still to be found, a significant feature of many recent issues has been the arrangement of motifs and lettering on white or tinted surfaces without any surrounding frame.

Both Finland and Sweden have flirted with photogravure or lithography in recent years, even commissioning the British firms of Harrison and De La Rue. Norway, on the other hand, used photogravure almost exclusively from 1937 onwards, but in recent years has been attracted to intaglio. The resulting stamps, especially those designed and engraved by K. Lökke-Sörensen, bear a striking similarity to the contemporary issues of Sweden.

Relatively few British stamps may be regarded as works of art, although the Post Office recently established a fellowship in minuscule design to explore the potential of stamps as an art form. There are, however, several examples of scenic stamps with an impressionist interpretation. These include David Bailey's set of four marking the Geographical Congress in 1964 and stamps by Andrew Restall in honour of the Forth Bridge in 1964. The stamps designed by David Gentleman are of a uniformly high standard of design and originality, though his recent work has veered towards realism and away from the symbolic

1. Iran, 3 rials, 1965

2. United Nations, 4 cents, 1961

3. Laos, 4 kip, 1963

Abstract designs are now being used more frequently for commemorative stamps: (1) Iranian Exhibition, Teheran, 1965; (2) United Nations series honouring the International Court of Justice, designed by Kurt Plowitz; (3) A. Freres produced a Daliesque motif for the Laotian stamp honouring UNESCO, 1963.

1. Saudi Arabia, 4 piastres, 1971
2. Ghana, 1 shilling, 1960
3. Singapore, 25 cents, 1969

Numerals and lettering have been effectively used as decorative motifs. In Ghana's Africa Freedom Day series, Willy Wind used each initial as the principal motif (2). Saudi Arabia's stamp has Roman capitals ornamentally treated in the manner of Kufic Arabic script (1), while Tan Siew Chiah's set for Singapore used numerals to simulate a block of flats (3).

treatment shown in his National Productivity Year series of 1962. Gentleman experimented with wood-cuts as the basis for stylized motifs, even when real subjects were depicted, and this is exemplified by his stamps for the International Lifeboat Conference (1963), Shakespeare (1964) and the Commonwealth Arts Festival (1965).

A young British designer whose work has appeared on the stamps of many Commonwealth countries (but not, surprisingly, of Britain) is Jennifer Toombs. Most of her designs have a solid appearance, induced by bleeding the colour into the perforations and doing away with the traditional white surround. Although much of her work has consisted of straight-forward pictorial designs, purely artistic motifs have included her Christmas series for Malawi (1967) and the UNESCO omnibus designs of 1966.

It is a sad fact, however, that the great philatelic public was not interested in the finer aesthetic qualities of stamp design. What was sought primarily were pretty pictures of certain well-defined themes, such as Sport, Space, Religion, Fauna and Flora, and the postal authorities, looking for ways of selling the most stamps to the most people, went to great lengths to pander to the thematic craze. Considerable in-genuity was shown in devising stamps which managed to incorporate several themes in a single design. Old Master paintings of the Nativity, for example, would cater to collectors of Art and Religion; stamps showing President Kennedy inspecting the 'Friendship 7' capsule (Ras al Khaima, 1965) would be purchased by collectors of the Space and Kennedy themes. The relevance of a subject to the country of issue might be slender—or utterly non-existent. As a result, there have been such ludicrous issues as the Innsbruck Winter Olympics series from the central African state of Burundi, where snowflakes are as rare as hen's teeth, or Old Master paintings of the Madonna and Child from the Moslem sheikhdoms of Arabia. Many countries with no direct stake in the space race have enjoyed vicarious participation by issuing stamps ex-tolling the latest Russian or American exploits. As stamps with even a remotely American connection are a sure-fire hit in the United States (and thus a useful earner of dollars), the American space exploits are rather better commemorated than those of the Soviet Union. This has gone to such lengths that even several countries in the Communist bloc (not-ably Czechoslovakia and Hungary) have produced stamps in honour of American astronauts—though none of America's allies has so far returned the compliment!

The subject matter of a stamp is no longer sufficient, it seems, to attract the interest (and money) of

Guinea, 1,200 francs, 1972

Umm al Qiwain, 25 naye paise, 1965

Gibraltar, 7 pence, 1969

Sierra Leone, 9 pence, 1964

Barbuda, 35 cents, 1971. This dependency of Antigua, which issued its own stamps from 1968 to 1972, produced a lengthy series portraying every British ruler since the Norman Conquest.

Left:
Free-form stamps were pioneered by Sierra Leone whose map-shaped stamps were recess-printed and lithographed by the Walsall Lithographic Company; backing paper protected the self-adhesive backs of these stamps. Gibraltar's New Constitution series of 1969, designed by A. G. Ryman, were perforated in the shape of the Rock.

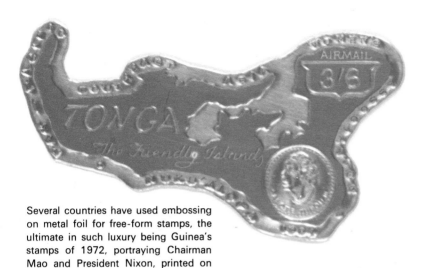

Several countries have used embossing on metal foil for free-form stamps, the ultimate in such luxury being Guinea's stamps of 1972, portraying Chairman Mao and President Nixon, printed on 22-carat gold foil set with gemstones.

Tonga, 3s 6d, 1964

Sierra Leone, 3 cents, 1965

2. Thessaly, 5 piastres, 1898

1. Tuva, 25 kopeks, 1936

3. Malta, 1s 4d, 1968

Unusual formats are increasingly common, though Thessaly, as long ago as 1898, was using octagonal stamps (2). The vignette, showing the railway bridge at Larissa, is almost completely lost in the welter of scrollwork and inscriptions. Tuva favoured diamond-shaped stamps in the Thirties (1), while rhomboids and irregular polygons have been employed recently by Malta (3).

1. Bhutan, 10 chetrums, 1970

2. Bhutan, 1.50 nultrums, 1968

3. Bhutan, 5 chetrums, 1969

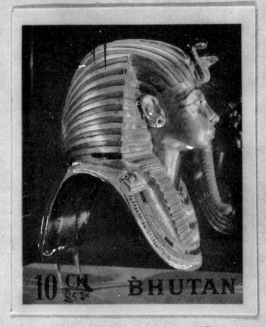

4. Bhutan, 10 chetrums, 1968

5. Bhutan, 5 nultrums, 1969

6. Russia, 20 kopeks, 1965

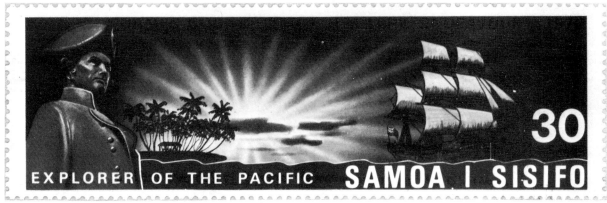

EXPLORER OF THE PACIFIC SAMOA I SISIFO 30

Excessively elongated horizontal designs have been a characteristic of several Samoan stamps since 1970, when this stamp was issued. Measuring 89 millimetres (including perforation edge), it commemorated Captain Cook and features a panoramic view of Pacific islands, together with a statue of the explorer and his ship *Endeavour*. Subsequent issues included the Interpex stamp of 1971 (84mm) and the Roggeveen series of 1972 (90mm).

Unorthodox materials have replaced conventional paper, providing some unusual gimmicks in stamp design. Russia used aluminium foil for a Space commemorative of 1965 (6), but Bhutan is the most prolific user of unusual substances, with silk (Buddhist prayer banners (5)), plastic relief printing (art series (4)), steel foil (Steel Industry series (3)), plastic simulating the surface of oil paintings (art series (2)), and prismatic-ribbed plastic creating a three-dimensional effect (Space, fishes and art series (1)).

philatelists. Traditional gimmicks, like miniature sheets or limited editions of stamps without perforations or in altered colours, have been used extensively but these are not enough to whet the jaded palate of the collector. Stamp producers have therefore been wracking their brains in recent years to find fresh angles. In 1970, for example, the Netherlands issued a set of stamps whose intricate patterns were designed by a computer. One gimmick, which has so far had only limited application, is to use substances other than paper on which to print stamps. In 1955 Hungary reprinted the 5 forint airmail stamp, showing the Matyas Rakosi metal works, on aluminium-surfaced paper to celebrate the Light Metal Industries International Conference in Budapest. Aluminium foil, used extensively in food packaging, was not really suitable for stamps so Hungary has not repeated the experiment. More recently, however, the Soviet Union has used aluminium foil in the production of several Space commemoratives, and this device was also used by Sharjah and Khor Fakkan for the Churchill commemoratives of 1966. Hungary used oilcloth to reprint the floral series of 1958 in a miniature sheet ostensibly honouring the International Philatelic Federation Congress in Brussels that year. It has been left to the remote Himalayan

kingdom of Bhutan (whose philatelic agency operates from Nassau, Bahamas) to issue stamps on the most unconventional substances. A series devoted to mythology (1968) was printed on silk, while a series featuring Old Masters released later the same year had a plastic surface simulating the texture of oil paint on canvas. Stamps issued in 1969 to publicize the steel industry were printed on thin steel plates. A series devoted to sculpture of antiquity, released in 1971, was made of plastic with a raised surface to simulate the three-dimensional quality of sculpture. This bas-relief effect was subsequently used for a series portraying world statesmen.

Three-dimensionalism has exercised the minds of stamp producers on other occasions. Anaglyptography, a form of typography using parallel, wavy vertical lines to create the effect of relief, was used by Austria for the high-value stamps of 1890 and 1899-1902, and by Australia for the King George V definitives of 1913, but it could only suggest three-dimensionality by an optical illusion. In 1956 Italy went a stage farther and issued two anaglyphic stamps, marking the first anniversary of admission to the United Nations Organization. The principal motif, a globe, was printed in red and green in two images which were slightly out of alignment, so that a three-dimensional effect would be achieved when the stamps were viewed through appropriately coloured spectacles. In the early fifties there was a vogue for books, magazines and films in 3-D assisted by green and red spectacles, so it was inevitable that the same gimmick should be extended to stamps. It was left to Bhutan again to provide the final solution. In 1967 a set of stamps celebrating space achievements was produced with laminated, prismatic-ribbed plastic surfacing. This three-dimensional effect was later used for stamps showing fishes and, more recently, Old Master paintings. The effect in the Art stamps was ludicrous; reminiscent of those tableaux of living art in which famous paintings are re-created as waxwork groups.

In 1963 Tonga issued a set of gold coins and then celebrated this fact by issuing stamps die-stamped on gold foil, reproducing the obverse and reverse of the coins. The stamps were circular in shape (the first truly circular stamps since the first Sind Dawks of 1852) and ranged in diameter from 42 mm to 80 mm—hence the derisive nickname of 'Tonga Beermats' given to them by collectors. They were immensely popular with philatelists and this induced Tonga to repeat the experiment with circular coin stamps in 1967. Similar circular coin stamps, embossed on gold or silver foil, appeared in Sierra Leone, Sharjah, Qatar, Umm al Qiwain and, of course, Bhutan, which has produced such curiosities on several occasions.

Tonga also issued metal-foil embossed stamps in other shapes. The Pan-Pacific and South East Asia Women's Conference was celebrated in 1964 by metal-foil stamps shaped like hearts or a map of Tongatapu and this may have been the cue for the Sierra Leone stamps of the same year (from the same printer, Walsall Lithographic Company) which were shaped like the map of the country. The stamps were die-stamped on specially coated paper and had motifs commemorating President Kennedy and the New York World's Fair superimposed on the map. The stamps, resembling old-fashioned scraps, were affixed to peelable backing paper. No 'lick' was required to stick the stamps on mail, and the world's first free-form, self-adhesive stamps were hailed (by the public relations men of Sierra Leone and Walsall Lithographic) as the greatest breakthrough since Rowland Hill devised the Penny Black. Both Sierra Leone and Tonga have produced a number of such stamps in recent years. It was soon realized that the reverse of the backing paper was an ideal place for commercial advertising, the idea being to sell the space to advertisers and thus defray the cost of producing these relatively expensive stamps.

Se-tenant strips simulating triptych paintings of religious subjects have been used for Christmas and Easter stamps. Gibraltar's 1969 Christmas stamps had rouletting as a means of separating the individual stamps, though conventional perforation was used for each strip as a whole (145 × 40mm).

The same technique has been applied by Taiwan to strips of up to six stamps in order to reproduce Chinese scroll paintings. Britain's strip of six stamps of 1966 featuring the Bayeux Tapestry has the superficial appearance of this technique, although the scenes depicted are not actually from contiguous portions of the tapestry.

Apart from multiple strips this practice is now being used increasingly in blocks of four or larger multiples, each unit bearing a portion of a picture, yet contriving to form a distinctive design in its own right. This approach is best suited to the reproduction of works (such as stained glass windows, tapestries and Breughel paintings), which contain a mass of detail and tiny vignettes within the structure of the whole.

Yugoslavia and Romania issued identical stamps for the inauguration of the Djerdap Hydro-Electric project, with values in the currencies of both countries. The stamps were jointly designed by B. Lazarovic (Yugoslavia) and E. Palade (Romania).

St. Lucia, Easter series, 1970
Composite stamps and se-tenant designs are now increasingly
common. St. Lucia's Easter series, designed by Victor
Whiteley, even simulated the staggered effect of the original
Hogarth Triptych. (95 × 65mm)

Dubai, Moon Landing, 1969
Dubai's Moon Landing series extended the triptych device to
a secular subject, linking stamps of different formats and
values. (127 × 45mm)

The French answer to these British gimmicks was to print stamps on actual gold sheets laminated to a paper backing. The metal-foil stamps of Tonga and Qatar, though simulating gold and silver, were actually produced from base metals. For Gabon, however, A. Revillard produced a sumptuous stamp in 22-carat gold, in memory of Albert Schweitzer (1965) and three years later improved on this with a similar stamp, in mourning for President Mba, with the national flag picked out in enamelled green, yellow and blue. The most recent of these confections was a set issued by Guinea in 1972 to mark the *rapprochement* between the United States and Communist China. Profiles of President Nixon and Chairman Mao flanked jewelled ping-pong bats.

An attempt to produce free-form shapes in sheets, with perforation in the orthodox manner, was made by the Bahamas in 1968 with a series featuring gold coins. The kidney-shaped stamps showed the obverse and reverse of the coins on gold-surfaced paper, with perforations following the curious outline of the stamps. The design would have looked better in a more conventional rectangular format, but no doubt that would have lacked the novelty value which helped to market the stamps. This idea was repeated the following year by Gibraltar, with a set of stamps shaped like the silhouette of the Rock. Malaysia and Malta have both experimented with oddly shaped stamps in recent years, though always keeping within practical bounds and using orthodox perforation. Triangles, diamonds, rhomboids and irregular polygons have been tried, but there is no evidence to suggest that such stamps sell any faster than conventional rectangles.

Printing stamps of different designs side by side in the same sheet has been tried on many occasions. In most cases two designs are used, printed alternately throughout the sheet. Australia, which favoured this device in the fifties, even produced stamps in threes, for a food production campaign in 1953. Multiple designs have long been a feature of Christmas stamps from Cuba, each stamp in the sheet depicting a different subject on the same basic theme. The worst excess of this kind, however, consisted of three denominations, each in sheets of twenty-five different designs, issued by Chile in 1948 to mark the centenary of Gay's handbook on Chilean flora and fauna. For years these stamps were banned from exhibitions under the auspices of the Federation Internationale de Philatelie, but such multiple designs are now commonplace. Britain used them successfully in 1966 to reproduce scenes from the Bayeux Tapestry, and more recently Formosa has reproduced ancient Chinese handscroll paintings in this way.

Bhutan, 1.25 nultrums, 'talking stamp', from the ser[ies] featuring the Bhutanese national anthem and re[com]mentaries on Bhutanese history. (67mm diam[eter]

Multiple designs have now given way [to composite] stamps, in which a group of four or more stamps forms a single picture, rather like a jigsaw puzzle. This idea originated in the Communist countries, but has also been used in recent years by West Germany. The United States adopted it in 1972 for the four 2 cent stamps depicting the Cape Hatteras National Seashore Park and repeated it the following year for the Boston Tea Party quartet. By keeping inscriptions and values to the outer margins the composite picture is left clear of extraneous matter; yet each quarter of the design has sufficient detail to tell a story or convey an idea on its own. Religious triptychs, reproduced on three adjoining stamps, have been popular for Christmas and Easter issues in recent years. St. Lucia even managed to simulate the staggered arrangement of the Hogarth Triptych on the Easter series of 1970.

The last word on philatelic gimmickry, however, must rest with Bhutan. In 1973 a set of stamps appeared on plastic, circular in shape and having a small hole in the centre. The design consisted of concentric grooves, and when placed on a record player the stamp gave out the reedy strains of the Bhutanese national anthem. The age of the talking stamp has arrived!

Books for further reading

AKERSTEDT, SVEN *Frimarkets Bok* Medens Forlags AB, Stockholm, 1957

BENNETT, RUSSELL AND WATSON, JAMES *Philatelic Terms Illustrated* Stanley Gibbons, London, 1972

BOGGS, WINTHROP S. *The Foundations of Philately* Faber, London and Van Nostrand, Reinhold, New York, 1956

EASTON, JOHN *British Postage Stamps Design* Faber, London, 1945
    Postage Stamps in the Making Faber, London, 1949
    The De La Rue History of British and Foreign Postage Stamps Faber, London, 1958

GENTLEMAN, DAVID *Design in Miniature* Studio Vista, London, 1972 and Van Nostrand, Reinhold, New York

GRAVESON, SAMUEL *Penny Postage Centenary* Postal History Society, London, 1940

HAVERBECK, HARRISON D. S. *The Commemorative Stamps of the British Commonwealth* Faber, London, 1955

HOUSEMAN, LORNA *The House that Thomas Built: the Story of De La Rue* Chatto and Windus, London, 1968

LOWE, ROBSON *Masterpieces of Engraving on Stamps* Postal History Society, London, 1940
    The Encyclopaedia of British Empire Postage Stamps, vols I–V Robson Lowe Ltd, London, 1949-74
    The British Postage Stamp of the Nineteenth Century National Postal Museum, London, 1968

MACKAY, JAMES *Commonwealth Stamp Design 1840-1965* British Museum, London, 1965
    The World of Classic Stamps Putnam, New York and Office du Livre, Fribourg, Switzerland, 1972
    The International Encyclopedia of Stamps International Publishing Corporation, London, 1970-2
    The Source Book of Stamps Ward Lock, London, 1974

NEW, ANTHONY S. B. *The Observer's Book of Postage Stamps* Frederick Warne, London, 1967

SUTTON, R. J. *The Stamp Collector's Encyclopaedia* (sixth edition revised by Kenneth W. Anthony) Stanley Paul, London, 1968 and International Publications Service, New York, 1970

TODD, THOMAS *Behind the Stamp Album* Duckworth, London, 1939
WATSON, JAMES *The Story of the Stamp* London, 1957

WILLIAMS, L. N. and M. *The Postage Stamp* Penguins, Harmondsworth and Baltimore, 1956
    Techniques of Philately Heinemann, London, 1969 and Transatlantic, New York, 1970
    Fundamentals of Philately American Philatelic Society, New York, 1969

Glossary

albino Colourless impression, caused accidentally by under-inking the printing plate, or deliberately used in embossing.

bed The table of a printing machine. The **forme** is laid on this for printing.

charity stamp Postage stamp bearing a premium in aid of charity; first adopted by the Australian states of Victoria and New South Wales in 1897.

cliché see **stereo**

commemorative stamp Postage stamp designed to commemorate an event or personality. The term is often used loosely to cover all postage stamps issued for special occasions or for a limited period.

composite stamps A pair, strip, block or other multiple of stamps which together compose a single picture or design. This device, pioneered in Eastern Europe in the late 1950s, is now widely used and permits the designer much greater scope.

coupon Label attached to postage stamps, but having no postal validity itself. Coupons may be found attached to stamps from booklet panes, bearing commercial advertising. In the 1930s Czechoslovakia introduced coupons alternating with stamps in sheets and bearing explanatory inscriptions or motifs relating to the stamps.

definitive stamp Stamp belonging to the ordinary or permanent series, as opposed to commemorative or charity stamps.

die The original or master engraving, in letterpress or intaglio printing, from which the multiple impressions of the plate are taken.

electro(type) Printing plate made by coating a mould electrolytically with copper.

forme Type, blocks etc. ready for printing, arranged and fixed in a chase or frame.

frame The border of the design, enclosing the **vignette** and often incorporating the inscriptions, **value tablet** and inset portraits.

fugitive inks Coloured inks which are liable to fade quickly if exposed to sunlight.

guilloche Intricate spiral pattern, often used on banknotes as a security device and occasionally found on stamps.

half-tone Reproducing light and shade photographically, using dots of different sizes. Also used to describe the photographs etc. reproduced in this way.

key plate Printing plate which can be used to print stamps of different values or even of different countries. Key plates were developed by De La Rue as an economic method of producing stamps for the numerous British colonies. Two plates were often used—a head plate containing impressions of the royal profile, and a duty plate containing the **frame** and the duty (i.e. value).

key type Standard design used by a number of territories, usually European colonies, the only variation being the name of the territory concerned. Key types were used extensively by Britain, France, Spain, Portugal and Germany for their overseas territories between 1879 and 1939 (though British key types survived as late as 1956).

miniature sheet Small sheet containing one or more stamps, usually with a decorative margin. Pioneered by Luxembourg in 1923, these sheets are designed mainly for collectors though they have nominal postal validity.

ogive The diagonal rib of a vault; a pointed window or arch.

omnibus issue Issue of stamps in uniform designs made in a group of countries simultaneously. Such stamps usually differ only in the name of the country and the denomination. They thus represent the **key type** principle applied to commemorative stamps.

overprint Inscription added to the design of stamps after the basic stamps have been printed. The term is restricted to inscriptions which do not alter the value of the stamp. An overprint may be applied to a stamp to change the scope of its validity (even the country in which it is used), to convert a stamp from one purpose to another (e.g. from **definitive** to **commemorative**, or from ordinary to airmail postage).

plate Device bearing impressions of the design, used to print stamps.

printer's ornament Decorative patterns, borders etc. supplied by the printer.

provisional Stamp altered by means of an **overprint** or by a **surcharge** and issued in times of emergency.

rouletting Rows of engraved dots for perforating paper etc.

screen A glass plate inserted in the camera to break a picture down into dots of different sizes to reproduce light and shade. See **half-tone**.

semi-postal American term for **charity stamp**—a more accurate description since it alludes to the fact that only part of the value expressed on such stamps has postal validity; the other part is devoted to charity.

se-tenant French expression denoting two or more stamps of different designs, values or colours, printed side by side on the same sheet.

spandrels The spaces in the design of stamps, between the central oval or circular motif and the rectangular lines of the **frame**. The spandrels were usually filled with intricate spiral or geometric patterns, partly for artistic effect and partly to defeat forgers.

stereo(type) Solid metallic plate for printing, cast from type or from a mould. Also called a cliché.

surcharge A form of **overprint** which alters the value of a stamp. Postage stamps are often surcharged with new values as a result of changes in postal rates.

tab A form of **coupon** with decorative motifs or inscriptions, found in the margins of Israeli stamps. Though Israel pioneered this device in 1948 and is the only country to use it consistently, other countries have issued stamps with similar devices (e.g. Zip Code cartoons on modern American stamps).

value tablet That portion of the design on which the numerals of value appear.

vignette The 'picture' part of pictorial stamps, as distinct from the **frame**.

Index

Numbers in italics refer to illustrations

A

Aaltonen, Waino, *138*
Aden, 124, *127*
Adler, C., *58*
Afghanistan, 51–2, 148
Agami Effendi Ali, *54*
Albania, 53, 67, 69, *139*, 156
American Bank Note Co., 28, 32, 37–8, *39*, 41, *42*, 43, 50, 79–80, 82, 124, 140, *141*
anaglyptography, 177
Angeli, Baron von, 69, *70*, 84
Angola, 65
Antigua, 32, *35*, 61, 121, *144*, *174*
Argentina, 42, 50, 96, *98*, 119, 168
Art Deco, 102–17, *139*
Art Nouveau, 87–101
Art Workers Guild, 93
Ascension, *123*, 124
Ash, John, *142*
Aspiotis Brothers, *139*, 140, 162
Aufseeser, Prof. Ernst, 106, *107*
Australia, 77, *120*, *142*, 148, *149*, 161, 177
Austria, 14, 21, 30, 57, 66, 68, 69, 95–6, *98*, 103, *105*, 132, 156, 161–2, 177
Austrian State Printing Works, Vienna, 68–9, *139*
Axster-Heudtlass, Prof. von, *132*
Ayala and Medrano, *49*

B

Baby type, *63*, 66
Bach, Guido, *80*
Baden, 32, *33*, 57, 77
Bahamas, 32, 37, 121, *122*, *166*, 177, 181
Bahrain, *122*
Bailey, David, 172
Balla, G., 110, *111*
Bamra, 19
Bang, Viggo, 172
Barbados, 30, *36*, 61, 82, *83*, 121, *124*
Barbuda, *174*
Barnard, James, 47
Barquitos, *49*
Barre, Desiré-Albert, 68
Jean-Jacques, *44*, 68
Bartlomiejczyk, E., *99*, 101
Basarab, L., *138*
Bauhaus Movement, 87, 103, *105*
Baum and Dallas, 49
Baumberger, O., 113
Bavaria, 25, 29, 32, *33*, 57, 96, *98*, 106, *108*, 151, 153, 156, 158
Beardsley, Aubrey, 87, 89
Beaune-Lambert process, 21
Bechuanaland Protectorate, *144*
Becker, E., 110
Belgian Stamp Printing Works, Malines, *67*, *88*, 134

Belgium, 28, 30, 55, *56*, *65*, 66, 68, *69*, 86, 87, *88*, 112, *134*, 145–6, 162
Bell, Charles, *26–7*, 60
Benda, J. A. R., 106, *107*
Bergedorf, 57
Bermuda, 29, 30, *61*, *71*, 119, *120*, *125*, *127*
Berry, James, *177*
Beutler, Jiri, *167*
Bhor, 46
Bhutan, 21, *176*, 177, 181
Bickel, Karl, *113*, 132
Bing, Samuel, 87
Blampied, Edmund, 160
Blanc, Joseph, 66, 89
Blazniks, I., 99
Bock and Cousins, 72, *73*
Bohm, J., 89, *92*
Bolivia, 42, *49*, 50, *114*, 116
Borov, N., *154*
Bosnia and Herzegovina, *66*, 69
Bradbury Wilkinson, 43, 44, 72, 77, 81–2, 89, 121, *125*, *138*, 162
Bramanti, B., 110, *111*
Brandt, Edgar, 112
Brazil, 29, 30, *31*, *40*, 42, 55, *101*, 116, 119
Bremen, 57
Britannia design, 30, 32, *36*, 47, 48
British American Bank Note Co., 43, 124
  Central Africa, *73*
  East Africa, 77, *78*
  Guiana, 20, 30, *42*, 43, 49, *83*, 84, 121, 124
  Honduras, *167*
  Museum, 14
  New Guinea, 121, *122*
  South Africa, 77, *78*
Brownell, F., *83*
Bruckmann of Munich, 153, 156
Brunei, 121, *122*
Brunswick, 57, *58*
Buenos Aires, *49*, 68
Buissert, L., 112
Bulgaria, 67, 69, 81, *110*, 112, *138*, 156, *158*, 171
Bull's Eyes, 29
burelage, *33*
Burne-Jones, Sir Edward, 89
Burundi, 173
Busag of Berne, *141*

C

Calcagnadoro, A., *101*
Calcutta Mint, 48
Cameroun, 128, *129*, 165
Canada, 21, 37–8, 41, 43, *83*, 84, 124, 165, 168
Canadian Bank Note Co., 124
Casha, J., *169*
Casse, E., *64*, 68
Cavallini, *14*, 16
Cape of Good Hope, 19, *26–7*, 30, 48, *60*, 61, *93*, *120*, 160
Cape Verde Islands, 65, 145
Cataldi, Pablo, *49*, 50
Cellini, G., 89, *94*
Central Lithuania, *99*, 109
Ceylon, 32, *35*, 37, 61, 124, *126*, 160
Chainbreakers design, *99*, 101
Chalmers, James, 13–14
Chalon, A. E., 32, *36*, 37, 77, 84
Channel Islands, *157*, 160

Cheffer, Henri, *130*, *134*
Cheverton, Benjamin, 16, 28
children's designs, *167*, 168
Chile, 37, *39*, *40*, *42*, 116, 181
China, 66, 84–5, *114*, 140, *170*, 181
Christmas Island, *149*
  stamps, 146, *149*, *178–80*
Cissarz, J. V., 106
City Despatch Post, 27–8
Claudius, M., *31*
Clayton, Robert, 48
Cleverley, Mark, *169*
coin profiles, *44*
Cole, Sir Henry, 16
Colombia, 50
combined printing processes, 25, 168–9
Confederate States of America, *34*, 52, 69, 70
Congo, *63*, 66, *83*
Consee, Oscar, 98
Continental Bank Note Co., 43, 140
Cook Islands, 76, *167*
Corbould, Henry, 16, *17*, 32, *35*, 44
Corrientes, *31*, 50
Costa Rica, *40*, 42
Cotton-reels, 30, 49
Courvoisier, S. A., 160–1
Craig, Edward Gordon, *99*, 109
Crane, Walter, 87, *88*
Cremona, E. V., *168*, 169
Crete, 66, 81
Croatia, *99*
Crown Agents, 32, 47, 143
Cuba, *33*, *170–1*
Cubism, 103, 116, *138*, 180
Curaçao, 66, 109
Curly Head type, *63*, 66, *135*
Cyprus, 121, 124, *125*
Czechoslovakia, 21, 87, 96, *98*, 100, 107, *139*, 148, 156, *158*, 162, *163*, *166–7*, 168–9, *170*, 173

D

Dachauer, Willi, 95, *98*, 103, *105*
Dahomey, 128
Dale, H. J., *125*
d'Annunzio, Gabriele, 101
Danzig, 106
Dardenne, M., 47
Delacryl, 25, 162
De La Rue, 19, 25, 32, *36*, 37, 43–4, 49, 59, 61, 65, 67, 69–72, *73*, *74*, 78, 79, *80*, *114*, *118*, 119–27, 140, 156, 160, 162, 172
Delpierre, J., *56*
Denmark, 29, 32, *33*, 96, 97, 112, *135*, 169–70
Depuis, D., 68
Derkinderen, Prof., 89
Deutsche Wertpapierdrückerei, *58*
die-stamping, *174–5*
Dingli, C., 95, *97*
direct plate printing *see* intaglio
discount postage, 30
Diveky, J., 89
Djibouti, *128*
Dog's Heads, 47
Dominica, 121, *122*, 160, *167*
dominical labels, 86–8
Dominican Republic, 116
Doms, A., *65*, 67
Dubai, *180*

Dubasov, I., *154*
Dubois, Alphée, 63
Dulac, Edmund, *144, 153*, 159
duplicating process, 20
Dürer, Albrecht, 21

E

Ecuador, 42, *49*, 85, *114*, 116
Egarter, Ferdinand, 14
Egypt, *54*, 66, 119, *120*, 156, *157*
Ehmcke, Prof., 106, *107*
Eichens, F. E., *56*
electrotypography, 19, 55, 79
Elmekki, Hatem, *168*, 169
El Salvador, 40, 42, 85
embossing, 20–1, 55, *174–5*
en epargne, 55
engine-turning, 14, *35, 36, 38*
Enschede of Haarlem, *65*, 66, 68, 72, *134*, 161, 162
Eritrea, *94*
Estavian, G., 81
Estonia, 96, *100*
etching, 21
Ethiopia, *64*, 68, 140, *141*
Eve, G. W., 93

F

Falkland Islands, *43*, 121, *122, 125*
Farrar-Bell, Michael, *157*
Federated Malay States, 119
Ferslew, M. W., *33*
Fiji, 76, 146–7
Fileki, S., *163*
Finland, 27, 57, 112–13, *139*, 146, 169, 172
Fiume, 101, *111*
Fournier, Heraclio, 161, 162
Fragoso, A., *135*
France, 14–15, 21, 28–9, *31*, *44*, *64*, 68, 73, 89, *102*, 109–10, *112*, 119, *127*, *130*, 143, 146, *148*, 151, 161–3, 165
Freedman, Barnett, *157*
free-form stamps, *174–5*, 181
French Government Printing Works, 65
    Guiana, *129*
    Guinea, 128, *129*
    Morocco, 128, *136*, 156, *158*
    Somali Coast, 128, *129*
Frere, Sir H. Bartle, 48
Freres, A., *172*

G

Gabon, *129*, 181
Gallen-Kallela, Akseli, *113*, 169
Gambia, *58*, 121
Games, Abram, *157*
Geiger, W., 106, *107*
Geneva, 29
Gentleman, David, *162*, 172–3
German–Austrian Postal Union, *33*, 77
Germania design, 89
Germany, 20, 24, 29, 57, 66, 77, 89, *93*, 106, *107*, 117, 119, 131–3, 145–7, 148, *166*, *170*, 181
Ghana, 165
Gibbons, Edward Stanley, 75
Gibraltar, 124, *174*, 181
Giesecke and Devrient, *58*, 69, 82
Gill, Eric, *144*, *158*, 159

Giori press, 131
Glimtzer, E., *170*
Goaman, Michael, 162
    Sylvia, *169*
Goat's Eyes design, 29
Goetz, Karl, *133*
Gold Coast, *62*, *73*, *157*, 159, 160, 165
Gomm, Sir William, 47
Granadine Confederation, *49*
Grasset, Eugène, 89, *90*
Grassi, V., *135*
Gray, Dr. John, 14
Great Britain *see* United Kingdom
Greece, *31*, *67*, 68, 69, 82, *83*, 119, *139*, 148, 168
Greig, Alexander, 27
Grenada, 32, *36*, 37, 61, 119, 160, 162
Gronowski, T., *112*
Gropius, Walter, 103
Guatemala, *40*, 42, 68, *81*
Gudjenov, D., *171*
Guedes, P., *135*
Guildhall Medal, *15*, 16
Guinea, *174*, 181

H

Ham, Thomas, *48*
Hamburg, *58*
Hamilton Bank Note Co., 85
Hanover, 57
Harrison and Sons, 156, *157*, 159–62, 172
    J.A.C., 19, *97*
    R.A., *142*
Hartz, S. L., *134*
Harvesters design, *137*
Hasper, W., *33*
Hawaii, 20, 49
Health stamps, *145–7*
Heath, Charles, 16, *17*, 44
    Frederick, 16, *17*, *35*, 44
Hejaz, *54*
Heligoland, *58*
heliogravure *see* photogravure
Hendrickx, H., *65*, *67*, 69
Hill, Sir Rowland, 13–16
Hjortzberg, Ole, 112
Hofman, P. A. H., 109
Hohenzollern types, *63*, 66
Honduras, 85
Hong Kong, *73*
Horta, *63*
Housa, Bedrich, *163*
Hulot, Anatole, 68
Humphrys, William, *17*, 32, *35*, *36*, 44
Hungarian State Printing Works, 69
Hungary, 69, 89, *92*, 113, *137*, 148, *149*, 173, 177
Hyderabad, *43*, 51

I

Iceland, 96, *97*
Inclinados, 29, *31*
India, *48*, 51–2, *67*, 121
Indonesia, 148
intaglio, 21, *24*, *34*, 26–45, 55
Ionian Islands, 32, *35*
Iran (*see also* Persia), *172*
Ireland, 113, *117*, *167*
Israel, 148
Italian Government Printing Works, 69–70

Italy, 57, 69–72, 89, *94*, 110, *111*, *112*, 132, *135*, 146, *170*, 177
Ivory Coast, 128, *129*

J

Jaipur, 51–2
Jamaica, 61, *62*, 79, 123, 124, *126*, 146–7
Jammu and Kashmir, *46*, 51
Jansson, Hammarsten, 169
Japan, 84–5, *114*, 140, *141*, 162
Jeens, Charles H., 32, *35*, *36*, 44
Jensen, Georg, 87
Jervis, H. C., *48*
Jhalawar, *46*, 51
Jirka, Ladislav, 169
Johore, *71*
Jones, Garth, 93
Jordan, *171*
Joubert, J. F., 19, 60
Jugendstil, 87, 96, 101
Jung, G., 103, *105*
Junk, R., 95, 103

K

Kaminski, Z., *110*, 112
Kashmir, 51
Kaulbach, F. A. von., *98*
Kazic, D., 162
Keatinge and Ball, *70*
key types, 61, *62–3*
Khor Fakkan, 177
King, R. J., 117
Kishangarh, 20, *46*
Kissling, R., *136*
Klein, R., *133*
Kobner and Lemkuhl, *31*
Konijnenburg, W. A., *109*
Korner, M., 106
Kosir, Laurenc, 14
Kraft, Guillermo, *114*
Krimpen, Jan van, *109*, *134*
Kuprianov, V., *100*
Kurz, L., *33*, *56*
Kuwait, 148

L

Labuan, *43*, 79
Lady McLeod stamp, 30
Lagos, 61
Lamb, Lynton, 160
Laos, *172*
Lapirot, M., 47
La Semeuse see Sower design
La Siracusa, *135*
Latvia, 96
Lauren, A., 169
Laurens, P. A., *130*
Lebeau, Chris, 109
Lebanon, 128, 156
Lebedev, *155*
Lee, W., *167*
Leeward Islands, *62*, 82
letterpress, 19–20, 54–73
Levinge, T. W., *35*
Liberia, 140, *141*
Liberty, Sir Arthur L., 101
Liechtenstein, 69, 96, 156
lithography, 24–5, 162–3
Lithuania, 96, *116*

Lökke-Sörensen, K., 172
Lombardo-Venezia, 30, 66
Long Island, 53
Louis, R., 130
Lübeck, 57, *58*
Luxembourg, *56*, *64*, 68, 145–6

M

Macao, 65, *144*
Macdonald Sisters, *96*
Mackennal, Sir Bertram, 93, *157*, 160
Mackintosh, Charles Rennie, 87, 89
Mackmurdo, A. H., *85*
Maclure, Macdonald and Co., 75, *76*
Mafeking, 53
Malawi, 148, 165, *167*
Malaysia, 181
Mali, 165
Malta, *80*, 95, 97, 123, 124, *168*, *175*, 181
Manley, F. D., *142*
Marshall Islands, *63*
Marussig, G., 101, *111*
Matabeleland, 20
Mathy, G. G., 106, *107*
Maura, B., *97*
Mauritania, *129*
Mauritius, 28, 30, 32, *36*, 47, 49, *62*, 160
Mecklenburg-Strelitz, *58*
Melnikov, K., *117*
Merson, Luc-Olivier, 66, 89, *92*
metal foil stamps, *174–6*, 177
meter franking, 165
Mexico, *40*, *49*, 50, *114*, 116, 165
Meyer, E., 68
  J. H., *58*
Middle Congo, *129*
Miller, Rev. Ernest, 53
miniature sheets, 148, *179*
Mitov, 81
Modena, 57, *59*
Monaco, 68
Montenegro, 69, *82*
Montserrat, 119, 121
Morris, William, 87
Mortensen, R., 172
Moser, Koloman, 95–6, *139*
Mouchon, Eugene, *64–5*, 66, 68, 82, 89
Mount Athos, *52*
Mozambique, 65
Mucha, Alfons, 87, *90–1*, 96, *100*, 101, 103
Müller-Rak, K., *133*
Mulready, William, *28*, *29*
Mulready wrappers, 27, *28*
multiple designs, 181
Munch, Edvard, *99*

N

Nairn, J., *170*
Naples, 57
Natal, *36*, 37, 61
National Bank Note Co., *39*, 41, 49
Naumann, C., *33*, *56*
Nelson, Harold, *152*, *153*
Nepal, 51–2
Nest, A. van, 87, *88*
Netherlands, 56, 66, 89, *95*, 109, *134*, 162, *167*, 168
  Antilles, *145*, *167*
  Indies, *63*, 66, *116*
Neu, P., *133*

Nevis, 43, 61
New Brunswick, 32, 38, *39*, *41*, 42
New Caledonia, 50
Newfoundland, 24, 32, 38, *39*, 41, 82, 123, *126*
New South Wales, 27, 30, 32, *35*, *48*, *71*, 75, *76*, 77, 82
New York City Despatch Post, 27–8
New Zealand, 32, *36*, 37, *71*, 72, 73, *80*, 81, 119, 121, 123, *124*, 127, 143, 145, *147*, 165, *170*
Nezière, J. de la, 128, *129*
Nicaragua, *40*, 42, 85
Niger, *129*
Niger Coast, 77, *78*
Nissen and Parker, 43
Noma, K., *141*
Noordzij, G., *167*
North Borneo, 77, *78*, 160
North Korea, *171*
Norway, *31*, 32, 132, *135*, *158*
Nossi-Bé, *63*
Nova Scotia, 32, *37*
Nyassa Company, *78*

O

Obrovsky, J., 96, *100*
Oldenburg, 57, *58*
omnibus issues, 143–5
Orange Free State, *71*, 72, 121, 160
Ortona, A., *110–12*
Oskan Effendi, 81
Otto of Gustrow, *58*, *71*
Oxenaar, R., *164*

P

Pacific Steam Navigation Co., 37
PAD Studio, *22*
Pakistan, 148
Panama, *141*
Papal States, 57, *59*
Papua New Guinea, *167*
Parma, 57
Paschetto, P., *135*
Paukert, J., *169*
Pekarak, K., *163*
Penny Black, 17, *134*
Penny Universal, *80*
Pereira, L., *83*
perforation, *25*
Perkins Bacon, 17, 21, *26–7*, 32, *35*, *36*, 37, 42, 43, 44, *51*, 52, *61*, 72, 82, 121, 124, 156, 161, *169*
Perkins, Jacob, 16
permit mailing, 165
Persia, *65*, 68–9, *158*
Peru, *40*, 50
Petit Poste, Paris, 14–15
Philippine Islands, *50*
photogravure, 21–3, 25, 153–63
Photogravure and Color Co., 163
photolithography, 25
photozincography, 24
Piel, J., *130*
Pipet, Matthew, *31*, 50
Pitcairn Islands, *169*
Plattner, W., *141*
Plowitz, Kurt, *173*
Poland, 27, 57, *99*, *110*
Poland, E., *100*

Portieltje, G., *86*, 87
Portugal, 20, 57, *58*, *63*, 65–6, *81*, 82, *83*, *116*, 127, 132, *135*, 145
Portuguese Guinea, *63*
  India, *63*, 65
postal stationery, 27
Postmasters' stamps, 27
Pre-Raphaelites, 86, 95
printing processes, *18*, 19–25
private posts, 27
Pro Juventute stamps, 145–6
propaganda stamps, *170–1*
Pro Patria stamps, 145–6
Prussia, 30, 55, *56*
Prussian State Printing Works, 55
Puerto Rico, *63*
Puyplat, J., *129*

Q

Qatar, 178, 181
Queensland, 32, 72, 77, *78*, 81
Questa, *23*, *177*

R

Radonicky, C. V., *59*
Rahikainen, Pentti, *153*, 169
Rapin, H., *102*
Ras al Khaima, 173
Rawdon, Wright, Hatch and Edson, 28, 37
recess-printing *see* intaglio
Red Cross stamps, 146
Regagnon, A., *130*
Reilly, Virgil, 77
Rembrandt, 21
Renner, J. F., *105*
Restall, Andrew, *153*, 172
Rethymno, *52*
Retzl, F., 103, *105*
Reunion, 20, 49–50, *129*
Revillard, A., 181
Rhodes, 110, *111*
Roberts, Samuel, 14
Robledo, A., 162
Romagna, 57, *59*
Romania, *31*, 68, 89, *95*, *107*, *138*, 148, 156, *158*, *179*
Rosetti, D. G., 89
Ross Dependency, *169*
rotogravure *see* photogravure
Roty, Oscar, 73, 89, *93*, 128, *130*
Ruandi-Urundi, 160
Ruet, L., *102*
Russia, 57, *58*, 84, *100*, 101, *104*, 117, 132, *136*, *137*, *154–5*, 165, *176*
Ruszczyc, F., *99*, 109
Ryman, A. G., *174*

S

Saar, *104*, 128, 146, 156
Saarinen, Eero, *139*, 169
Sage, Jules-Auguste, 68
St. Christopher, *61*, 121
  Helena, 32, *35*, 121, *122*, 123, *125*, 161
  Kitts-Nevis, 119, 121, *123*, 125
  Lucia, 32, *126*, *180*, 181
  Pierre and Miquelon, *101*
  Thome and Prince Islands, 65
  Vincent, 32, *35*, 37
Salgado, J. V., 82

Samoa, 76, *177*
San Marino, *94*
Sardinia, 16, 20, 57, *58*
Saudi Arabia, *173*
Savialov, Victor, *154*
Saxony, 57, *58*
Schantz, P. von, *172*
Scherff, E., 106, *107*
Schilling, H. G., *56*
Schirnböck, Ferdinand, *67*, 153, 156
Schwarzer Einser, 29
Scott, F., *162*
Scott, J. Walter, 75
Seahorses design, *97*, 121
security underprints, 29
Seebeck issues, 85
Semar, Sepp, 106
Senefelder, Alois, 24
Senegal, 128
Serbia, *59*, *64*, 68, *141*
se-tenant stamps, *178–80*
Seychelles, *62*, *160*, 161
Sezession, 95, *139*
Sharjah, 177, 178
Sherborn, C. W., 93
Sherwin, 47
Sicily, *56*, 57
Sierra Leone, 21, *62*, 118, 124, *174–5*, 178
Sievier, Robert, 20
Sind Dawks, *48*
Singapore, *167*, *173*
Slovenia, *99*, 101
Somerset House, 15, 20
South Africa, 124, *126*, *127*, 143, 156
South Australia, 32, 37, *73*, 77, *78*
Sower design, *73*, *93*, 119, 128, *130*
Spain, 19, 30, *50*, *56*, 66, 81, 82, *97*, 127, 132, *135*
Stacey Wise, 16
Stage, Mads, *172*
Stanton, Colonel, 121
stereotypes, 19
Stevens, Francis W., 14
Stile Liberty, 87, *94*
Stobie, J. R. R., *157*, 160
Stone, Reynolds, *153*, 160
Straits Settlements, *62*
Sturman, E., *120*
Sudan, 121, *122*
Sungei Ujong, *120*
surface-printing *see* letterpress
Surinam, 66, *109*
Survey of Egypt, Cairo, *54*, 159
Svab, J., *166*
Svabinsky, Max, *169*
Svengsbir, Jiri, *169*
Svolinsky, Karel, *168*
Sweden, 16, 19, 32, 112, 132, *135*, 168, 169–72
Switzerland, 20, 21, 30, 113, *116*, 132, *136*, 151
Syria, 128, *130*, 156

T

Tablet design, *63*, 65, 127
taille douce see intaglio
talking stamps, 181
Tan Siew Chiah, *173*
Tasmania, 32, 61, *62*, 77, 79, *80*, 123

Thailand, *71*, 72
Thessaly, *175*
Thevenin, M., *92*
Thiele, H. H., *33*, 97
three-dimensional stamps, *176*, 177–8
Thurn and Taxis, *33*
Tibet, 51–2
Tiffany, Louis C., 87
Timor, 65, *83*, *144*
Tin Hat design, *134*
Tobago, *61*
Togo, *129*, 165
Tonga, 21, 79, *80*, *175*, 178
Toombs, Jennifer, *166*, *169*, 173
Toorop, Jan, *95*, *96*, 106, *109*
Toppan, Carpenter, Casilear and Co., 41
Transvaal, *71*, 72, 84, *85*
Treasury Competition, 16
Treffenberg, Curry Gabriel, 16
Trinidad, 30, 32, *36*, 43, 48, *74*, 121, *123*, 124, *127*
Tripolitania, *101*
Triquerat, Sergeant, 50
Triumph, K., *100*
Tunisia, *64*, 68, *168*
Turkey, 30, 51, 66, 69, 81–2
Turks Islands, 32, *35*, 37, 61
Tuscany, 57
Tuva, *175*
typography *see* letterpress
type-set stamps, 19–20, 49–50, 55
typewritten stamps, 19, 53

U

Uganda, 53, *53*
Ukraine, *99*, 101
Umm al Qiwain, *175*, 178
Uniform Penny Postage, 13–16
United Kingdom, 11–16, 25, 27, 30, 32, 41, *44*, *59*, *60*, 68, 72, *97*, 121, 143, *144*, 146, *153*, *157*, 162, 165, 172
United Nations, 151, *166*, 169, *172*
United States, 16, 21, 27, *39*, 41, 49, 55, 69, 75, *81*, 82, 93, *114*, 116, 127, 148, *149*, *150*, *156*, 162–3, 165, *170*, 173, 181
Universal Postal Union, 30, 89, 112
Upper Senegal, *129*
Upper Silesia, *93*
Uruguay, 50, 75, *76*, 81, 101, 116

V

Van der Vossen, A., 109
Van Diemen's Land (*see also* Tasmania), 32, *36*
Vaugirard, *130*, 143, 156
Vavpotic, I., *99*
Vella, G., 95
Venezuela, 50, 116, *171*
Vepsaleinen, Olavi, 169
Veth, J., *134*
Vibert, P. E., 113
Victoria, 17, 30, 32, *48*, 72, 77, 81
Vietnam, *171*
Villayer, Renouard de, 14–15
Virey Brothers, *56*
Virgin Islands, 160
Vurtheim, J., *56*, *71*, 72

W

Wadhwan, 51
Waldraff, Paul, 89
Wallace, Robert, 14
Walsall Lithographic Co., 21, *174–5*, 178
Waterlow and Sons, *42*, 43–4, 49, 77, *78*, 79, *80*, 81, 84–5, 121, 123, 140, 160
Werner, Anton von, 89
Western Australia, 37, 48, 61
Whiteley, Victor, 161
Whiting, Charles, *12*, *15*, 16, 20
Wiener, Charles, *58*
Wilding, Dorothy, *153*, *157*
Willcocks, Sir James, *125*
Wind, Willy, *173*
Windsor, Henry T., 27
Wohlfahrtsmarken, 145–7
Woodblocks, 48
Wright, E. A., 140
Württemberg, 27, 57, 77, 106, *108*, 131, 151
Wyon, Williams, *15*, 16–17, *35*, 44

Y

Yemen, 148
Yugoslavia, *141*, *163*, 168, *179*

Z

Zanzibar. 66, *79*
Zarrin, R., *100*, 101
Zerritsch, F., 103
Zietara, V., *108*
Zürich, 29